Excel® for Accountants

Conrad Carlberg

CPA911 Publishing, LLC
Philadelphia PA

Excel for Accountants

ISBN Number 978-1-932925-01-2

Published by CPA911 Publishing, LLC 2007

Copyright 2007 CPA911 Publishing, LLC

CPA911 is a Registered Trademark of CPA911 Publishing, LLC.

Table of Contents

Acknowledgments

Cover Design: Matthew Ericson

Production: InfoDesign Services (www.infodesigning.com)

Indexing: After Words Editorial Services (www.aweditorial.com)

From the Author

As this book was written, in late 2006, I was still exploring a beta version of Excel 12, which is part of Office 2007. I realized that I had to make a crucial decision: whether or not the book's figures and instructions should take account of Excel 12's radically different user interface. After I regained my composure and got back on my chair, I saw that my decision required a sober explanation, and here it is.

Excel 12 – along with the other Office 2007 applications – has dispensed with the menu structure that's been around since Excel was MultiPlan. The thinking at Microsoft was that there just had to be a more intuitive way of grouping tasks than the old menu structure. People were confused by looking for tasks that had to do with files in a File menu; tasks that had to do with editing in an Edit menu; and so on.

So Microsoft came up with the Ribbon, a toolbar that stretches across the top of the worksheet. The Ribbon has several tabs, similar to the tabs often found at the top of a dialog box. In Excel's case, the standard tabs are Sheet, Insert, Page Layout, Formulas, Data, Review and View. These tabs organize tasks in a much more intuitive fashion than the old menus. For example:

To select a font, you use the Sheet tab. Or you use the Page Layout tab. It depends. If you want to name a cell or range, you use the Formulas tab. If you want to set Excel options such as whether to recalculate automatically or manually, you don't use a tab – you use something called the File button.

We wanted to get this book published before the end of the current presidential administration, so I decided not to cover the interface changes introduced in Excel 12. I'm depending on the fact that most people who might read this book have clients who use an earlier version of Excel. (Many corporations still use Office 97, because it's a major undertaking to move to a more recent version in a networked environment, and the benefits of an upgrade don't clearly justify the costs.)

But if you or your clients have acquired Excel 12, you'll still find this book useful for accounting matters. The tools, formulas and functions discussed here work in Excel 12 as they always have. You might have a more difficult time finding them in Excel 12, but I'm told they're all still there somewhere.

Conrad Carlberg

Download the Example Files

You can download the Excel workbooks that contain the original data for all the examples and worksheet figures that appear in this book. The files are available for downloading at **www.cpa911publishing.com**. Click the Navigation Button labeled Downloads.

The files are compatible with all versions of Excel from Office 97 through Office 2003. Excel 12 (in Office 2007) will also open the files but will want to save them in a new format, with a different extension; usually .xlsx or .xlsm.

Chapter 1

Using Lists in Excel

Defining a List

Sorting Lists

Filtering lists

Managing a List

Using the Data Form

You put data into an Excel worksheet so that you can chart it, or analyze it, or get its total, or turn it into a report, or for any of a dozen different reasons. But you don't do it for fun. So if you're serious about it, you should know how to organize the data: how to lay it out, how to label it, when to keep it separate from other information, how to edit it, and so on.

Defining a List

Wearing my Excel consultant hat, I've seen some pretty strange ways of laying out data on a worksheet. Granted, the people who designed those worksheets had what they thought were pretty good reasons for their layouts. Sticking totaling rows into the middle of what is in effect a database probably seemed like a good idea at the time.

Still, we all encounter worksheets with strange arrangements of data. One that you've probably run across occurs when someone pastes an existing report from an accounting package into a worksheet. A layout that works well for a report can be spectacularly useless as the basis for an analysis or a chart. See Figure 1-1 for an example.

	A	B	C	D	E	F	G	H
1		**Northwest Region**						
2	March 2003							
3		Towels	$ 58,221.64					
4		Area rugs	$ 57,541.41					
5		Slipcovers	$ 53,330.55					
6		Placemats	$ 48,000.61					
7								
8	Subtotal, March 2003		$ 217,094.21					
9								
10	April 2003							
11		Towels	$ 54,491.18					
12		Area rugs	$ 50,829.70					
13		Slipcovers	$ 57,531.81					
14		Placemats	$ 36,324.01					
15		Tablecloths	$ 52,676.73					
16								
17	Subtotal, March 2003		$ 251,853.43					
18								
19	May 2003							
20		Towels	$ 55,183.67					
21		Area rugs	$ 36,940.23					
22		Slipcovers	$ 17,169.76					
23								
24	Subtotal, Mary 2003		$ 109,293.66					
25								

H ◀ ▶ ▶H \ **Regional Report** ⁄ ◀

Figure 1-1 Excel doesn't know where to find the values that it should use.

Suppose you wanted Excel to show you the total of the figures in Column C for Towels plus those for Tablecloths in the Northwest region. You'd have to create a formula like this one:

=C3+C11+C20+C15

You find yourself pointing-and-clicking at cells and ranges instead of using something quick and simple like this:

=SUM(C2:C6)

List Layout

But you can use a simple formula like that one if you've set up your figures properly — and in Excel, that usually means in the form of a *list*. Figure 1-2 shows what an Excel list looks like.

	A	B	C	D	E	F	G	H
1	Date Sold	Region	Product	Sales				
2	March-03	Northeast	Area rugs	$ 47,924.49				
3	June-03	Northeast	Area rugs	$ 12,777.93				
4	April-05	Northeast	Area rugs	$ 21,798.71				
5	May-05	Northeast	Area rugs	$ 30,404.28				
6	July-06	Northeast	Area rugs	$ 11,825.77				
7	February-03	Northeast	Placemats	$ 57,656.37				
8	July-04	Northeast	Placemats	$ 19,378.49				
9	September-05	Northeast	Placemats	$ 48,967.02				
10	March-04	Northeast	Slipcovers	$ 14,799.90				
11	June-04	Northeast	Slipcovers	$ 10,746.93				
12	August-04	Northeast	Slipcovers	$ 36,402.82				
13	September-04	Northeast	Slipcovers	$ 37,438.96				
14	January-05	Northeast	Slipcovers	$ 6,429.15				
15	June-05	Northeast	Tablecloths	$ 47,807.36				
16	October-03	Northeast	Towels	$ 46,287.41				
17	November-03	Northeast	Towels	$ 21,855.43				
18	February-05	Northeast	Towels	$ 2,544.17				

Regional Product Sales

Figure 1-2: This layout makes it much easier to do something as simple as totaling.

The data you see in Figure 1-2 is arranged so that it's easy to total. For example, to get the total of the sales dollars, just type this in a blank cell *outside* column D:

=SUM(

Then, click the D at the top of column D, and press enter. Your formula will now look like this:

=SUM(D:D)

NOTE: Don't enter the formula itself in Column D because you'll get a circular reference error: the result of the formula would depend on the formula itself.

> **NOTE**: *SUM(D:D) is a quick-and-dirty formula. If you have an extraneous numeric value somewhere else in column D, it will be part of the total that's calculated by the SUM function. It's usually better to specify the cells, not just the column: for example: SUM(D2:D55) to get the total of the values in cells D2 through D55.*

It happens that the arrangement of data shown in Figure 1-2 conforms to the requirements of an Excel list:

- Each row represents a different transaction. (In this case, anyway. You could also use the list to keep track of your kangaroos; in that case, each row would represent a different kangaroo.)
- Each column represents a different variable (or *field*, which is just another term for the information you're putting in the column).
- Each column is headed by the name of the variable.

That's it. If your data conforms to the requirements bulleted above, you have a list. And Excel agrees with you.

What does a list buy you? Quite a bit, in fact:

- Some things that you'd like to use Excel for just can't be done without data structured as a list; this chapter discusses a couple of examples and you'll find more in later chapters.
- Other things can be done without a list, but only with more effort, sometimes a lot more effort. The SUM situation discussed in the prior section is a good example.

Still, a list is not really a formal structure in Excel. An Excel workbook has all kinds of formal structures — things that you use and manipulate — such as worksheets, charts, menus, cells, rows and so on. These structures are built into what's called the *Excel object model*.

> **NOTE**: *I won't have much to say about the Excel object model in this book. It's only a little less complicated than a detailed outline of FASB regulations.*

And you won't find an object like a list in that object model. It's informal, and yet something with a list structure is needed if you want to:

- Create a pivot table or pivot chart
- Use the Data Form
- Use Excel's AutoFilter
- Use tools like Histogram and Moving Average
- Copy data from a worksheet and paste it into a true database (and vice versa)
- Look up a value in a table (for example, a commission rate based on product sold and revenue recognized)

…as well as do other Excel tasks.

So if you set up your data as described in this section, you'll make your life with Excel a lot easier — starting with sorting the data.

Sorting Lists

Excel enables you to sort on up to three keys simultaneously. This means that you might sort a company's costs first on cost center, then on vendor within cost center, and then on invoice date within cost center and vendor. Each of these (in the example, cost center, vendor and date) is what is usually termed a key.

Sorting on One Key

More frequently, though, you find yourself sorting on just one key. The next few figures show how this works.

The list in Figure 1-2 started out sorted by Region, then by Product, and then by Date Sold. Suppose you wanted to change the sorting priority, and sort the information solely by Date Sold. You can ignore Region and Product, and get your date-only sort by taking these steps:

1. Select any cell in the Date Sold column. (This step isn't a necessary one, but it can make things easier in Step 3.)

2. Choose Sort from the Data menu. The dialog box shown in Figure 1-3 appears.

3. Start by selecting only one sort key. Because you started in Step 1 by choosing Date Sold, that's the field that Excel proposes as the sort key.

4. Click OK.

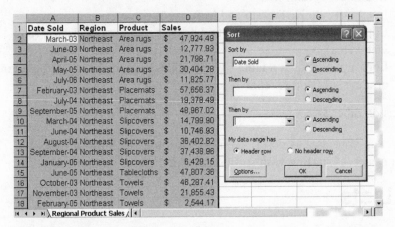

Figure 1-3: The Options button gives you additional sorting tools, such as left-to-right instead of top-to-bottom.

Figure 1-4 shows the result.

	A	B	C	D
1	Date Sold	Region	Product	Sales
2	February-03	Northeast	Placemats	$ 57,656.37
3	March-03	Northeast	Area rugs	$ 47,924.49
4	April-03	Northwest	Area rugs	$ 57,541.41
5	May-03	Southeast	Area rugs	$ 11,635.33
6	June-03	Northeast	Area rugs	$ 12,777.93
7	July-03	Northwest	Placemats	$ 48,000.61
8	August-03	Northwest	Slipcovers	$ 53,330.55
9	September-03	Southeast	Placemats	$ 40,304.51
10	October-03	Northeast	Towels	$ 46,287.41
11	November-03	Northeast	Towels	$ 21,855.43
12	December-03	Southwest	Towels	$ 34,755.95
13	January-04	Northwest	Towels	$ 58,221.64
14	February-04	Northwest	Tablecloths	$ 52,676.73
15	March-04	Northeast	Slipcovers	$ 14,799.90
16	April-04	Southeast	Slipcovers	$ 31,901.87
17	May-04	Southeast	Tablecloths	$ 4,165.40
18	June-04	Northeast	Slipcovers	$ 10,746.93

Regional Product Sales

Figure 1-4: The list is now sorted in ascending Date Sold order. Within any particular date, the records are in their original order.

TIP: *If you're sorting on one field only, you can get the same result by selecting any cell in the Date Sold column and then clicking the Sort Ascending button on the main toolbar*

With the records sorted in ascending date order, earliest to most recent, you can sensibly use a chart to show how revenues have moved over time. See Figure 1-5.

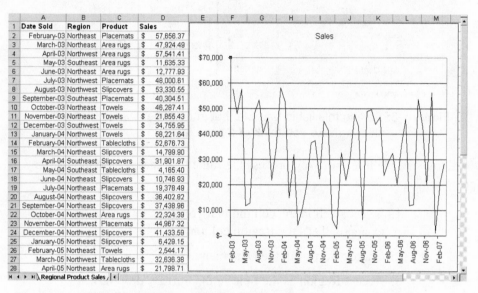

Figure 1-5: With your list sorted in date order, it's easy to create a chart that shows the data as a time series.

Sorting on Multiple Keys

In practice, you don't often find a reason to sort on more than one key at a time. One reason is that you seldom need to look at the order of records in secondary keys. Another is that tools such as pivot tables do a better job of grouping records than pure sorting does.

But Excel lets you sort on as many as three keys, so here's a look at how you might sort first on Region, then on Product, then on Date Sold. Figure 1-6 shows the unsorted records.

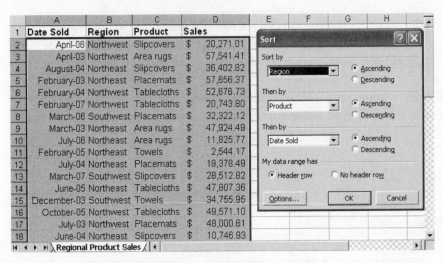

Figure 1-6: Sorting this list is feasible, but in time these situations will always make you think of a pivot table.

You start the three-sort-key process the same way that you do the one-key process:

1. Select a cell in the column that you want to sort on first; in this example, that's the Region column.

2. Choose Sort from the Data menu.

3. Accept Region as the field in the Sort By drop-down.

4. Click the second drop-down (refer back to Figure 1-3), the first of the two that are labeled Then By. Choose Product from the drop-down list.

5. Click the third drop-down (again, refer back to Figure 1-3), and choose Date Sold from the drop-down list.

6. Click OK.

NOTE: *The Sort Ascending button on the main toolbar doesn't handle multiple sort keys — just one, the selected column. If you want to sort on more than one key, use the method shown here.*

As you see in Figure 1-7, the full list has been sorted first by Region; then, within each value of Region, by Product; and finally, within each combined value of Region and Product, by Date Sold.

	A	B	C	D	E	F	G	H
1	Date Sold	Region	Product	Sales				
2	March-03	Northeast	Area rugs	$ 47,924.49				
3	June-03	Northeast	Area rugs	$ 12,777.93				
4	April-05	Northeast	Area rugs	$ 21,798.71				
5	May-05	Northeast	Area rugs	$ 30,404.28				
6	July-06	Northeast	Area rugs	$ 11,825.77				
7	February-03	Northeast	Placemats	$ 57,656.37				
8	July-04	Northeast	Placemats	$ 19,378.49				
9	September-05	Northeast	Placemats	$ 48,967.02				
10	March-04	Northeast	Slipcovers	$ 14,799.90				
11	June-04	Northeast	Slipcovers	$ 10,746.93				
12	August-04	Northeast	Slipcovers	$ 36,402.82				
13	September-04	Northeast	Slipcovers	$ 37,438.96				
14	January-05	Northeast	Slipcovers	$ 6,429.15				
15	June-05	Northeast	Tablecloths	$ 47,807.36				
16	October-03	Northeast	Towels	$ 46,287.41				
17	November-03	Northeast	Towels	$ 21,855.43				
18	February-05	Northeast	Towels	$ 2,544.17				

ℍ ◄ ▶ ℍ \ Regional Product Sales / ◄

Figure 1-7: In Excel sorts, numbers come before letters.

In management accounting situations, sorting on more than one key usually occurs when you want a report distributed in sections. In the example shown in this section, a CFO might want to show sales by date, within product — just as it was sorted in the last set of steps — but have a different report distributed to each regional sales manager. The best way to handle that is to do the three-key sort just as shown above, and then to split the report physically into regions with page breaks.

TIP: *Insert a page break in a worksheet by selecting a row where you want the break, then choosing Page Break from the Insert menu. The page break appears above the row you selected.*

Unsorting a List

There's one particular popular report layout that makes me nuts. It uses a blank line to separate one category from the next. Even though they may be helpful when it comes to *reading* a report, I can't stand dealing with those blankety-blank blanks when it comes to analyzing or charting the data. They do nothing but get in the way. Figure 1-8 has an example.

	A	B	C	D	E	F	G	H	I
1	Year	Region	Product	Sales					
2									
3	2003	Northeast	Area rugs	$ 124,731.18					
4			Placemats	$ 126,001.88					
5			Slipcovers	$ 105,817.76					
6									
7	2004		Tablecloths	$ 47,807.36					
8			Towels	$ 148,086.71					
9									
10	2003	Northwest	Area rugs	$ 79,865.80					
11			Placemats	$ 142,385.89					
12			Slipcovers	$ 115,035.15					
13			Tablecloths	$ 267,057.45					
14			Towels	$ 101,230.92					
15									
16	2003	Southeast	Area rugs	$ 46,387.55					
17			Placemats	$ 46,527.86					
18									
19	2004		Slipcovers	$ 31,901.87					
20			Tablecloths	$ 4,165.40					
21									
22	2003	Southwest	Area rugs	$ 1,028.55					
23			Placemats	$ 32,322.12					

Regional Sales Report

Figure 1-8: The problem is to remove the blank rows and leave everything else as is.

I use Excel to sort the blank rows out of the data, like this:

1. Type **Row** into cell E1. This isn't necessary but it helps keep things clear.

2. In E2 enter **2.** In E3 enter **3**.

3. Select E2:E3. Put your mouse pointer over the Fill Handle in the lower right corner of E3, hold down the mouse button, and drag down into the final row (In Figure 1-8, that's row 23). You now have a new field, named Row, in your list.

4. Sort the list, using Sales (or another field or fields) as the sort key. The field to choose is one that has a value in all rows *other* than the ones that are blank in all columns.

5. You'll find that the blank rows have been sorted to the bottom. In Excel sorts, blank values come after everything else.

6. Delete the blank rows at the bottom. You can do that in two steps, just by dragging through their row headers and choosing Edit → Delete. (But do this only if you feel compulsive about it; the blank rows are now out of the way, so you can forget about them.)

7. Re-sort the remaining records according to the values in the Row column. This puts the list back in its original order.

NOTE: Excel uses the term AutoFill for the dragging operation described in Step 3 of the instructions to sort blank rows out of the data. As with nearly every operation in Excel, there are several ways to do it, but this one is probably the cleanest if you sort on more than one column.

Filtering Lists

When you filter a list in Excel, you're saying that there are some records that you don't want to pay attention to for the time being. You want Excel to leave them out of an analysis (for example, it ignores them when you use the SUM function), or omit them from a chart, or not show them on the worksheet at all.

It's important to keep in mind that phrase in the prior paragraph, "for the time being." In most cases you can filter some records to ignore them temporarily, and then when you're ready you can bring them back into play.

There are a couple of different approaches to filtering in Excel; one is simple and virtually automatic, and the other is a little more complicated and you have to stay involved with what's going on.

AutoFiltering Excel Lists

In keeping with this chapter's main topic, you'll find that it's easier to filter records that are in a list than records that are just hanging around the worksheet. Take a look at Figure 1-9.

	A	B	C	D	E	F	G	H	I
1	Name	Year	Quarter	Gross	FWH	FICA	Net		
2	Lenny	2006	Q1	$ 7,140.17	$1,146.90	$ 535.51	$ 5,457.76		
3	Howell	2006	Q1	$13,731.34	$3,696.19	$1,029.85	$ 9,005.30		
4	Beu	2006	Q1	$ 3,309.52	$ 568.14	$ 248.21	$ 2,493.17		
5	Daniell	2006	Q1	$ 7,429.55	$2,571.26	$ 557.22	$ 4,301.07		
6	Cummins	2006	Q1	$ 9,755.32	$3,132.27	$ 731.65	$ 5,891.41		
7	Tafoya	2006	Q1	$15,812.80	$3,056.27	$1,185.96	$11,570.57		
8	Neil	2006	Q1	$28,280.54	$3,920.09	$2,121.04	$22,239.41		
9	Bell	2006	Q1	$20,409.24	$6,210.50	$1,530.69	$12,668.05		
10	DeFratis	2006	Q1	$12,566.97	$2,652.60	$ 942.52	$ 8,971.84		
11	McCleary	2006	Q1	$17,672.22	$ 961.22	$1,325.42	$15,385.58		
12	Marble	2006	Q1	$28,303.50	$8,188.72	$2,122.76	$17,992.02		
13	Rouse	2006	Q1	$15,824.32	$1,013.14	$1,186.82	$13,624.36		
14	Garber	2006	Q1	$ 3,554.07	$1,152.74	$ 266.56	$ 2,134.78		
15	Rodgers	2006	Q1	$29,500.18	$9,299.19	$2,212.51	$17,988.48		
16	Kohout	2006	Q1	$12,022.35	$3,961.06	$ 901.68	$ 7,159.61		
17	Sikorski	2006	Q1	$17,529.95	$1,253.50	$1,314.75	$14,961.70		
18	Blanch	2006	Q1	$14,847.62	$2,041.46	$1,113.57	$11,692.59		
19	Lenny	2006	Q2	$16,151.84	$2,388.69	$1,211.39	$12,551.76		
20	Howell	2006	Q2	$11,849.12	$1,669.86	$ 888.68	$ 9,290.58		
21	Beu	2006	Q2	$29,809.68	$8,576.89	$2,235.73	$18,997.07		
22	Daniell	2006	Q2	$ 4,740.68	$ 230.60	$ 355.55	$ 4,154.52		
23	Cummins	2006	Q2	$14,113.24	$1,372.95	$1,058.49	$11,681.80		

Figure 1-9: A year-to-date salary report for Castor Oil Corporation.

Because the report is set up as an Excel list, it's very easy to focus on just a subset of records. Take these steps:

1. Select any cell in the list.

2. Choose Data→Filter→AutoFilter.

3. Drop-down arrows appear at the head of each column, adjacent to each list header.

4. Click the drop-down arrow for the field you want to use for filtering, and choose the value that you want to keep. (Other options like Top Ten are discussed later in this chapter.)

That's it. If you chose, for example, Q2 in the Quarter field, Excel displays only those records in the list that have Q2 in Quarter's column.

TIP: When you head into a parking space, it's nice to know how you're going to get out. To turn off the AutoFilter, choose Data → Filter → AutoFilter — it's just a toggle.

Figure 1-10 shows the list, filtered for Q1 using AutoFilter.

	A	B	C	D	E	F	G	H
1	Name	Year	Quarter	Gross	FWH	FICA	Net	
2	Lenny	2007	Q1	$ 7,140.17	$ 1,146.90	$ 535.51	$ 5,457.76	
3	Howell	2007	Q1	$ 13,731.34	$ 3,696.19	$ 1,029.85	$ 9,005.30	
4	Beu	2007	Q1	$ 3,309.52	$ 568.14	$ 248.21	$ 2,493.17	
5	Daniell	2007	Q1	$ 7,429.55	$ 2,571.26	$ 557.22	$ 4,301.07	
6	Cummins	2007	Q1	$ 9,755.32	$ 3,132.27	$ 731.65	$ 5,891.41	
7	Tafoya	2007	Q1	$ 15,812.80	$ 3,056.27	$ 1,185.96	$ 11,570.57	
8	Neil	2007	Q1	$ 28,280.54	$ 3,920.09	$ 2,121.04	$ 22,239.41	
9	Bell	2007	Q1	$ 20,409.24	$ 6,210.50	$ 1,530.69	$ 12,668.05	
10	DeFratis	2007	Q1	$ 12,566.97	$ 2,652.60	$ 942.52	$ 8,971.84	
11	McCleary	2007	Q1	$ 17,672.22	$ 961.22	$ 1,325.42	$ 15,385.58	
12	Marble	2007	Q1	$ 28,303.50	$ 8,188.72	$ 2,122.76	$ 17,992.02	
13	Rouse	2007	Q1	$ 15,824.32	$ 1,013.14	$ 1,186.82	$ 13,624.36	
14	Garber	2007	Q1	$ 3,554.07	$ 1,152.74	$ 266.56	$ 2,134.78	
15	Rodgers	2007	Q1	$ 29,500.18	$ 9,299.19	$ 2,212.51	$ 17,988.48	
16	Kohout	2007	Q1	$ 12,022.35	$ 3,961.06	$ 901.68	$ 7,159.61	
17	Sikorski	2007	Q1	$ 17,529.95	$ 1,253.50	$ 1,314.75	$ 14,961.70	
18	Blanch	2007	Q1	$ 14,847.62	$ 2,041.46	$ 1,113.57	$ 11,692.59	
36								
37								

Castor Salary Summary

Figure 1-10: Notice that some row numbers are missing.

Figure 1-10 suggests how AutoFilter does its work: the records that don't conform to the filter that you specify are hidden. Their rows are modified to have a height of zero — this is the same as selecting a row or rows and then choosing Format → Row → Hide.

NOTE: *If you are already up on pivot tables, you might know this, but just in case: You can't use AutoFilter (or the Advanced Filter, for that matter) on a pivot table, even though it might look like an Excel list.*

Using AutoFilter Options

Figure 1-11 is Figure 1-9, repeated here for convenience. The AutoFilter has already been selected and you see the options available from the Column D drop-down.

Apart from the first three items in the drop-down list, there are only individual values. As you saw earlier, you can select one of those values to filter out all records that do not have that value in Column D.

	A	B	C	D	E	F	G
1	Name	Year	Quarter	Gross	FWH	FICA	Net
2	Lenny	2006	Q1		$1,146.90	$ 535.51	$ 5,457.76
3	Howell	2006	Q1		$3,696.19	$1,029.85	$ 9,005.30
4	Beu	2006	Q1		$ 568.14	$ 248.21	$ 2,493.17
5	Daniell	2006	Q1		$2,571.26	$ 557.22	$ 4,301.07
6	Cummins	2006	Q1		$3,132.27	$ 731.65	$ 5,891.41
7	Tafoya	2006	Q1		$3,056.27	$1,185.96	$11,570.57
8	Neil	2006	Q1		$3,920.09	$2,121.04	$22,239.41
9	Bell	2006	Q1		$6,210.50	$1,530.69	$12,668.05
10	DeFratis	2006	Q1		$2,652.60	$ 942.52	$ 8,971.84
11	McCleary	2006	Q1		$ 961.22	$1,325.42	$15,385.58
12	Marble	2006	Q1		$8,188.72	$2,122.76	$17,992.02
13	Rouse	2006	Q1		$1,013.14	$1,186.82	$13,624.36
14	Garber	2006	Q1		$1,152.74	$ 266.56	$ 2,134.78
15	Rodgers	2006	Q1		$9,299.19	$2,212.51	$17,988.48
16	Kohout	2006	Q1	$ 12,022.35	$3,961.06	$ 901.68	$ 7,159.61
17	Sikorski	2006	Q1	$ 17,529.95	$1,253.50	$1,314.75	$14,961.70
18	Blanch	2006	Q1	$ 14,847.62	$2,041.46	$1,113.57	$11,692.59
19	Lenny	2006	Q2	$ 16,151.84	$2,388.69	$1,211.39	$12,551.76
20	Howell	2006	Q2	$ 11,849.12	$1,669.86	$ 888.68	$ 9,290.58
21	Beu	2006	Q2	$ 29,809.68	$8,576.89	$2,235.73	$18,997.07

Gross dropdown list: (All), (Top 10...), (Custom...), $3,309.52, $3,554.07, $4,740.68, $5,350.93, $5,732.45, $6,950.20, $7,140.17, $7,429.55, $9,386.44, $9,755.32, $9,979.07, $10,554.00, $11,849.12, $12,022.35, $12,566.97, $13,361.29, $13,731.34

Castor Salary Summary

Figure 1-11: The All, Top Ten and Custom items have special results.

The other three items work as follows:

- (All)... This option restores all the original records in the list: it un-filters them.
- (Top Ten)... This option lets you select an ordered subset of the records.
- (Custom)... This option enables you to specify more complex filtering criteria than simply choosing a particular value in the list.

If you select the Top Ten option, you next see the dialog box shown in Figure 1-12.

You have the following options:

- The drop-down on the left, where Top is now selected, also lets you choose Bottom.
- The box in the center, where 10 is now selected, lets you supply any number between 1 and 500.

- The drop-down on the right, where Items is now selected, also lets you choose Percent.

	A	B	C	D	E	F	G	H
1	**Name** ▾	**Year** ▾	**Quarter** ▾	**Gross** ▾	**FWH** ▾	**FICA** ▾	**Net** ▾	
2	Lenny	2006	Q1	$ 7,140.17	$1,146.90	$ 535.51	$ 5,457.76	
3	Howell	2006	Q1	$ 13,731.34	$3,696.19	$1,029.85	$ 9,005.30	
4	Beu	2006	Q1	$ 3,309.52	$ 568.14	$ 248.21	$ 2,493.17	
5	Daniell	2006	Q1	$ 7,429.55	$2,571.26	$ 557.22	$ 4,301.07	
6	Cummins	2006	Q1	$ 9,755.33	$3,132.27	$ 731.65	$ 5,891.41	
7	Tafoya	2006	Q1				70.57	
8	Neil	2006	Q1				39.41	
9	Bell	2006	Q1				68.05	
10	DeFratis	2006	Q1				71.84	
11	McCleary	2006	Q1				85.58	
12	Marble	2006	Q1				92.02	
13	Rouse	2006	Q1				24.36	
14	Garber	2006	Q1	$ 3,554.07	$1,152.74	$ 266.56	$ 2,134.78	
15	Rodgers	2006	Q1	$ 29,500.18	$9,299.19	$2,212.51	$17,988.48	
16	Kohout	2006	Q1	$ 12,022.35	$3,961.06	$ 901.68	$ 7,159.61	
17	Sikorski	2006	Q1	$ 17,529.95	$1,253.50	$1,314.75	$14,961.70	
18	Blanch	2006	Q1	$ 14,847.62	$2,041.46	$1,113.57	$11,692.59	
19	Lenny	2006	Q2	$ 16,151.84	$2,388.69	$1,211.39	$12,551.76	
20	Howell	2006	Q2	$ 11,849.12	$1,669.86	$ 888.68	$ 9,290.58	
21	Beu	2006	Q2	$ 29,809.68	$8,576.89	$2,235.73	$18,997.07	

Top 10 AutoFilter

Show

Top | 10 | Items

OK | Cancel

◄ ◄ ► ►◄ \ Castor Salary Summary ◄ ►

Figure 1-12: Use these options to define your Top Ten. They remain selected until you change them, even across instances of Excel.

What you get depends in part on what's in the list:

- If all the items in the column are text (for example, the letters A through H and the word Management) then selecting Top Ten has no effect.
- If the items in the column are a mix of numeric and textual values, then only the numeric values will be shown by the Top Ten option.
- The number of items that the filter can display can be no greater than the number of numeric values in the column. For example, if the column contains 1, 2, 3 and D, choosing Top 10 and specifying 5 values will display 1, 2 and 3 only.

- If you choose to display Percent instead of Items, you will get the top (or bottom) X Percent in the list, subject to the limits on text values and maximum counts I just mentioned.

Entr'acte: Deciding to Use AutoFilter

AutoFilter is a convenient way to look at a subset of your list, and it's quick to set up. The drop-down makes it easy to focus on records that have a particular value in a column. But as a practical matter, you're probably not going to have much use for more advanced AutoFilter features, such as Custom filtering.

As you'll see in the next section, it's entirely feasible to use AutoFilter's Custom criteria to focus on, say, office revenues for 2005 in the Northwest region. But setting up AutoFilter to do that takes a little time, and when you subsequently want to look at office revenues for 2005 in the Southwest region, you'll have to rebuild your Custom filter. That extra time and effort tends to defeat the purpose of something intended to be a handy tool.

It's much easier to use Advanced Filter or, better yet, a pivot table to do that kind of analysis. Both are based on lists, just like AutoFilter, and they take about as long to set up. But once you've done the setup, you have the results you want — to continue the present example, you have office revenues for each year in each region — and you don't need to rebuild anything when your interest shifts from one region to another.

So: think of AutoFilter as a quick-and-dirty way of getting a look at a subset of data: it's great for ad hoc peeks into a list. But even though Excel provides the tools to make it more complex, resist the temptation. You'll save a lot of time and energy in the long run, and you can save your best swear words for Microsoft itself, rather than its innocent products.

Now that's off my chest, I can move on the AutoFilter's Custom filter with a clear conscience, knowing that you'll skip it if you want to.

Using the Custom Criteria

With a list set up and the AutoFilter drop-downs visible, click one of the drop-downs and choose Custom from the drop-down list. You see the dialog box shown in Figure 1-13.

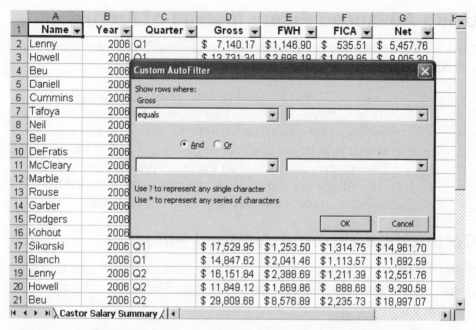

Figure 1-13: You can specify two operators (e.g., greater than and less than) and two corresponding values for this field.

There are twelve operators you can choose from in the left hand drop-downs. We won't enumerate them here (if you're interested, you can check by clicking one of the drop-downs) beyond mentioning that they include:

- Equals
- Is less than
- Is greater than

You can do the same with another field in your list, and then the custom criteria act as though they were connected by an *and*. Therefore, you could set up a custom criterion for the Region field that calls for Region to equal "Northwest" and one for the Product field that calls for Product to not equal "Towels." That would give you sales in the Northwest for products other than towels.

And when you wanted to look at sales of towels in the Southeast, you do it over again, changing the Region and Product custom criteria.

Using Advanced Filters Instead of AutoFilter

There are some things you can do with Excel's Advanced Filters that you can't do with AutoFilter. Here they are:

- Copy the filtered list to some other place on the worksheet.
- Show unique records only. This can be helpful if you want to find out if you have duplicate records (the filtered list will normally be shorter than the original) but it won't help you find the duplicates.
- Use complex criteria to filter the list. As you've already seen, AutoFilter gives you selection criteria to work with, but the Advanced Filter's criteria can be more sophisticated.

Getting More from Advanced Filter

One of the strongest points of the Advanced Filter is the ability to filter unique records only. Suppose that these are the names of regions as they exist in your list:

- Northwest
- Northeast
- Southwest
- Southeast
- Southeast

Notice that there are two instances of Southeast. Although you can't see it here, one of them is followed by a blank space. Apparently, someone mistyped the name of the region, or some really esoteric glitch took place inside the black box.

TIP: This is a great reason to use Data Validation, which allows you to create drop-downs in cells. The drop-downs limit the possible entries to those that you want to allow. Choosing Data → Validation walks you through the process.

You wouldn't know that this had happened — that is, an extra version of Southeast sneaking into your list — without either poking around for one, or using a tool such as Advanced Filter (or pivot tables) that highlight the presence of an erroneous value. Using Advanced Filter, you arrange for a shorter list consisting of the original list's unique values.

Here's how to filter for unique values in your list:

1. Select a cell in the list.

2. Choose Filter from the Data menu.

3. Choose Advanced Filter from the Filter menu.

4. In the Advanced Filter dialog box (see Figure 1-14) verify the List Range address.

5. Click the Copy to Another Location option button. The Copy to box becomes enabled.

6. Click in the Copy to box, and then click in the cell where you want the filtered list to begin.

6. Fill the Unique Records Only checkbox.

7. Click OK. You'll get the result shown in Figure 1-15.

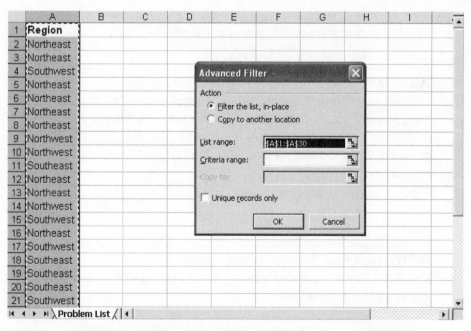

Figure 1-14: The list's range is filled in automatically if you start by selecting a cell inside the list.

	A	B	C	D	E	F	G	H	I
1	**Region**		**Region**						
2	Northeast		Northeast						
3	Northeast		Southwest						
4	Southwest		Northwest						
5	Northeast		Southeast						
6	Northeast		Southeast						
7	Northeast								
8	Northeast								
9	Northwest								
10	Northwest								
11	Southeast								
12	Northeast								
13	Northeast								
14	Northwest								
15	Southwest								
16	Northeast								
17	Southwest								
18	Southeast								
19	Southeast								
20	Southeast								
21	Southwest								

Problem List

Figure 1-15: Notice that the Advanced Filter copies not only the records but also the column header to the new location.

WARNING: *If you use the Advanced Filter to copy filtered records to another location, be sure there's no data already in the columns you want to use. If you're copying the result into columns C and D and there's anything anywhere in those columns, it will be lost — and you can't Undo the results of the operation.*

NOTE: *Your new location — the location to which you want Excel to copy the filtered data — must be on the same worksheet as the original list.*

As Figure 1-15 showed, there is at least one record in your list that's supposed to be grouped with other Southeast region records, but it isn't; the trailing blank tells Excel that it's a different region.

Now that you know that there is such a record (or records), you can take a couple of simple steps to find it. Probably the quickest is to start by sorting your list on Region — the record with the trailing blank after "Southeast" will sort to the bottom of other Southeast records.

However, you don't yet know how many such records there are. So, after sorting on Region, you might want to take these steps:

1. Select a cell that's outside the list, but in the same row as the first Southeast record — which we'll assume is in cell A40.

2. Enter this formula: =**LEN(A40)** which returns the number of characters in the value found in A40. (LEN stands for *length*.) In this case, it should return 9, the number of characters in Southeast.

3. Autofill the LEN formula down until you reach the row with the final Southeast value.

4. Edit any versions of the Southeast value where the LEN function does not return 9. In particular, a value with a trailing blank would return 10: nine for the visible characters plus one for the trailing blank.

How Excel decides that records are unique is partly a function of how many columns are in the list that you filter. Using the data in the present example:

- If your list consists only of Region, there will be four unique records — one for each region. Of course, if you had another region, say Central, you'd get five unique records.
- If your list consists of Region and Year, you'll have up to twenty unique records: four regions times five years. If there's no record for a given year in a given region, that maximum of twenty will drop to an actual of nineteen.
- If your list consists of Region, Year and Product, you'll have a maximum of 4 X 5 X 5 = 100 unique records.
- Finally, if your list consists of Region and Revenue, it's likely that your list of unique records will be identical to your original list — except in the unlikely situation where two or more regions have exactly the same revenue.

Complex Criteria

Even if you're not interested in unique records in your list, you can still make use of the Copy To Another Location option. But in that case you'll want to specify some criteria for the filter — otherwise, your filter will trivially return all the records in your list.

There are two general steps for setting up criteria for Advanced Filter:

- Choose a range of cells at least one column away from your list. In the first row of that range, put the names of fields in your list that you want to filter on. This is the first row of your criteria range.
- Below the name of each field in the criteria range, enter the values that you want to keep: that is, the values that you want to filter for.

Figure 1-16 shows an example.

	A	B	C	D	E	F	G	H	I	J	K	L	M
1	Year	Region	Product	Sales		Region	Year		Year	Region	Product	Sales	
2	2003	Northeast	Area rugs	$47,924.49		Northwest	2005		2005	Northwest	Tablecloths	$32,636.38	
3	2003	Northeast	Area rugs	$12,777.93					2005	Northwest	Tablecloths	$43,008.21	
4	2005	Northeast	Area rugs	$21,798.71					2005	Northwest	Tablecloths	$49,571.10	
5	2005	Northeast	Area rugs	$30,404.28									
6	2006	Northeast	Area rugs	$11,825.77									
7	2003	Northeast	Placemats	$57,656.37									
8	2004	Northeast	Placemats	$19,378.49									
9	2005	Northeast	Placemats	$48,967.02									
10	2004	Northeast	Slipcovers	$14,799.90									
11	2004	Northeast	Slipcovers	$10,746.93									
12	2004	Northeast	Slipcovers	$36,402.82									
13	2004	Northeast	Slipcovers	$37,438.96									
14	2005	Northeast	Slipcovers	$ 6,429.15									
15	2005	Northeast	Tablecloths	$47,807.36									
16	2003	Northeast	Towels	$46,287.41									
17	2003	Northeast	Towels	$21,855.43									
18	2005	Northeast	Towels	$ 2,544.17									
19	2006	Northeast	Towels	$23,661.65									
20	2006	Northeast	Towels	$53,738.05									
21	2003	Northwest	Area rugs	$57,541.41									

Filter with Criteria

Figure 1-16: You can avoid typing errors in the criteria range by copying and pasting from the original list.

In Figure 1-16, the criteria range is F1:G2. The names of the fields in the list that Excel should use as criteria for filtering are in F1:G1. The values of those two fields that Excel should filter for are in F2:G2. These two criteria fields are treated as if they were connected by an AND; Return any records where the Region is Northwest and the Year is 2005. The filtered list has been copied to another location, starting in cell I1.

You'll have less use for an implied OR connector in a criteria range, but here's how to make one. Suppose, strangely, that you want to return any records that are either from the Northwest region *or* from year 2005. Put those two criteria in the same columns as before, but in different rows. Figure 1-17 shows how to do this.

	A	B	C	D	E	F	G	H	I	J	K	L	M
1	Year	Region	Product	Sales		Region	Year		Year	Region	Product	Sales	
2	2003	Northeast	Area rugs	$47,924.49		Northwest			2005	Northeast	Area rugs	$21,798.71	
3	2003	Northeast	Area rugs	$12,777.93			2005		2005	Northeast	Area rugs	$30,404.28	
4	2005	Northeast	Area rugs	$21,798.71					2005	Northeast	Placemats	$48,967.02	
5	2005	Northeast	Area rugs	$30,404.28					2005	Northeast	Slipcovers	$ 6,429.15	
6	2006	Northeast	Area rugs	$11,825.77					2005	Northeast	Tablecloths	$47,807.36	
7	2003	Northeast	Placemats	$57,656.37					2005	Northeast	Towels	$ 2,544.17	
8	2004	Northeast	Placemats	$19,378.49					2003	Northwest	Area rugs	$57,541.41	
9	2005	Northeast	Placemats	$48,967.02					2004	Northwest	Area rugs	$22,324.39	
10	2004	Northeast	Slipcovers	$14,799.90					2003	Northwest	Placemats	$48,000.61	
11	2004	Northeast	Slipcovers	$10,746.93					2004	Northwest	Placemats	$44,967.32	
12	2004	Northeast	Slipcovers	$36,402.82					2006	Northwest	Placemats	$29,338.22	
13	2004	Northeast	Slipcovers	$37,438.96					2006	Northwest	Placemats	$20,079.74	
14	2005	Northeast	Slipcovers	$ 6,429.15					2003	Northwest	Slipcovers	$53,330.55	
15	2005	Northeast	Tablecloths	$47,807.36					2004	Northwest	Slipcovers	$41,433.59	
16	2003	Northeast	Towels	$46,287.41					2006	Northwest	Slipcovers	$20,271.01	
17	2003	Northeast	Towels	$21,855.43					2004	Northwest	Tablecloths	$52,676.73	
18	2005	Northeast	Towels	$ 2,544.17					2005	Northwest	Tablecloths	$32,636.38	
19	2006	Northeast	Towels	$23,661.65					2005	Northwest	Tablecloths	$43,008.21	
20	2006	Northeast	Towels	$53,738.05					2005	Northwest	Tablecloths	$49,571.10	
21	2003	Northwest	Area rugs	$57,541.41					2006	Northwest	Tablecloths	$12,167.81	

Filter with Criteria

Figure 1-17: The filtered list is copied to another location, to avoid hiding rows as AutoFilter does.

You can even mix-and-match ANDs and ORs. With Southwest in F2, 2005 in G2, and Southeast in F3, you'll get records from the Southwest in 2005 (the AND), as well as records from Southeast regardless of their Year (the OR) — that is, (Southwest AND 2005) OR Southeast.

Figure 1-17 showed the filtered list copied to a new location. If, instead, you choose to filter the list in place, Excel hides the rows that don't conform to your criteria, just as with AutoFilter. The easiest way to get those rows back is to choose Data → Filter → Show All.

Managing a List

There's a way of managing lists that first showed up in Excel 2003. It offers little you can't do in earlier versions, but it does bring some existing capabilities together in one place. If you're new to lists, that can be handy.

Suppose you have your data laid out as in Figure 1-17, shown earlier. Click any cell in the list and choose List from the Data menu. You'll see a shortcut menu that has only one useful item: Create List. As soon as you select that item, you see the window shown in Figure 1-18.

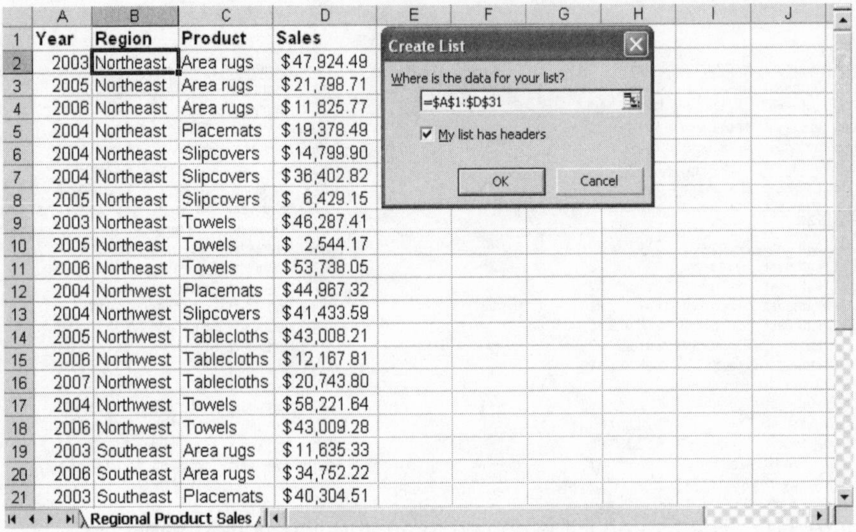

Figure 1-18: If you take the advice given in this chapter about setting up lists, your list will have headers.

Confirm the range address of your data, and if necessary correct it (you can drag through the correct range on the worksheet). Accept or correct Excel's guess about whether your list has headers, and click OK. You'll see the result shown in Figure 1-19:

Figure 1-19 shows that Excel automatically adds the following elements to your list:

- Filter drop-downs (so you don't have to select AutoFilter to get them)
- A border around the outside of your list. This border might help you analyze the data more effectively, but I can't think how.
- A row where you can enter a new record. You can do this at the bottom of any list, but this row has an asterisk.

- List headers, if you didn't supply them yourself. The headers get the names Column1, Column2, Column3 and so on, so it's a good idea to specify them before you formally create the list.
- A *total row*, which you can toggle on-and-off (it's off at first). This can be a time-saver, so let's look at it a little more carefully.

	A	B	C	D	E	F	G	H	I	J
1	Year ▾	Region ▾	Product ▾	Sales ▾						
2	2003	Northeast	Area rugs	$ 47,924.49						
3	2005	Northeast	Area rugs	$ 21,798.71						
4	2006	Northeast	Area rugs	$ 11,825.77						
5	2004	Northeast	Placemats	$ 19,378.49						
6	2004	Northeast	Slipcovers	$ 14,799.90						
7	2004	Northeast	Slipcovers	$ 36,402.82						
8	2005	Northeast	Slipcovers	$ 6,429.15						
9	2003	Northeast	Towels	$ 46,287.41						
10	2005	Northeast	Towels	$ 2,544.17						
11	2006	Northeast	Towels	$ 53,738.05						
22	2005	Southeast	Placemats	$ 6,223.35						
23	2004	Southeast	Slipcovers	$ 31,901.87						
24	2004	Southeast	Tablecloths	$ 4,165.40						
25	20	List		▾ ×						
26	20	List ▾ Σ Toggle Total Row								
27	2007	Southwest	Slipcovers	$ 20,512.02						
28	2005	Southwest	Tablecloths	$ 43,836.76						
29	2003	Southwest	Towels	$ 34,755.95						
30	2005	Southwest	Towels	$ 46,704.67						
31	2006	Southwest	Towels	$ 45,841.13						
32	✱									
33	Total			$ 536,421.58						
34										

H ◀ ▶ H \ Regional Product Sales ⟨ ◀

Figure 1-19: Rows 12 through 21 have been hidden to make room for special rows at the bottom of the list.

First, though, note that some aspects of the list disappear when you activate a cell outside the list. The AutoFilter drop-downs disappear, and the border around the list, while it stays there, is no longer bold, and the new-record row — the one with the asterisk — disappears.

Handling the Total Row

So does the List toolbar — disappears, that is. It was shown in Figure 1-19. To get at the List toolbar, just click inside the list.

TIP: *If you still don't see the List toolbar after clicking inside the list, choose Toolbars from the View menu, fill the check-box next to List, and click OK.*

Figure 1-19 showed the toolbar's Toggle Total Row button. If you don't see the Total Row as the list's final row, click the Toggle Total Row button, and the Total Row should appear.

If your list has a column with at least one numeric value, that column defaults to Sum as its total. A column that contains no numeric value has no default total. However, you can set it to show Count as its total by following these steps:

1. Click the cell that would contain a total if its column were not all text values. In Figure 1-19 that cell could be B33 or C33.

2. A drop-down appears immediately at the right side of the cell. Click the drop-down to display the totals that are available to you. If you want to know the number of text values in that column of the list, choose Count.

By default, the left-most column in your list has the word **Total** in the Total Row. You can override this with the cell's drop-down and choosing anything, including **None**, from the list.

Using the Totals

There are nine options in the Total Row's drop-down list:

- None: Leave the cell blank.
- Average: Show the mean of the numeric values in the column. (Because the term "average" is sometimes used to mean different things, let's be explicit: here, it means the total of the numeric values divided by the number of numeric values.)
- Count: Show how many values are in the column.
- Count Nums: Show how many *numeric* values are in the column. If your column contains 12, 8, B, 27, 365 and Fred, Count Nums returns 4.

- Max: Show the largest numeric value in the column.
- Min: Show the smallest numeric value in the column.
- Sum: Show the total of the numeric values in the column. This is the default total for a column with numeric values.
- StdDev: Show the standard deviation of the numeric values in the column. I've been using Excel for over 20 years, including the years since Excel 2003 was released, and I've *never* seen anyone use the Total option for standard deviation on a list.
- Var: Show the variance (the square of the standard deviation) of the numeric values in the column. Getting the variance of a list's column is even rarer than the standard deviation. Okay, that's less than zero, but you know what I mean.

Totals in the Status Bar

These options go a little farther than the options you can get from the Status Bar. What's the Status Bar got to do with it? Well, first, the Status Bar is the horizontal bar at the bottom of the Excel window, the one that's normally just beneath the sheet tabs, with the word "Ready" at its left. Figure 1-20 shows the Status Bar.

Ready	CAPS NUM SCRL

Figure 1-20: If you put a toolbar at the bottom of the Excel window, it will separate the worksheet tabs from the Status Bar.

The Status Bar can tell you some useful things. Notice in Figure 1-20 that these abbreviations appear on the status bar:

- CAPS
- NUM
- SCRL

They mean that at the time the figure was created, Caps Lock was on, Num Lock was on, and Scroll Lock was on. It's a quick way to tell what keyboard options you've selected. When I press 9 on my keyboard's numeric keypad, and the Excel window scrolls up a page, instead of putting **9** in the active cell, a quick glance at the Scroll Bar tells me that I forgot to turn on Num Lock.

But that's incidental to what we're talking about. Try this:

1. Select a group of cells that contain some numbers — cells that are adjacent and in the same column (B1:B5, for example), or the same row (maybe B2:F2), or that are in a range such as C10:F16. (This step isn't really necessary but it makes things a little clearer.)

2. Right-click anywhere on the Status Bar. You'll see a menu pop up, with the names of various totals you can choose from.

3. Choose one of the totals — say, Max. The maximum number in the group of cells you selected in Step 1 appears in the Status Bar.

The same sort of thing happens if you choose any of the six options in the menu you saw in Step 2. So, what's to choose from if you want a total from a list (by using the Data → List command, discussed in the prior section) or to see it on the Status Bar? There are two points to choose from:

- You don't have as many options on the Status Bar. The list totals give you the standard deviation and the variance. Like me, you might not regard this as a compelling reason to use a list for calculating measures of dispersion.
- Using the Status Bar, your data don't have to be laid out in a list. The numbers can be scattered all over the sheet. If you take a notion that you want the total of 2006 revenue, 2005 inventory turns, and 2003 EBITDA, just make sure you've selected Sum for the Status Bar totals (Step 3, above) and then select the cells, one by one, wherever they are on the worksheet.

TIP: To select several cells that are not adjacent, hold down the Ctrl key as you click in the cells.

Getting Rid of a List

By "getting rid of a list," I don't mean the data; just the bells and whistles that Excel adds when you use Create List. On either the List toolbar or in the menu you get by choosing Data → List, you'll find a Convert to Range command. All this item does is remove the drop-down arrows, border, and so on — items it added when you used Data → List → Create List.

Using the Data Form

In Excel, a *data form* is a special kind of window that opens in response to something you do, such as clicking a custom button. The data form pops up and someone starts entering data. When he or she is through, the data is saved on a worksheet. Figure 1-21 shows this situation.

	A	B	C	D	E	F	G	H
1	Year	Region	Product	Sales				
2	2003	Northeast	Area rugs	$47,924.49				
3	2005	Northeast	Area rugs	$21,798.71				
4	2006	Northeast	Area rugs	$11,825.77				
5	2004	Northeast	Placemats	$19,378.49				
6	2004	Northeast	Slipcovers	$14,799.90				
7	2004	Northeast	Slipcovers	$36,402.82				
8	2005	Northeast	Slipcovers	$ 6,429.15				
9	2003	Northeast	Towels	$46,287.41				
10	2005	Northeast	Towels	$ 2,544.17				
11	2006	Northeast	Towels	$53,738.05				
12	2004	Northwest	Placemats	$44,967.32				
13	2004	Northwest	Slipcovers	$41,433.59				
14	2005	Northwest	Tablecloths	$43,008.21				
15	2006	Northwest	Tablecloths	$12,167.81				
16	2007	Northwest	Tablecloths	$20,743.80				
17	2004	Northwest	Towels	$58,221.64				
18	2006	Northwest	Towels	$43,009.28				
19	2003	Southeast	Area rugs	$11,635.33				
20	2006	Southeast	Area rugs	$34,752.22				
21	2003	Southeast	Placemats	$40,304.51				

Enter Sales Data

Year: 2007

Product
- ⦿ Towels   ○ Area rugs   ○ Placemats
- ○ Tablecloths   ○ Slipcovers

Region
- ⦿ NW   ○ NE   Sales: |
- ○ SW   ○ SE   [OK] [Cancel]

Enter New Data

Figure 1-21: A moderately experienced developer can develop a form like this in just a few minutes.

What you see in Figure 1-21 is a *custom data form*. It's one that someone experienced in Excel constructs and ties to a worksheet, so that when the user hits the OK button, Excel takes the data in the form and writes it to the sheet. There are plenty of good reasons to arrange the entry of data with a data form. For example:

- Checking the data on the form for validity
- Displaying some fields (or some records) for certain users, and other fields or records for other users — usually in a context that requires different levels of security

• Situations where there are so many fields that it's clumsy to display them all on one form and several tabs are needed. (Excel's Options form is one example.)

An experienced developer can create and test the form shown in Figure 1-21 in no time. But Excel provides you with a built-in Data Form that offers some of the functionality of a custom form. Figure 1-22 shows how the Data Form looks with a list I've used extensively in this chapter. In this case, because the custom form in Figure 1-21 is pretty rudimentary, the Data Form in Figure 1-22 has much *more* functionality than does the custom form.

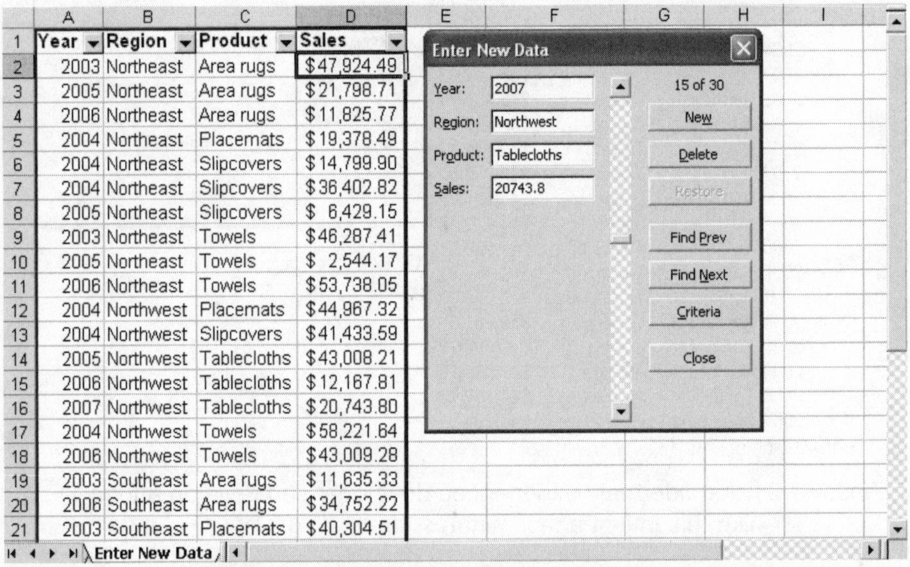

Figure 1-22: The Data Form's name, on its title bar, is by default the same as the name of the active worksheet.

Before looking at the individual capabilities, notice how difficult it is to create the form:

1. Click in a cell in your list.

2. Choose Form from the Data menu.

That's all that's needed to get the form you see in Figure 1-22. It's a good way to impress someone who doesn't know that Excel can do this for you.

Now, here's what you or your data entry person can do with the data form:

- You can tell how many records are in your list, and which record is active, by looking just above the New button.
- Move through the records using the scroll bar (just left of the buttons).
- Establish a new record at the bottom of the list by clicking New.
- Delete the current record by clicking Delete.
- Revert to original values that you've edited in the current record, by clicking Restore. The Restore button is dimmed until you make a change to a value. You can't Restore a record that you've Deleted. (Instead, close the data form, and then close the workbook. *Do not* save changes when you're prompted. Lastly, re-open the workbook.)
- Go to the prior record, by clicking Find Prev (short for *previous*). If you have established selection criteria by clicking the Criteria button, this takes you to the closest prior record that qualifies according to the criteria.
- Go to the next record, by clicking Find Next. The criteria act in the same way as with Find Prev, except that Find Next takes you to the following qualifying record.
- Establish selection criteria, also known as *filters*, by clicking the Criteria button.
- Close the Data Form by clicking the Close button.

If you click the Criteria button, you see something very similar to the data form; the main difference is that the boxes will be empty. Type the values that you want to select in the appropriate boxes: for example, to select the Northwest region and the Towels product, type Northwest into the Region box and Towels into the Product box.

Chapter 2

Pivot Tables

The Purpose of Pivot Tables

Getting Data Summaries

Building Pivot Tables

Too Much Information: The Data Cache

Using Named Ranges as Data Sources

Now that you've taken a look at lists, as Excel defines them, you're ready to start putting them to work as sources of data. Chapter 1 mentioned some of the ways that you can use lists to set up financial analyses that are more sophisticated than just looking at transactions. One of those ways is by means of a pivot table. A pivot table is *the most powerful and flexible* method of data analysis and synthesis available in Excel.

The Purpose of Pivot Tables

We're often confronted with a mass of data that probably has some interesting patterns in it — but there's so much detail that it's almost impossible to tell the forest from the trees. A 50-page detail report of expenses by cost center is hard enough to deal with, but it can become a real headache if someone needs to total up the costs by vendor.

That's the sort of thing that pivot tables are intended to do for you. You build a pivot table on a set of detail records, and Excel summarizes the data in whatever way you specify. Any field in the data — for example, cost center, vendor, PO number, invoice month, and so on — can be used to summarize the information.

And the pivot table can be thought of as either an ad hoc report, ideal for data snooping, or a standard periodic summary. You can change the summary categories from, say, month of the year to another variable such as vendor name just by dragging a button on the worksheet. Your summaries can be any statistic you wish, although it's likely that you'll find yourself arranging for sums, counts and averages more often than the others available.

Since Excel 2000, pivot tables have come with another feature, pivot charts. Although pivot charts have some useful features, they tend to be less flexible than standard Excel charts, and therefore this book does not cover pivot charts in much detail. I believe that you'll be a good bit better served if you base standard Excel charts on pivot tables, as shown in Chapter 4, than if you use pivot charts.

You might have noticed that I'm referring here to "pivot tables," not "PivotTables." The latter usage, which jams the two words together, is a neologism brought to you by Microsoft. They're a Microsoft product and Microsoft can call their products whatever they want. But I don't have to compound the felony, and I think that "PivotTable" is jarring, and this book calls them "pivot tables."

I may as well be up front about this: I'm a big fan of using pivot tables to analyze information such as financials and operational data. Pivot tables have some problems, including a few that make me nuts (for example, recent versions of Excel have *forced* the user into pivot charts if they want to show pivot data summaries graphically). But I think you'll find, if you haven't already, that pivot tables' advantages outweigh their drawbacks by a long chalk.

There are so many advantages, in fact, that I'm going to spend the first several sections of this chapter describing some of them, before I get into the issue of actually building a pivot table. So, if you're impatient to get on with it, skip to the section named Building Pivot Tables.

Getting Data Summaries

As part of its discussion of lists in Excel, Chapter 1 discussed data summaries, or *totals*. I don't much care for the term "totals," because it implies summation. In ordinary English, when you total some things, you add them up. So, although Excel's developers and marketers probably found the term "total" convenient, it's misleading. There's much more you can do with what I'll call *summaries* than just look at numeric totals.

Data Summaries

A data summary isn't part of how the structure of a pivot table is defined. It *is* the way that you choose to look at the data in the pivot table. The pivot table in Figure 2-1 is one in which the user has chosen to look at numeric totals — the data will look familiar to you if you've worked your way through Chapter 1's material on lists.

	A	B	C	D	E	F	G	H	I
1	Sum of Sales								
2	Region ▼	Total							
3	Northeast	$ 261,128.96							
4	Northwest	$ 263,551.65							
5	Southeast	$ 128,982.68							
6	Southwest	$ 233,002.00							
7	Grand Total	$ 886,665.29							
8									
9									
10									

Regional Sales Totals

Figure 2-1: This pivot table shows the sum of the sales for each region.

Sometimes you'll be interested in the *average* of the sales for each region (or product, or accounting period, or sales manager, or whatever). Figure 2-2 shows the difference due to looking at averages instead of sums.

Notice that the pivot tables shown in Figures 2-1 and 2-2 don't differ in structure. They both show information about sales dollars according to sales region, and each region appears in a different row of the pivot table. The main difference between the two pivot tables is that one shows sales dollars as sums, and the other shows sales dollars as averages.

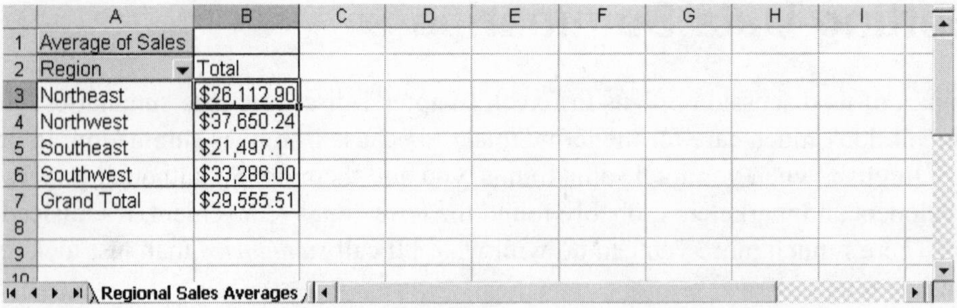

	A	B	C	D	E	F	G	H	I
1	Average of Sales								
2	Region ▼	Total							
3	Northeast	$26,112.90							
4	Northwest	$37,650.24							
5	Southeast	$21,497.11							
6	Southwest	$33,286.00							
7	Grand Total	$29,555.51							
8									
9									
10									

Ⅰ ◀ ▶ ▶Ⅰ \ Regional Sales Averages / ◀

Figure 2-2: The structure of the pivot table is unchanged by showing averages rather than sums.

Besides sums and averages, there are several other summaries that you can choose. In the context of reporting sales figures on a region-by-region basis, these other summaries are listed below.

- Count: The number of values that Excel finds in the data source. Continuing the current example, the pivot table could show you the number of records for each region. This summary does not distinguish between numeric and other types of values, such as text.
- Max and Min: The largest (or the smallest) numeric value that Excel finds. In this case, you would see the numerically largest sales value recorded for each region, or the smallest, depending on whether you choose Max or Min.
- Product: The product of all the values Excel finds for a given region. Not to say that one doesn't exist, but I've never seen this summary put to a good use.
- Count Nums: The number of *numeric* values found for each region. But if you have a mix of numeric values and other types of values in the same field — which is the only reason for using Count Nums — then there is some question whether you've defined the field properly.
- StDev and StDevp: The standard deviation of, in the present example, the sales figures found for each region. There's an argument for getting these summaries if you're developing a *confidence interval* on sales for each region, or if you're preparing a statistical process control analysis (most often used in manufacturing applications). The difference between StDev and StDevp depends on whether you regard the values as coming from a sample (use StDev) or a population (use StDevp).

- Var and Varp: Var is the square of StDev, and Varp is the square of StDevp. Both are measures of the variance of a set of numbers. It's possible to argue that these summaries would be useful if you're working on an Analysis of Variance. But it's a stretch.

These data summaries apply only to the field that you choose to treat as a *data field*. A pivot table's structure consists not only of data fields, but also of *row fields*, *column fields*, and *page fields*.

We've established that the data summary you choose doesn't determine the structure of the pivot table. In Figures 2-1 and 2-2, for example, all the information is in the same cells; the only difference is the summary values that appear in cells B3:B6. What *does* make a difference to a pivot table's structure is how you use row fields and column fields.

Row Fields

A pivot table's row field contains a different value in each row, and the pivot table reserves one row for the field's name. So, in Figure 2-2, the row field occupies cells A3:A6, with the Region field's name in cell A2. The values you see in cells A3:A6 are called *items*.

A pivot table can handle thousands of items (the upper limit has increased with every release since Excel 95). In theory, you could have a field called Age In Weeks, which could take on every value from 1 to, say, 4680, and it could be a field in a pivot table, with one row for each week. Of course, while there might be a situation in which you would want to see a summary value for each of 4680 items in a field, it's hard to imagine a realistic one.

NOTE: *There's another type of field that you can put in a pivot table called a column field, discussed in its own section later in this chapter. Instead of a different item in each row, a column field has a different item in each column. Virtually all of what this section says about row fields applies to column fields as well. However, because of the way we're used to viewing tables, it's usual to put things such as subtotals in their own rows rather than in their own columns, and that implies the use of a row field rather than a column field.*

Multiple Row Fields

A pivot table such as the one shown in Figure 2-2 can give you a good, quick overview of your data (and you can also use it for a giggle test: if you can look at the pivot table without giggling, chances are that you've acquired and accounted for the underlying transactions correctly). Often, though, you're interested in more than just one field. Figure 2-3 shows a pivot table that summarizes Sales by Region *and* by Product.

	A	B	C
1	Sum of Sales		
2	Region	Product	Total
3	Northeast	Area rugs	$ 81,548.97
4		Placemats	$ 19,378.49
5		Slipcovers	$ 57,631.87
6		Towels	$ 102,569.63
7	Northeast Total		$ 261,128.96
8	Northwest	Placemats	$ 44,967.32
9		Slipcovers	$ 41,433.59
10		Tablecloths	$ 75,919.82
11		Towels	$ 101,230.92
12	Northwest Total		$ 263,551.65
13	Southeast	Area rugs	$ 46,387.55
14		Placemats	$ 46,527.86
15		Slipcovers	$ 31,901.87
16		Tablecloths	
17	Southeast Total		$ 124,817.28
18	Southwest	Area rugs	$ 1,028.55
19		Placemats	$ 32,322.12
20		Slipcovers	$ 28,512.82
21		Tablecloths	$ 43,836.76
22		Towels	$ 127,301.75
23	Southwest Total		$ 233,002.00
24		Area rugs Sum	$ 128,965.07
25		Placemats Sum	$ 143,195.79
26		Slipcovers Sum	$ 159,480.15
27		Tablecloths Sum	$ 119,756.58
28		Towels Sum	$ 331,102.30
29	Grand Total		$ 882,499.89
30			

Product Sales within Region

Figure 2-3: Notice that Region now has subtotals, identical to the regional totals in Figure 2-1.

With the Regional subtotals, you can see both the total for the Product within the Region, and the total for the Region. I'll get into this issue more in the section on building pivot tables, but for now you should know that:

- Excel provides subtotals automatically when you call for two or more row fields. The automatic subtotals are for the outer row field or fields (in Figure 2-3, that's Region).
- The default subtotal is Sum (for most numeric fields; the default is Count for a field that has even one text or date value), but you can get any summary statistic listed above in the section titled Data Summaries.
- You can suppress subtotals entirely if you want, and this can be best if you're basing a chart on a pivot table.
- Subtotals are not automatic for the innermost row field (in Figure 2-3, that's Product). You can, however, get what Excel calls *block totals* for the innermost field. Figure 2-3 gives an example, in cells C24:C28.

Sorting a Row Field's Items

Many of the tasks you handle with values that are stored on the worksheet in the normal fashion can also be done with data in a pivot table. But you usually have to take a somewhat different route if you're using a pivot table's fields.

One example is sorting. To sort values in, say, a list, you select a cell in the list and choose Sort from the Data menu (see Chapter 1 for more information.) But you take a different approach, depending on the Excel version you're using, to sorting items in a pivot table. Figures 2-4 and 2-5 show how this is done.

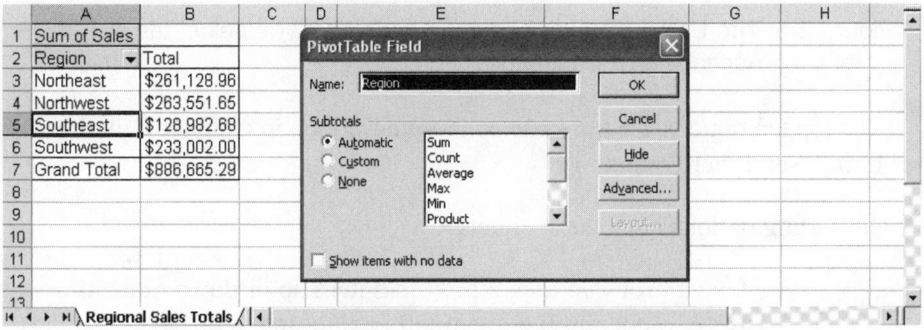

Figure 2-4: You can take care of several pivot field tasks by starting with Field Settings.

1. Right-click any cell in a row field (or in a column field or page field, which I talk about later on in this chapter). Do *not* select a data field first if you want to set sorting or top ten options.

2. Select Field Settings from the shortcut menu.

3. The PivotTable Field dialog box appears, as shown in Figure 2-4. Click the Advanced button.

4. Figure 2-5 shows your options as to sorting and top ten settings. Select the options you prefer and click OK.

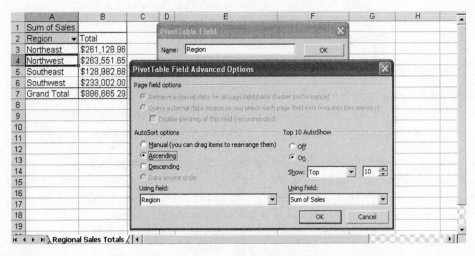

Figure 2-5: The Using Field dropdown is enabled if you select the Ascending or Descending sort.

(The top ten options are the same as those described in Chapter 1, in the section titled Using AutoFilter Options.)

The sorting options have these effects:

- *Manual.* You can drag a row field item up or down into a different row (or a column field item left or right into a different column). The associated data field items will follow their row field item. All you have to do is click a row field item, move your cursor over the cell's top or bottom edge, hold down the mouse button and drag.

- *Ascending*. The row field items will sort themselves automatically in ascending order. If you add a new record to the pivot table's data source, and that new record contains a row item not yet in the pivot table, Excel adds it to the pivot table in ascending row field order (but not immediately: see the section on the Data Cache later in this chapter).
- *Descending*. This option has the same effect as choosing Ascending, except that the order in which the items appear in the pivot table is reversed.

The Using Field dropdown is disabled unless you choose the Ascending or the Descending sort option. Then, it becomes enabled, and you can choose which field — either the selected row field or the data field — to use as your sort key.

NOTE: *If you choose to use the data field as the sort key, Excel will sort by the data field's grand total across columns.*

To summarize your sorting options:

- You can sort manually, by dragging a row field item.
- You can sort automatically, either ascending or descending.
- If you choose to sort automatically, the sort key can be either a row field (e.g., 2000, 2001, 2002, etc.) or a data field (e.g., $50,285.17 , $170,545.02, $180,907.69, etc.)

TIP: *You can also sort a pivot table by selecting a row field item and choosing Sort from the Data menu. However, if you do it that way, the field will not automatically re-sort when it encounters new data.*

Grouping Row Values

What if you want to use a *numeric* variable as a row field? So far, this chapter's examples have used text variables as row fields: Northwest and Southeast, for example, are items in the Region field, and the Product field has items like Towels and Placemats.

But you might have an interest in an analysis that uses Sales as a row variable. For example, you might want to know how many records in the underlying data source have between $0 and $10,000 in sales, between $10,000 and $20,000, and so on.

But Sales is a numeric variable, and can easily have thousands of distinct values — you don't want a pivot table to give you a different row field item for each distinct value of sales dollars.

The solution is to *group* on the numeric field Sales so as to create categories of values. Figure 2-6 shows a pivot table with the row field Sales first ungrouped, and then grouped.

	A	B	C	D	E	F	G	H	
1	Sum of Sales			Sum of Sales					
2	Sales ▾	Total		Sales ▾	Total				
3	$ 1,028.55	$ 1,028.55		1028.55-11028.55	$ 20,390.62				
4	$ 2,544.17	$ 2,544.17		11028.55-21028.55	$ 90,551.10				
5	$ 4,165.40	$ 4,165.40		21028.55-31028.55	$ 50,311.53				
6	$ 6,223.35	$ 6,223.35		31028.55-41028.55	$ 210,439.49				
7	$ 6,429.15	$ 6,429.15		41028.55-51028.55	$ 403,012.86				
8	$ 11,635.33	$ 11,635.33		51028.55-61028.55	$ 111,959.69				
9	$ 11,825.77	$ 11,825.77		Grand Total	$ 886,665.29				
10	$ 12,167.81	$ 12,167.81							
11	$ 14,799.90	$ 14,799.90							
12	$ 19,378.49	$ 19,378.49							
13	$ 20,743.80	$ 20,743.80							
14	$ 21,798.71	$ 21,798.71							
15	$ 28,512.92	$ 28,512.92							

Figure 2-6: The first pivot table's analysis is completely redundant.

See the section named Grouping on a Purely Numeric Field, later in this chapter, for information on how to make the grouped pivot table more readable, and interpretable, than it is in Figure 2-6.

NOTE: *It's unfortunate, but when you group on a numeric field that would normally have a special format such as Currency or Accounting, the dollar signs and the thousands separators are lost in the process of grouping. (What actually happens is that the numeric values are converted to text labels such as 10000-20000, and Excel isn't sophisticated enough to apply the numeric format to a text value.)*

There are other grouping methods available for a numeric row field. For example, dates and times are numeric fields in Excel. Figure 2-7 has another pair of before-and-after pivot tables that show how you could group individual dates into months.

	A	B	C	D	E	F	G	H	I	
1	Sum of Sales									
2	Sales Date ▼	Total								
3	1/15/2007	$47,924.49								
18	7/21/2007	$31,901.87		Sum of Sales						
19	7/27/2007	$27,172.95		Sales Date ▼	Total					
20	7/31/2007	$19,378.49		Jan	$47,924.49					
21	8/1/2007	$44,967.32		Feb	$84,444.17					
22	8/5/2007	$34,752.22		Mar	$132,764.84					
23	8/7/2007	$21,798.71		Apr	$57,424.76					
24	8/31/2007	$34,755.95		May	$36,402.82					
25	9/11/2007	$28,512.82		Jun	$93,068.32					
26	9/15/2007	$46,287.41		Jul	$78,453.31					
27	10/17/2007	$43,009.28		Aug	$136,274.20					
28	10/18/2007	$40,304.51		Sep	$74,800.23					
29	10/21/2007	$2,544.17		Oct	$85,857.96					
30	11/6/2007	$58,221.64		Nov	$59,250.19					
31	11/20/2007	$1,028.55		Grand Total	$886,665.29					
32	Grand Total	$886,665.29								
33										

Ⅰ ◄ ► Ⅰ \ Monthly Sales ⁄ | ◄

Figure 2-7: Compare, for example, the two September sales in the first
pivot table with the one grouped value in the second.

There are plenty of ways to aggregate dates and times — for example, by some number of days that you specify (such as seven for a weekly analysis), or by quarter, or by year, or by month within year, and so on. And you can combine the grouping factors: for example, quarter within year.

TIP: *One problem with the grouping feature is that it can't handle missing data. If you have dates as your row field's items, and if even one of them is missing, Excel will display the error message* Cannot Group That Selection. *There's no help for it, other than to delete the record with the missing value, or to make a value up. If you do either one of those, start over with a new pivot table: the old pivot table will remember that there was a problem, and won't believe you even if you make up a value and refresh the data cache (see the section on the Data Cache).*

Pivoting a Pivot Table

This book hasn't yet discussed what's pivotal about a pivot table. The term "pivot table" is more marketing hype than functional description, but it's true that pivot tables can and do pivot.

> *TIP*: Excel and Microsoft insist on the term "pivottable" without the space. If you're looking up a pivot table's attributes in a Help document, or at a Microsoft web site, you might want to search both for "pivot table" and "pivottable".

Figure 2-8 shows a pivot table, before and after pivoting.

	A	B	C	D	E	F	G	H	I	J
1	Sum of Sales			Sum of Sales	Region ▾					
2	Region ▾	Total			Northeast	Northwest	Southeast	Southwest	Grand Total	
3	Northeast	$ 261,128.96		Total	$ 261,128.96	$ 263,551.65	$ 128,982.68	$ 233,002.00	$ 886,665.29	
4	Northwest	$ 263,551.65								
5	Southeast	$ 128,982.68								
6	Southwest	$ 233,002.00								
7	Grand Total	$ 886,665.29								
8										

◄ ► ►I \ Regional Sales / ◄ |

Figure 2-8: The second pivot table is identical to the first, but the row field has been *pivoted* so that it's a column field.

Figure 2-8 is shown only to introduce the notion of pivoting a pivot table. You would seldom create a pivot table with a row field and then pivot the table so that it became a column field (unless you're using Excel 97 and you want to group a column field: if so, first group it as a row field and then pivot it so it's a column field).

To pivot the table as shown in Figure 2-8, you would take these steps:

1. Move your mouse pointer over cell A2, labeled Region. The pointer turns to crossed double-arrows.

2. Hold down the mouse button and drag the Region label to the right of cell A1, labeled Sum of Sales.

3. Release the mouse button. When you do so, the table pivots.

In fact, the pivot capability is not one that you'll have much use for. On rare occasions, I've had reason to pivot a table, to change it from a table with two row fields to one with a row field and a column field (see Figure 2-9 for an example), but the only other reason I can recall had to do with creating a figure for a book.

	A	B	C	D	E	F	G	H	I
1	Sum of Sales	Region ▼							
2	Year ▼	Northeast	Northwest	Southeast	Southwest	Grand Total			
3	2003	$ 94,211.90		$ 51,939.84	$ 34,755.95	$180,907.69			
4	2004	$ 70,581.21	$144,622.55	$ 36,067.27		$251,271.03			
5	2005	$ 30,772.03	$ 43,008.21	$ 6,223.35	$ 90,541.43	$170,545.02			
6	2006	$ 65,563.82	$ 55,177.09	$ 34,752.22	$ 78,163.25	$233,656.38			
7	2007		$ 20,743.80		$ 29,541.37	$ 50,285.17			
8	Grand Total	$261,128.96	$263,551.65	$128,982.68	$233,002.00	$886,665.29			
9									

H ◄ ► H \ Annual Sales by Region ∕ ◄

Figure 2-9: The blank cells represent missing data: for example, the
Northeast region had no sales during 2007 .

It's true that pivoting a table has limited usefulness, but there are plenty of good reasons to plan the design of a pivot table as shown in Figure 2-9. That structure can be more informative visually, and it turns out to be a good way to design a table for use with Excel's Lookup functions, such as VLOOKUP.

Column Fields

Column fields give you the same functionality that you get with row fields: they're just oriented so that each item occupies a different column, instead of a different row. In particular, with both types of field you get:

- Subtotals (optional, and recommended only if you have more than one column field, or more than one row field)
- Grouping
- Sorts and Top Ten

The main differences between column fields and row fields are their orientation on the worksheet, and the relatively small number of columns on the worksheet available to handle a column field's items.

The choice of whether to orient a field as a row field or a column field is usually a matter of personal preference, and it might depend on the kind of data in the field. For example, suppose that the field in question contains dates or times. We're accustomed to seeing dates and times progress from left to right in tables and charts, so you might decide to arrange the pivot table so that, say, January's dollars appear in Column B, February's in Column C, March's in Column D and so on, as in Figure

2-10. (Yes, you could use a data table in the chart, but it wouldn't be formatted as currency.)

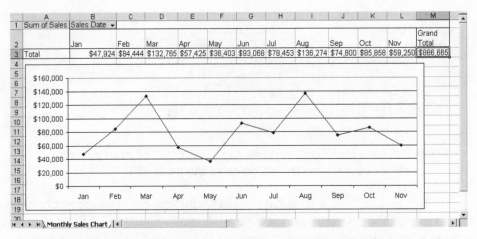

Figure 2-10: Your figures *could* be in rows instead of columns, but the chart is easier to compare to the worksheet data with this orientation.

Another reason to orient a field as a column rather than as a row is that you might have two fields to show, and you'd like to use one as a row field and the other as a column field, as shown previously in Figure 2-9.

TIP: You can make a pivot table as complicated as you wish. For example, it's entirely possible to build one that has multiple row fields and multiple column fields. But always keep in mind the needs and capabilities of your clients. A lot of good research done during the 1970s showed that a user's ability to mentally process the data in a table plummets with every added layer of complexity.

Page Fields

A *page field* in a pivot table is a structural element, as are row fields and column fields. But its use is conceptually different: you use a page field to select which records the pivot table will display. Figure 2-11 shows an example of three pivot tables. Each has a page field, Year, and each uses the page field differently: one shows all records, one shows only the records from 2006, and one shows only those from 2007.

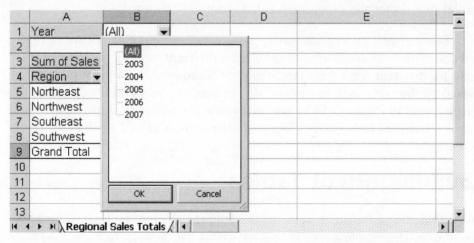

	A	B	C	D	E	F	G	H	I
1	Year	(All) ▼		Year	2006 ▼		Year	2007 ▼	
2									
3	Sum of Sales			Sum of Sales			Sum of Sales		
4	Region ▼	Total		Region ▼	Total		Region ▼	Total	
5	Northeast	$ 261,128.96		Northeast	$ 65,563.82		Northwest	$ 20,743.80	
6	Northwest	$ 263,551.65		Northwest	$ 55,177.09		Southwest	$ 29,541.37	
7	Southeast	$ 128,982.68		Southeast	$ 34,752.22		Grand Total	$ 50,285.17	
8	Southwest	$ 233,002.00		Southwest	$ 78,163.25				
9	Grand Total	$ 886,665.29		Grand Total	$ 233,656.38				
10									

Regional Sales by Year

Figure 2-11: You use a page field to filter for only those records that belong to a particular item in that field.

As I mentioned in Chapter 1, even though you can use lists and Excel's filters to analyze one field in terms of another field, your first thought in these situations should be of pivot tables. They make it very easy for you to focus on one item of a field, if you treat that field as a page field. All you have to do to change from one item to another is use the page field's dropdown arrow (see Figure 2-12).

	A	B	C	D	E	
1	Year	(All) ▼				
2			(All)			
3	Sum of Sales		2003			
4	Region ▼		2004			
5	Northeast		2005			
6	Northwest		2006			
7	Southeast		2007			
8	Southwest					
9	Grand Total					
10						
11						
12			OK	Cancel		
13						

Regional Sales Totals

Figure 2-12: Select the item you want to filter for and then click OK.

You can use more than one page field at once, as seen in Figure 2-13.

	A	B	C	D	E	F	G	H	
1	Product	Towels ▾							
2	Year	2006 ▾							
3									
4	Sum of Sales								
5	Region ▾	Total							
6	Northeast	$ 53,738.05							
7	Northwest	$ 43,009.28							
8	Southwest	$ 45,841.13							
9	Grand Total	$ 142,588.46							
10									

◄ ◄ ► ►◄ \ Region Totals by Product, Year / | ◄

Figure 2-13: The page fields act as though they were connected by
ANDs.

In Figure 2-13, you see the sales of Towels during 2006 in each Region
for which qualifying records exist..

In my own business, I have several clients who want to see financials, particularly operating expenses, on a monthly basis — but they prefer not to have
to manipulate a pivot table's page fields to choose a date range. So we provide
an Excel workbook for each fiscal year, with a different worksheet for each
month. On each worksheet is a pivot table (and a chart based on that pivot
table) that shows the expenses for that month.

Some clients appreciate this approach, because they don't care to fool
around with drop-down arrows to select a different date range: it's easier to
select a different worksheet tab. However, although all the pivot tables are
based on the same data source, we do not base the pivot tables on one another
(look ahead to Figure 2-14 to see how you'd get a start on doing that). The reason is discussed later in this chapter, in the section named Page Field
Problems.

Building Pivot Tables

Now that you've looked at some of the features of pivot tables, it's time to
build one. The simplest way is to start with a list, as seen in Figure 2-14.

In Figure 2-14, you see the list that several pivot table examples in this chapter are based on. To build a pivot table from that list, take these steps:

1. Click any cell in the list. This step isn't necessary but it makes things easier.

2. Choose PivotTable and PivotChart Report from the Data menu to start the Pivot Table Wizard.

3. For this example, accept the default choices of Microsoft Excel List or Database, and PivotTable. Click Next to see the wizard's second step.

4. In Figure 2-15, notice that the list's address appears in the Range box. If you begin by selecting a cell in the list, Excel finds its boundaries for you; otherwise, you have to supply the address yourself. Verify the address and click Next to go the third and final step of the wizard, shown in Figure 2-16.

5. You'll often want a pivot table to appear on a new worksheet, to avoid the visual clutter of the list, so just click Finish. (But see a Tip on that topic later in this chapter.)

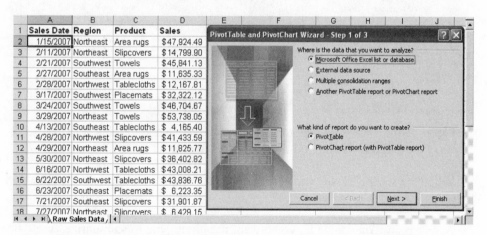

Figure 2-14: You need a list structure if you want to build a pivot table from figures on a worksheet.

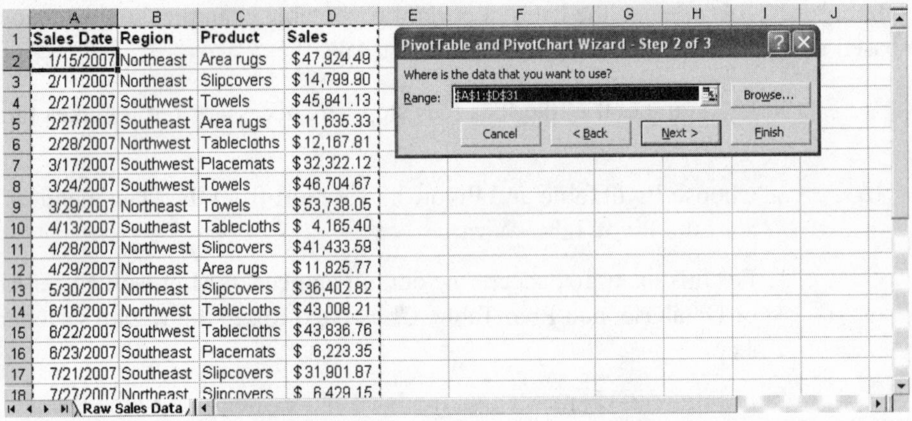

Figure 2-15: This is why it's smart to start by selecting a cell in the list.

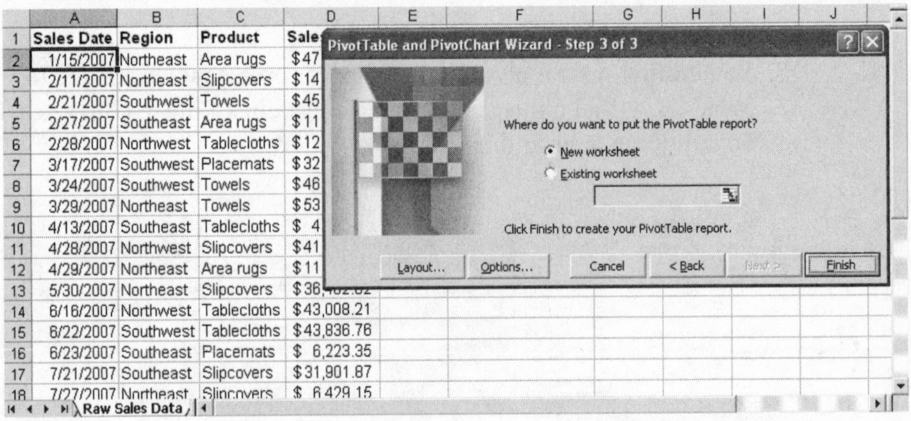

Figure 2-16: Click the Layout button if you're more comfortable with the Excel 97 method of designing the pivot table.

When the wizard closes you see the table schematic and the field list shown in Figure 2-17.

At this point you decide how you want the pivot table to summarize your data. Suppose that you wanted to view the sum of sales dollars for each of four regions. In that case:

1. Click and drag the Region button in the PivotTable Field List box into the area on the worksheet labeled Drop Row Fields Here.

2. Click and drag the Sales button from the PivotTable Field List box into the area on the worksheet labeled Drop Data Items Here.

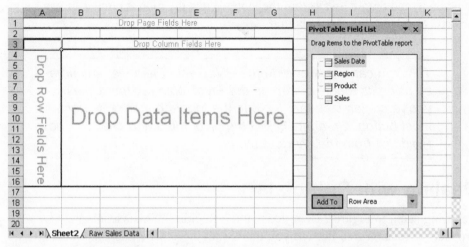

Figure 2-17: The schematic for the pivot table appears on the work-sheet (prior to Excel 2000, it was on a dialog box).

TIP: *The moment that you drag a field into the Data area, Excel assumes that you're through designing the table and it removes the schematic from the worksheet. It's usually a good idea to add row fields (and column and page fields too, if you're using them) before you put a field in the Data area.*

Creating Multiple Row Fields

Earlier in this chapter (specifically, in Figure 2-3), I showed a pivot table that breaks down Sales dollars by Region *and* by Product. That's easy to do: after adding Region, and while the PivotTable Field List box is still open, take these steps:

1. Click the Product button.

2. Make sure that Row Area appears in the dropdown at the bottom of PivotTable Field List box.

3. Click the Add To button.

If you prefer, you can add any field to the pivot table by means of the Add To button, rather than dragging a button onto the table schematic. However, if you want to remove a field from a pivot table, it's best to click the grey button with the field's name on it, and drag it away from the table. When the mouse pointer grows a stylized red X, release the mouse button.

TIP: *You can show or hide the PivotTable Field List any time by using its toggle button on the PivotTable toolbar. Unless you've customized that toolbar, the toggle button is its rightmost button. Or, right-click in the pivot table and choose Show Field List from the shortcut menu.*

Dealing with Subtotals

Referring again to Figure 2-3, notice that the Region field has a subtotal across Product for each Region item. If you don't want those subtotals, take these steps:

1. Select any Region item, such as Northwest, and click the Field Settings button on the pivot table toolbar. Or, you can right-click any Region item and choose Field Settings from the shortcut menu.

2. The PivotTable Field dialog box shown in Figure 2-18 appears.

3. Click the None button under Subtotals, and then click OK.

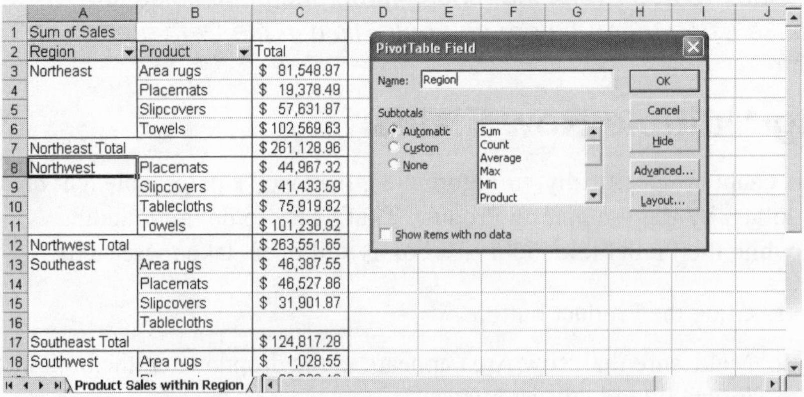

Figure 2-18: Some of the buttons in the dialog box differ if you start by selecting a Data field.

> *TIP: If you are going to base an Excel chart on a pivot table (that's different from building a pivot chart), you should probably first remove the pivot table's subtotals.*

Of course, you can also use the PivotTable Field dialog to reset subtotals to Automatic. *Automatic* in this context means that if the Data field is exclusively numeric, the subtotal summary defaults to Sum. If there's even one text value in the Data field, the subtotal summary defaults to Count.

> *TIP: I don't think you're going to have much use for this, but just so you know: When you choose the Custom subtotal button, you can select the subtotal summary that you want to use: Sum, Count, Average, etc.*

Grouping Numeric Fields

Earlier, in this chapter's section called Grouping Row Values, I mentioned that you can cause a pivot table to group numeric values into categories that are useful for analysis. (It helps to remember that you group those values *after* you've built the pivot table.) This section shows you how to do that.

Grouping on a Purely Numeric Field

Suppose that you want to take a look at the number of sales a company makes, according to the sales revenue for each sale. Using the list shown earlier in Figure 2-14, you could use the pivot table wizard just as described in this section, except that you would treat the Sales field in the list as both a row field and a data field.

> *TIP: This approach, using the same field as both a row field and a data field, is a good way to familiarize yourself with a new set of transactions. For example, I often look at the count of various items by using something such as Product as a row field and also as a data field, with the summary set to Count.*

A pivot table with a row field that has individual numeric items — especially sales or cost figures — is often uninformative. You can learn more if you take these steps:

1. Right-click any cell in the row field.

2. From the shortcut menu, choose Group and Show Detail (your version of Excel might show Group and Outline instead) and choose Group from the submenu.

3. You'll see the Grouping dialog box shown in Figure 2-19. The quickest move now is to accept the default values and click OK. If you do, you'll see the pivot table shown in Figure 2-20.

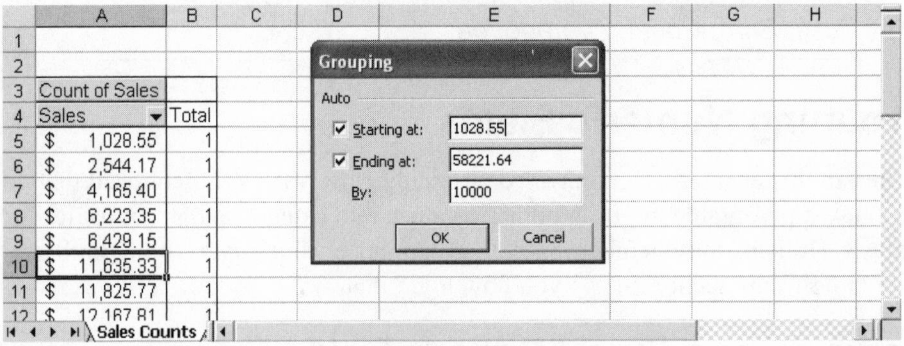

Figure 2-19: If the checkboxes are filled, Excel figures the minimum and maximum values for you.

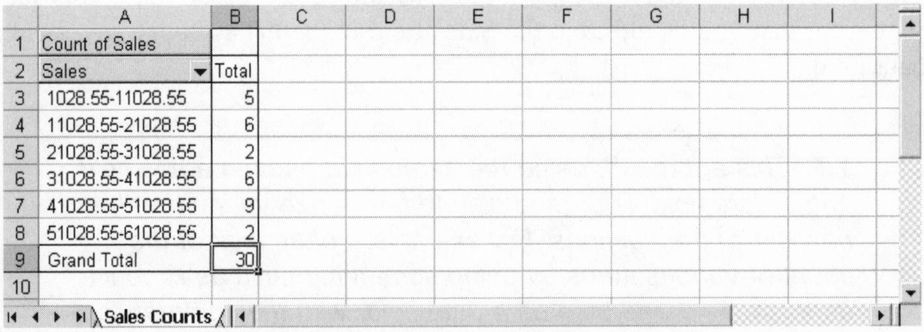

Figure 2-20: This sort of analysis gives you a way to determine where most of the sales are coming from.

You can clean up the pivot table some if you specify your own values in the Grouping dialog box. My tendency with this data would be to set the Minimum to zero and the Maximum to 60,000. This gets rid of the decimal points in the row field, and makes the categories a little easier to conceptualize (see Figure 2-21).

	A	B	C	D	E	F	G	H	I	J
1	Count of Sales									
2	Sales ▼	Total								
3	0-10000	5								
4	10000-20000	5								
5	20000-30000	3								
6	30000-40000	5								
7	40000-50000	10								
8	50000-60000	2								
9	Grand Total	30								
10										

Figure 2-21: Cleaning up the automatic groupings improves readability.

Grouping on a Date or Time Field

Things are somewhat different if you group a row field that shows dates or times. Figure 2-22 shows a pivot table with Sales Date as the row field, before grouping.

	A	B	C	D	E	F	G	H
1						Sum of Sales		
2	Sales Date	Region	Product	Sales		Sales Date ▼	Total	
3	1/15/2007	Northeast	Area rugs	$47,924.49		1/15/2007	$47,924.49	
4	2/11/2007	Northeast	Slipcovers	$14,799.90		2/11/2007	$14,799.90	
5	2/21/2007	Southwest	Towels	$45,841.13		2/21/2007	$45,841.13	
6	2/27/2007	Southeast	Area rugs	$11,635.33		2/27/2007	$11,635.33	
7	2/28/2007	Northwest	Tablecloths	$12,167.81		2/28/2007	$12,167.81	
8	3/17/2007	Southwest	Placemats	$32,322.12		3/17/2007	$32,322.12	
9	3/24/2007	Southwest	Towels	$46,704.67		3/24/2007	$46,704.67	
10	3/29/2007	Northeast	Towels	$53,738.05		3/29/2007	$53,738.05	
11	4/13/2007	Southeast	Tablecloths	$ 4,165.40		4/13/2007	$4,165.40	
12	4/28/2007	Northwest	Slipcovers	$41,433.59		4/28/2007	$41,433.59	
13	4/29/2007	Northeast	Area rugs	$11,825.77		4/29/2007	$11,825.77	
14	5/30/2007	Northeast	Slipcovers	$36,402.82		5/30/2007	$36,402.82	

Figure 2-22: Because the Sales Date field is measured by day in the underlying list, the pivot table automatically gives the field a different item for each distinct day.

As before, begin by right-clicking a cell in the row field, and then choose Group and Show Detail → Group. Excel recognizes the row field as a date field and shows you a different Grouping dialog box (see Figure 2-23).

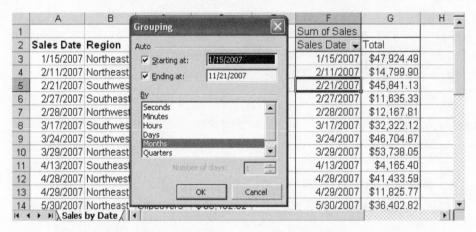

Figure 2-23: Excel enables the Number of Days spinner if you choose Days from the listbox.

You can select more than one grouping level: for example, choose Month *and* Year to get month within year. Choose one or more grouping levels and click OK. Figure 2-24 shows the result of grouping by months.

	A	B	C	D	E	F	G	H
1						Sum of Sales		
2	Sales Date	Region	Product	Sales		Sales Date ▾	Total	
3	1/15/2007	Northeast	Area rugs	$47,924.49		Jan	$47,924.49	
4	2/11/2007	Northeast	Slipcovers	$14,799.90		Feb	$84,444.17	
5	2/21/2007	Southwest	Towels	$45,841.13		Mar	$132,764.84	
6	2/27/2007	Southeast	Area rugs	$11,635.33		Apr	$57,424.76	
7	2/28/2007	Northwest	Tablecloths	$12,167.81		May	$36,402.82	
8	3/17/2007	Southwest	Placemats	$32,322.12		Jun	$93,068.32	
9	3/24/2007	Southwest	Towels	$46,704.67		Jul	$78,453.31	
10	3/29/2007	Northeast	Towels	$53,738.05		Aug	$136,274.20	
11	4/13/2007	Southeast	Tablecloths	$ 4,165.40		Sep	$74,800.23	
12	4/28/2007	Northwest	Slipcovers	$41,433.59		Oct	$85,857.96	
13	4/29/2007	Northeast	Area rugs	$11,825.77		Nov	$59,250.19	
14	5/30/2007	Northeast	Slipcovers	$36,402.82		Grand Total	$886,665.29	

⊮ ◂ ▸ ⊯ \ Sales by Date / ◂

Figure 2-24: You can group a row field or a column field, but not a page field.

Too Much Information: The Data Cache

Every pivot table has a supporting component called the data cache, or just *the cache*. The data that the pivot table summarizes is stored in the cache. In a sense, the cache is redundant, because it contains all the information that you have in the pivot table's data source (so far in this chapter, the only data source we've discussed is a worksheet list, but there are other sources we have yet to get to). The cache is useful largely because it stores the data in a format that the pivot table can use quickly and efficiently.

That's about as much as you really need to know about the cache: basically, that it's there. Unless you're thirsty for more information, skip ahead to the next section. But if you want to know a bit more, read on: you'll see some reasons that pivot tables behave as they do.

What's in the Cache?

If you've used pivot tables before, you've probably noticed that when you change the underlying data (for example by adding or deleting records, or adding a new field) the pivot table doesn't automatically update. This is different from Excel's normal behavior. Usually, when you change data in a worksheet, formulas and charts that are based on the data update immediately and automatically.

Things are different with pivot tables. When you add data to your underlying data source, you have to tell Excel to update (or refresh, or recalculate — use whatever term you're most comfortable with) the pivot table.

TIP: You refresh a pivot table by selecting one of its cells and choosing Refresh Data from the Data menu (you can also use the pivot table toolbar, or right-click a cell in the pivot table and use the shortcut menu).

When you refresh a pivot table's data, what you're actually doing is refreshing the cache: you're adding new records to it, or deleting them, or adding a field. Once the cache is refreshed, the pivot table automatically updates to reflect the change you've made.

The presence of the cache dates back to the 1990s, when pivot tables were first introduced in Excel. At the time, disk storage space was relatively hard to come by on personal computers. Internal disks tended to offer only a few megabytes of capacity. So Excel tried to offer some ways for you to save space.

One of those ways was (and still is) to save a workbook containing a pivot table *without* the cache. This made for a smaller workbook file, but it also meant that any time you updated the underlying data source, Excel had to rebuild the cache. It's the old tradeoff: time for space, just like in chess.

Internal disks are now much, much larger than they were in the 1990s and there's much less reason to worry about a bigger file due to the presence of a pivot table cache. There are excellent reasons to keep the cache in the file, though, and we'll look at some of them next.

How the Cache Helps

Beyond being just a place to store a pivot table's underlying data, the cache can help you in other ways, as described in the following sections.

Discarding the Underlying Data

Suppose that you build a pivot table from an Excel list, as we've done in this chapter's examples. The underlying data in the list might be confidential on a record-by-record basis, but not in the aggregate. For example, you might want to build a pivot table that summarizes regional sales figures, and the table is based on a list of individual records for specific sales reps. You'd prefer not to have that list hanging around so that people can view it.

Once you've built the pivot table from the list, all the list's data is stored in the cache, and you can afford to get rid of the list. You can clear the range that it occupies, or — if it's on a different worksheet than the pivot table — you can just delete the worksheet.

Because all the data's in the cache, you can rearrange the pivot table (for example, changing a row field to a page field), change the subtotals, change the data summary from, say, Sum to Count, and so on. The underlying list is not needed for that kind of operation.

Does it feel like you're taking a chance by throwing out the underlying data? Are you concerned that your data is floating away with the bathwater? Don't stress: you can bring the list back by double-clicking the pivot table's Grand Total cell. Excel responds by inserting a new worksheet and writing all the original, underlying data in the form of an Excel list. Excel can do that because the cache has all the necessary information: field names, field values and records.

For this to work, you have to have a particular option set; it's the default option, so it will be set properly unless someone has deselected it. If you right-click a cell in a pivot table, one of the menu items you see is Table Options (see Figure 2-25). Select that item and be sure that the Enable Drill to Details checkbox is filled.

If you don't see the Grand Total cell, you can get the table to show it by taking these steps:

1. Right-click any cell in the pivot table.

2. From the shortcut menu, choose Table Options. The dialog box shown in Figure 2-25 appears.

3. Fill both the Grand Totals for Columns and the Grand Totals for Rows checkboxes.

4. Click OK.

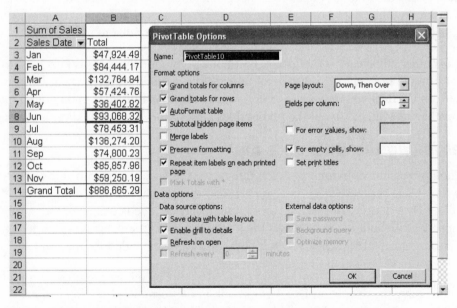

Figure 2-25: To get rid of the cache, clear the Save Data with Table
            Layout checkbox.

Now you will find a cell in the bottom row and rightmost column of the pivot table that's labeled Grand Total. Double-click that cell to get a new worksheet with the data in it as a list.

Basing One Pivot Table on Another

Again referring back to Figure 2-14, notice that one of your options for an underlying data source is Another PivotTable or PivotChart Report. All this means is that if you already have one pivot table in the active workbook, you can use its *cache* as the basis for another pivot table.

Why would you want to do that? Well, not everyone has your level of expertise in using pivot tables. Although you could bring up the Field List and use it to change the structure of an existing pivot table, you want to accommodate the benighted client who doesn't yet know how.

So you might arrange to show the same data, analyzed in two or more different ways, in two or more different tables. You can make your task easier, and at the same time guard against mistakes, by building the next table — and subsequent tables — based on the first one. That means that all the pivot tables you build in this fashion will be based on the same data set. You won't have to worry about getting 150 records into one pivot table, and 149 into another due to a misclick.

Another advantage is that if you build one pivot table based (say) on a worksheet list, and build all the other pivot tables on that first one, then when you want to refresh the data you only have to do it once. That one refresh is enough to update the cache that's shared by all the pivot tables, and so they will all update as a result.

Retrieving the Data as a List

It's not immediately obvious, and you might want to keep this in your hip pocket: If you look back at Figure 2-14, you see that one of your choices as a data source is External Data Source. In practice, an External Data Source is usually either a true database (a file built using Access, Oracle, or any other true database management system) or a text file (such as the soft copy of a report intended for the printer).

If you've built a pivot table using a true database as the data source, you probably don't have the data in an Excel workbook in the form of a list. You can get it there, if you want, by double-clicking the Grand Total cell, just as described earlier, even though the underlying data isn't a list. It's the cache that enables you to do this.

How the Cache Hurts

Well, the cache doesn't really hurt. But there are some things you have to be careful of. Mainly, these occur when you have two or more pivot tables that share the same cache.

Recall that one of your options when you start building the pivot table is to indicate that the data you want to use is in another pivot table (or pivot chart). You can select that option in Step 1 of the pivot table wizard. When you do, Excel displays a dialog box that shows what pivot tables already exist in the active workbook. Select one of them, and your new pivot table will share a cache with the existing pivot table.

> *TIP: This is just one good reason to supply a descriptive name for each pivot table using the Table Options dialog box shown in Figure 2-25.*

The problem arises because some structural changes that you make to one pivot table can turn up in another, as discussed next.

Grouping Problems

Suppose you want one pivot table to show costs by quarter, and you design it so that it does so. You want another pivot table to show costs by month, to make a point about seasonality in a company's cost patterns. You decide to base the second pivot table on the first.

But if you do, you won't be able to group the two pivot tables differently, one by quarter and one by month. As soon as you group one by month, the other automatically groups itself by month. And when you group the other pivot table by quarter, the first one follows suit.

The solution in this sort of situation is to base both pivot tables on the same data source, but to avoid basing one pivot table on the other. When you do so for the second of the two (or more) pivot tables, Excel alerts you that your new pivot table will consume less memory if you base it on the existing pivot table. You can choose Yes to base it on the existing table, and No to keep the tables separate.

If you want to base two or more pivot tables on the same data, but group them differently, you should choose No, so as to keep them separate. Now you will be able to choose different grouping levels for the different tables.

Page Field Problems

You can safely ignore this section if you're using Excel 2000 or a later version. Many companies, however, even in 2007, continue to use Excel 97. (And many of them have very good reasons for living in the past. The conversion of hundreds — to say nothing of thousands — of workstations from Office 97 to a later version is a complex and expensive project.)

If you are using Office 97, be aware that there is a problem with page fields. If you have several pivot tables on different worksheets and refresh them periodically, it can happen that two or more pivot tables wind up with the same selection in their page fields. Therefore, you might have to deal with a pivot table on a worksheet named January that selects January records, and another pivot table on a worksheet named February that also selects January records.

This can be embarrassing, and the solution is the same as suggested in the prior section: base all the pivot tables on the same data source, but don't base them one another. The final major section in this chapter, Using Named Ranges as Data Sources, has a recommendation that makes it much easier to base several pivot tables on the same data source.

Refreshing the Cache Automatically

Later in this chapter, in the section named Building and Refreshing a Pivot Table From a Dynamic Range, this book describes how you can arrange for a pivot table's underlying data range to redefine itself automatically. As new data on, say, costs comes into the workbook, you don't need to tell pivot tables to look further into the worksheet to find the most complete set of information.

But redefining the reference to the data source is only half the job. The other half is getting the pivot table to refresh itself based on that new data. There are several ways to do this. One is by hand: all you need to do is right-click any cell in the pivot table and choose Refresh Data from the shortcut menu.

But you have to remember to do that; it's all too easy to assume that the pivot table contains the most current information and forget that you haven't refreshed it. So consider doing something to refresh the table automatically.

Refreshing the Pivot Table When You Open the Workbook

One way to arrange for an automatic refresh is to select an option that forces a refresh. If you right-click a cell in a pivot table, a shortcut menu appears, and one of its items is Table Options. Select that item to see the dialog box shown earlier in Figure 2-25.

Clearly, there are many options you can set using this dialog box. The one that's pertinent to this section is Refresh on Open. Fill this checkbox to get Excel to refresh the pivot table when you open the workbook.

WARNING: Don't forget to save the workbook after you've selected this option. If you don't, the option will keep the value it already had — and if the checkbox was cleared (that's the default) then the pivot table won't automatically refresh when you open the workbook.

With this option set, Excel refreshes the pivot table while it is opening the workbook, before it turns control over to the user. For most situations, that could very well be all you need. If you open the workbook that contains the pivot table only occasionally you'll want the pivot table to have refreshed itself — new data could easily have been put in the workbook since you last opened it.

And if all you do is take a quick look at what the pivot table displays when you open the workbook, you're in good shape. Only in exceptional cases could you have the workbook open while a different user is updating the data source.

The Problem Cases

There are two general situations that could cause a pivot table's underlying data to change without your knowledge, and I'll go over those in this section.

The Shared Workbook

One such case occurs when the workbook is *shared*. (A workbook is shared when more than one user at a time can have it open and save changes to it. This is done using Tools → Share Workbook.) You cannot edit — or even build — a pivot table in a shared workbook, not even if you're the only one who has the workbook open.

NOTE: This is just one of several reasons that I urge my clients not to use shared workbooks. One of the other reasons is that they have a tendency to hang — to quit responding to user input — when they get fairly large. You do not want a workbook with a lot of data in it to hang.

In a shared workbook, another user could easily edit a pivot table's data source, and you would not necessarily know that had happened.

External Data Sources

The other case occurs when a pivot table is based on an external data source. The most typical external data sources are text files, other Excel workbooks, and true databases. ("Most typical" is a relative term, though, because the majority of pivot tables are based on worksheet lists.) You build a pivot table that's based on an external data source starting with the pivot table wizard's first step (covered earlier in this chapter).

You would not necessarily know that another user had updated the pivot table's data source when that source is located in a database or in a different Excel workbook. That's why you might find useful another checkbox in the Table Options dialog box.

Refer back to Figure 2-25, and notice the checkbox labeled Refresh Every X Minutes. The checkbox, and the associated spinner, are enabled only if the pivot table is based on an external data source. You can use this checkbox and the spinner to cause Excel to refresh the pivot table as frequently as you wish from the external data source. But use a little caution, at least: if the pivot table is based on a large amount of data, it's possible to clog up a network with frequent, possibly unnecessary refreshes.

> *TIP*: Perhaps the slickest way to design a pivot table is to keep the underlying data set in a true database, such as SQL Server, Oracle or Access. Then base the pivot table on that database, using the External Data Source option in step 1 of the pivot table wizard. If you do this, you leverage the data management and retrieval strengths of the database and the analysis and graphic display strengths of Excel.

Using Named Ranges as Data Sources

Excel has a way of referring to a collection of cells on a given worksheet. Such a collection is called a *range*, and it's every bit as important as a list. A range can consist of a single cell, such as cell D5 — in fact, a cell *is* a range in a formal sense. A range can also consist of thousands of cells, such as the range A1:Z500.

Ranges are in some ways less formal than lists, and in some ways more so. For example, you can put any sort of data in a range and orient it as you like. A list — to be a list — requires that you have field names in the first row, that each subsequent row represent a different record, and that each column contain a different field.

But ranges are much more forgiving. You'd have to be irrational to do it, but you could put a record in one row of a range, and another record in one of the range's columns. A range, in other words, has all the flexibility of the worksheet it's on as to what goes where: that's all up to you.

On the other hand, a defined range has a couple of things that a list doesn't. One is a *name*: all defined ranges have names, like PhoneList or Q4Actuals. The other is an *address*: Excel requires that an address, like D5 or A1:Z500, be associated with the name of the defined range. (In contrast, recall from Chapter 1 that lists don't have names, and although they occupy cells they don't have specific cell addresses.) All defined ranges must have names, and those names must be associated with cell addresses.

Creating a Named Range for an Aging Report

One useful example, seen in Figure 2-26, is a named range for an aging report.

	A	B	C	D	E	F	G	H	I
	A1	▼		fx	Acct				
1	**Acct**	**Amount**	**Sales Date**	**Past Due**		**Closing Date:**	**12/31/2007**		
2	34401	$6,260.33	11/27/07	34					
3	18747	$6,613.43	11/26/07	35					
4	86243	$3,149.04	11/22/07	39					
5	34897	$3,959.03	11/17/07	44					
6	99578	$9,035.72	11/4/07	57					
7	48287	$1,752.94	10/29/07	63					
8	59476	$3,955.75	10/18/07	74					
9	60097	$3,039.39	10/12/07	80					
10	16987	$ 758.83	10/7/07	85					
11	48064	$1,833.85	10/6/07	86					
12	82675	$9,959.65	10/2/07	90					
13	56910	$2,747.88	9/28/07	94					
14	77493	$3,155.85	9/27/07	95					
15	18508	$7,941.37	9/27/07	95					
16	44094	$1,120.03	9/24/07	98					
17	23425	$5,407.36	9/16/07	106					
18	26287	$8,137.89	9/13/07	109					
19	37005	$2,155.39	9/2/07	120					
20	45207	$4,924.56	9/1/07	121					
21	29082	$1,195.40	8/29/07	124					
22	53605	$2,755.99	8/25/07	128					
23	80510	$7,357.35	8/25/07	128					

H ◀ ▶ H \ **Aging Report** / ◀ |

Figure 2-26: Of course, you can create a named range from any set of cells, not just an aging report.

Here's how to create a range named AgingReport:

1. Select the cells in the range you want to name. In Figure 2-26, that's A1:D23. (We'll ignore the closing date information in F1:G1, but of course you could include it.)

2. Choose Insert → Name → Define to see the dialog box shown in Figure 2-27.

3. In the Names in Workbook box, type a descriptive name, such as AgingReport.

4. Click OK.

You now have a range named AgingReport in the active workbook. You can use it as input to a pivot table (instead of typing the cell references in the second step of the pivot table wizard — refer back to Figure 2-15 — you can just type the name of the range).

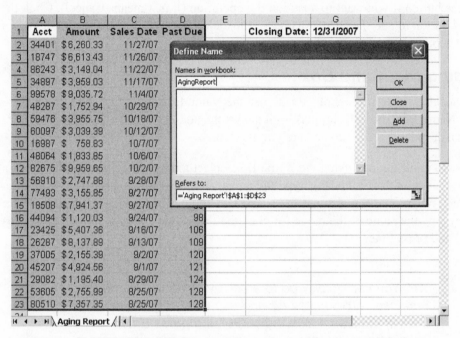

Figure 2-27: There are other ways to add a named range, but this gives you the most control.

There are many other ways to use a named range, and most of them have to do with using the name instead of typing a cell reference such as A1:D23. It's easy to forget or to miskey a cell reference; if you chose a good name for the range, such as ChartOfAccounts, it's harder to forget or miskey.

Before you start looking into using a named range as input to a pivot table, following are a few basics about named ranges to bear in mind:

Embedding Blanks

The name of the range can't contain embedded blanks. It would be nice to name a range *Aging Report*, but Excel won't let you. If you find it jarring to see the two words run together in *AgingReport*, consider using an underscore instead of a blank space: *Aging_Report*.

Getting Out of the Dialog Box

Notice the other buttons on the Define Name dialog box in Figure 2-27. Click the Close button if you want to abandon the operation (it just means Cancel). Click the Add button to add the current name — the dialog box will stay open so that you can add another named range.

Using the Name Box

A quicker way to name a range is to use the Name Box. In Figure 2-26, you can see the Name Box above Column A — it shows the address of the active cell, A1, and it has a dropdown arrow immediately to its right.

To name a range using the Name Box, select a range of cells that you want to name, click in the Name Box, type the name, and press Enter. That creates the named range. You can also use the Name Box to go to that range: click in the Name Box, type the name of the range (or click the dropdown arrow and select it from a list) and press Enter.

> *TIP: You can quickly go to a cell by using the Name Box. Suppose you're in cell A1 and you want to go to cell Z90. Click in the Name Box, type Z90, and press Enter.*

Another helpful feature of the Name Box is that if you have selected a named range, the name of the range appears in the Name Box. In Figure 2-26, if you had already named the range AgingReport, and subsequently selected that range, its name would appear in the Name Box.

> *NOTE: This feature of the Name Box does not, unfortunately, apply to dynamic range names, which are discussed next.*

Static and Dynamic Named Ranges

The prior section described one type of named range — a static range, the type that is best known. ("Best known" is another relative expression, of course. An educated guess is that perhaps 10% of those who use Excel frequently have even heard of a named range.)

A static named range is static because it doesn't change without your help. It doesn't move, and its dimensions don't change. Left to its own devices, a static range that consists of 24 rows and 10 columns will always have 24 rows and 10 columns.

But what if you have use for a range that can grow or shrink as a function of the number of values it contains? For example, to return to the account aging report in Figure 2-26, what happens when another account becomes past due? You add it to the range of data that's currently in A1:D23, of course, but now the data would occupy A1:D24, and the range name still refers to A1:D23. If you used the range name AgingReport in an analysis, you'd miss the 23rd record (in the 24th row).

The Refers To Box

Have another look at Figure 2-27, in particular the Define Name dialog box. Notice at the bottom of its window is a box labeled Refers To. That box contains this information:

='Aging Report'!$A$1:$D$23

There are some points of interest about that entry:

- It begins with an equal sign. Thus, it has aspects similar to a formula in a worksheet cell. In particular, it can be calculated and recalculated.
- It begins with the name of the worksheet where the range is located. Because the name of the worksheet in this case has a blank in it (between "Aging" and "Report"), Excel puts single quotes around it.
- Excel separates the name of the worksheet from the cell address with an exclamation point. This convention occurs elsewhere in Excel, such as in charts.
- The range address, $A$1:$D$23, is an absolute reference. The column designations, A and D, and the row designations, 1 and 23, are each preceded by dollar signs. These dollar signs anchor the address, making it fixed, absolute, static.

You can tinker with this definition of where to find the range named AgingReport. In particular, you can make the definition sensitive to the number of accounts that should be included in the named range — so that when a new account is added, the range's definition expands to include the new account. Then the named range is no longer static, it's dynamic.

And we're now getting close to the reason I've stuck all this stuff about named ranges in the middle of a chapter on pivot tables. *If you base a pivot table on a dynamic named range, you don't need to change the range address of the pivot table's input data: it changes automatically as new data becomes available.* If you use pivot tables extensively to synthesize, analyze and chart, for example, your clients' operating costs and revenue sources, the ability to get them to update their addresses automatically is huge.

Basing a pivot table on data in a dynamic named range doesn't by itself completely solve the problem of updating a pivot table with new data. You still have to refresh the pivot table. But that too can be automated, as you saw earlier in this chapter's section titled Refreshing the Cache Automatically.

When you can automatically change the address of the input data and automatically refresh the pivot table, you're in a position to hand your client a valuable resource. Or, if you prefer to keep it to yourself, you've arranged to save yourself a lot of time and grief going forward.

A couple of additional tools are needed to make a named range dynamic: the OFFSET function and the COUNTA function.

The OFFSET Function

OFFSET is a worksheet function that directs Excel's attention from one cell to another, but it's also useful in the definition of a dynamic named range. Here's the OFFSET syntax as you might use it on a worksheet:

=OFFSET(*celladdress,rows,columns*)

For example:

=OFFSET(A1,1,2)

This example tells Excel to return a value in a cell that

- is *offset* from cell A1 — that is, a cell that is removed from A1 by some number of rows and some number of columns. (In this example, A1 is the function's first argument.)

- is found one row below A1 (1 is the second argument in the function)
- is found two columns to the right of cell A1.

Here's another example:

=OFFSET(C2,5,4)

The second example tells Excel to return a value in a cell that

- is offset from cell C2.
- is found five rows below C2.
- is found four columns to the right of cell C2.

Finally, a special case — it will look trivial at first, but it turns out to have plenty of uses, including dynamic named ranges:

=OFFSET(A5,0,0)

This usage calls for an offset of zero rows and zero columns from cell A5 — that is, it refers to cell A5 itself.

The OFFSET Function in a Named Range

Suppose you want to name a worksheet range that starts in cell A1 and ends in cell D4. As we've seen, the usual definition of that range — shown in the Refers To box of the Define Name dialog — would be:

=$A$1:$D$4

But you could also type this into the Refers To box:

=OFFSET($A$1,0,0,4,5)

Here, the OFFSET function refers to cell $A$1, and just as in the last example it offsets zero rows and zero columns, so it includes A1 itself. But there are two more arguments that we haven't looked at yet: the numerals 4 and 5.

They tell Excel that the reference that OFFSET should return is to have four rows and five columns. Formally, these are optional arguments, but they're necessary if you're to get a range that consists of multiple cells when the basis (here, $A$1) is one cell only. In their absence, Excel assumes one row and one column. That is, the following two examples are equivalent:

=OFFSET($A$1,0,0)
=OFFSET($A$1,0,0,1,1)

So, suppose you entered this in the Refers To box of the Define Name dialog:

=OFFSET($A$1,0,0,4,5)

Then the range you're defining would occupy A1:E4. That's the range that

- is offset zero rows from A1.
- is offset zero columns from A1.
- occupies four rows.
- occupies five columns.

The problem is that the range is still static. It always occupies four rows and five columns and starts in cell A1. You're about to make it dynamic, though.

Making the Range Name Dynamic

It's wise to back up a moment to review the purpose of all this stuff. The problem is to get a pivot table to react automatically after new information enters the worksheet range that contains its underlying data. The pivot table might be getting the total of revenues for each month — then, when a sales region reports its total revenue for the current month, that information goes into a worksheet list and we want the pivot table to add that revenue to its analysis.

What you can do is *count* the number of records in the list. Suppose that the list occupies cells A1:B25. A new record arrives, stating that $100,000 in revenue was recognized in November. The value *November* goes into cell A26 and *$100,000* goes into B26. The list has expanded by one row.

Suppose that you want the worksheet to keep track of the number of records in the list. In cell C1, say, you could enter this formula:

=COUNTA(A:A) - 1

That formula counts the number of values in Column A, and subtracts 1 from that. The reason for subtracting 1 is that one value in Column A is the list's column header — something such as the word "Month".

TIP: There are a couple of counting functions in Excel. One is COUNT, which counts the number of numeric values in a range of cells. The other is COUNTA, which counts the number of values in a range of cells, regardless of whether the values are numeric or text. COUNTA is used here because it's more general, but COUNT often works just as well. You know the nature of your data better than I do.

Now you're ready to define a dynamic range name. The definition uses the COUNTA function as an argument to the OFFSET function — the result of COUNTA tells OFFSET how many rows to include in the named range. For a dynamic range name that starts in cell A1 and has four columns, the Refers To box would have:

=OFFSET($A$1,0,0,COUNTA($A:$A),4)

This definition probably looks more intimidating than it really is. Try interpreting it piecemeal, from the inside out, and begin by assuming that you have values in the range A1:A5 and nowhere else in Column A. (For the purpose of this example, it doesn't matter whether there are values in columns B through D, but as a practical matter you'd usually have values in those columns, associated with values in Column A.)

In that case, this part of the definition:

COUNTA($A:$A)

calculates the number of values found in Column A — under the assumption in the last paragraph, that's 5. Substituting into the full definition you get:

=OFFSET($A$1,0,0,5,4)

That is, the range that is offset from A1 by zero rows and zero columns, and that contains five rows and four columns: using standard Excel notation, A1:D5.

Now suppose that you add new data to that range, in cell A6 (and perhaps B6:D6). If you do, the COUNTA function returns 6, not 5: it's sensitive to the number of values it finds. The definition adjusts to:

=OFFSET($A$1,0,0,6,4)

and the range name's definition contains six rows instead of five: A1:D6. You've defined a dynamic range name.

Try it yourself by taking these steps:

1. Enter, say, four values in A1:A4.

2. Choose Insert → Name → Define.

3. In the Names in Workbook box, type a name such as **DynamicRange**.

4. In the Refers To box, type =OFFSET($A$1,0,0,COUNTA($A:$A),4)

5. Click OK.

6. Click in the Name Box and type the name you chose in Step 3.

7. Press Enter.

Excel will select the cells defined by columns A through D, and by as many rows as you have values in Column A.

WARNING: *Keep any extraneous values (or formulas) out of the column whose values you're counting. Suppose you have a simple "q" in cell A957. That's a value in Column A, and if you're defining your dynamic range using a count of the number of values in the column, you would wind up with one more row in the dynamic range than you really want.*

Now, enter another value in a blank cell in Column A, and repeat steps 6 and 7, above. Excel will select one row more than it did before.

Before you leave this section, be sure you follow the rationale for all this — which might well seem like a bunch of handwaving from some deranged geek. By defining a dynamic range name, you can arrange for the range's dimensions (usually, its number of rows) to be automatically recalculated when new data is added. In turn:

• Any charts that depend on that range name will also automatically redraw.

• Any formulas that depend on values in the named data range will automatically recalculate.

- Any pivot tables that depend on values in the named data range will automatically grab the new data when they are refreshed — which can also be done automatically.

Building and Refreshing a Pivot Table From a Dynamic Range

In this chapter's section titled Building Pivot Tables, you saw how you could make reference to a range of cells occupied by a list, that would serve as the underlying data for the pivot table. That section mentioned that you could select a cell in the list prior to starting the pivot table wizard with Data → PivotTable and PivotChart Report.

If you do so, Excel determines the boundaries of the list and proposes the range it occupies as the pivot table's data source. If you do not begin by selecting a cell in the list, you must identify the range address of the list by typing it, or by dragging through the range with your mouse.

If you base the pivot table on a dynamic range name, then (both at the outset and later on) you don't need to bother with that. Just type the name of the range in the Range box that you see in Step 2 of the pivot table wizard, and proceed just as before. Figure 2-28 starts an example of how this is done.

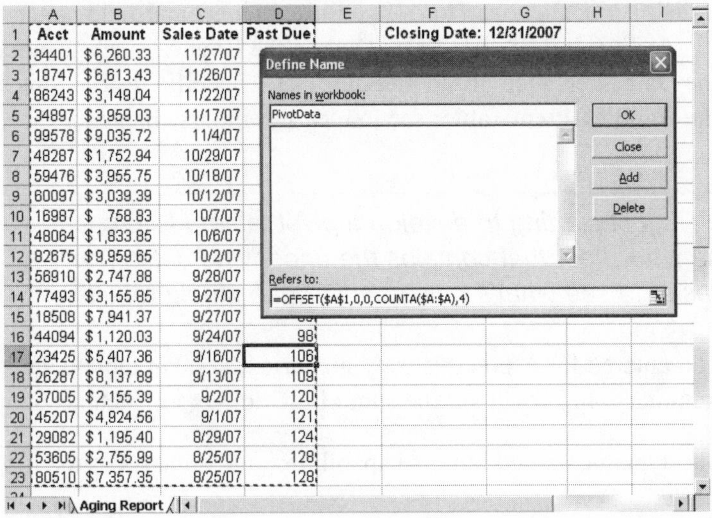

Figure 2-28: Note the defined name of the range, and what it refers to.

It's usual (if not strictly necessary) to begin by selecting a range of cells when you're defining a static range name. But with a dynamic range name, it's pointless to do so because you're setting the range up so that it will redefine itself.

In Figure 2-28, the user has not selected a range of cells, but has chosen Insert → Name → Define. Now take the following steps:

1. In the Names in Workbook box, type a name such as **PivotData**.

2. In the Refers To box, type
   =OFFSET($A$1,0,0,COUNTA($A:$A),4)

3. Click OK to get the name defined.

4. Choose Data → PivotTable and PivotChart Report.

5. In Step 1 of the pivot table wizard, accept the defaults of Excel List and PivotTable. Click Next.

6. In Step 2 of the *wizard*, type into the Range box the name, perhaps **PivotData**, that you used in Step 1 of *this list*. Click Next.

7. In Step 3 of the wizard, make your own choice about where to locate the pivot table, and click Finish.

8. The schematic appears on the worksheet, and the PivotTable Field List dialog box shows up too. If you use the data and field names shown in Figure 2-28, add Sales Date to the Row Area and Amount to the Data Area, then group on Sales Date. Specific instructions are in the Building Pivot Tables section, earlier in this chapter.

TIP: *When I'm just starting to develop a pivot table, I like to put it on the worksheet that contains the underlying data. That makes it easier to see what's going on if I get a stupid result.*

If all the data you entered for Amount is truly numeric, the pivot table defaults to Sum as the data summary, and you'll get the sum of the dollars for each account.

Now, to test your dynamic named range's capabilities, add a record to the list, as shown in Figure 2-29.

	A	B	C	D	E	F	G	H	I
1	Acct	Amount	Sales Date	Past Due		Closing Date:	12/31/2007		
2	34401	$6,260.33	11/27/07	34					
3	18747	$6,613.43	11/26/07	35		Sum of Amount			
4	86243	$3,149.04	11/22/07	39		Past Due ▼	Total		
5	34897	$3,959.03	11/17/07	44		31-60	$30,604.88		
6	99578	$9,035.72	11/4/07	57		61-90	$21,300.41		
7	48287	$1,752.94	10/29/07	63		91-120	$30,665.77		
8	59476	$3,955.75	10/18/07	74		121-150	$16,233.30		
9	60097	$3,039.39	10/12/07	80		Grand Total	$98,804.36		
10	16987	$ 758.83	10/7/07	85					
11	48064	$1,833.85	10/6/07	86					
12	82675	$9,959.65	10/2/07	90					
13	56910	$2,747.88	9/28/07	94					
14	77493	$3,155.85	9/27/07	95					
15	18508	$7,941.37	9/27/07	95					
16	44094	$1,120.03	9/24/07	98					
17	23425	$5,407.36	9/16/07	106					
18	26287	$8,137.89	9/13/07	109					
19	37005	$2,155.39	9/2/07	120					
20	45207	$4,924.56	9/1/07	121					
21	29082	$1,195.40	8/29/07	124					
22	53605	$2,755.99	8/25/07	128					
23	80510	$7,357.35	8/25/07	128					
24	92848	$1,587.33	11/30/07	31					
25									

Aging Report

Figure 2-29: Adding the record expands the range name's definition by one row.

Lastly, right-click anywhere in the pivot table and choose Refresh Data from the shortcut menu. You should see the pivot table summary update to reflect the presence of the new record.

Chapter 3

Common Sizing Using Worksheets

The Rationale for Common Sizing

Common Sizing Income Statements

Other Uses of Common Sizing

Because of its ability to calculate and recalculate formulas, Excel is an ideal application for common sizing financial statements. You have several tools available to help with different purposes for common sized statements: for example, you might create a common sized statement that can recalculate as new information comes to hand, or one that is static — that is, one that has values only, and no formulas.

This chapter begins by discussing the rationale for common sized statements. That may seem pretty basic, but I've met many accountants who are unfamiliar with the concepts involved. (If the idea is old hat to you, by all means skip ahead to the section titled Common Sizing Income Statements.) The chapter then goes on to describe how you can use Excel to common size income statements and balance sheets, to make comparisons with earlier accounting periods or with another company or even an entire industry.

The Rationale for Common Sizing

We're all so used to looking at income statements and balance sheets that are denominated in dollars that seeing one denominated in percentages seems a little odd. But when you look at a common sized financial report that shows percentages, you find that it makes a lot of sense.

The idea itself is pretty straightforward. Suppose that you're looking at an income statement. Many of the values shown there — especially on an income statement that's been structured to support management decisions — are driven by net sales. Salaries, COGS and virtually any other variable cost, even fixed costs — in a rationally-managed company all of these rise and fall, if only eventually, with net sales.

So it's sensible to look at how dollars are allocated to various cost categories as a percentage of net sales, something to which they react. A company might have $10,000,000 in net sales in 2007 and pay $2,000,000 in salaries. Another company in the same business sector might have $30,000,000 in net sales for the same year and pay $10,000,000 in salaries.

One company pays 20% of its net sales in salaries, and the other pays 33%. With very small firms — say, those with less than $1,000,000 in annual net sales — that difference wouldn't jump out at you. Just sending a CFO to jail for six years could easily account for the difference.

But with companies that have tens of millions of dollars in annual net sales, the difference between 20% and 30% for salaries is probably worth taking a quick look. You might find something of interest, or problematic — or nothing at all — but at least your attention was directed to a difference that's a little bit unusual.

It would be more difficult to notice that difference if you were simply looking at raw dollars, especially if you're looking through income statements for 20 or 30 companies. With net sales or revenues all over the ballpark, it's hard to tell if anything's out of whack.

But when you've common sized the statements, you eliminate the effect of one principal source of variation: net sales measured in raw dollars. With everything on the income statement cast in terms of percent of net sales, it's much easier to make comparisons between companies. And that, of course, puts you in a position to assess how two or more companies differ in terms of how they structure their costs.

There are various sources of income statements and balance sheets, available for particular business sectors and already common sized. One source, for example, is Risk Management Associates at http://www.rmahq.org/RMA, which sells common sized reports. This is one way to compare a particular company in which you are interested with a larger number of companies in the same general line of business.

It's not necessary to limit the comparison to one company and another, or one company and an entire sector. It can be helpful to look at a comparative income statement that describes the activities of one company at different points in time, usually consecutive accounting periods. In that case, of course, you would express all costs from, say, 2006 in terms of percentage of net sales for 2006, and all costs from 2007 in terms of net sales for 2007. Once you've removed the effect of variation in net sales, you can easily see the change in cost allocation from year to year.

Common Sizing Income Statements

You have a choice, early in the process of common sizing an income statement, as to whether you want the common sized statement to be fixed or changeable. If it's fixed, that means you'll see the same percentages whether or not you get new numbers for the original income statement: such a common sized statement stores fixed percentages.

On the other hand, if the common sized statement is changeable, you can see the percentages change as new data arrives. It's changeable because you've stored the percentages as formulas, and if you get more information about costs or sales, the common sized statement recalculates its formulas and show you updated percentages.

Probably, the best time to "freeze" a common sized statement is at the end of the accounting period it covers, after adjusting entries have been made and the only further change would be restatements. Bear in mind, though, that you can always convert the statement back to formula-based common sizing by going back to the original statement.

The Mechanics: Using Formulas

Figure 3-1 shows an ordinary income statement. (It's highly simplified and condensed for reasons of space.) This section describes how to create a common sized income statement that's based on formulas, and retains them.

	A	B	C	D	E	F	G
1	Net Sales		$ 3,414,926				
2	Cost of Goods Sold		1,866,171				
3	Gross Profit		1,548,755				
4	Operating Expenses						
5		Travel & Entertainment	89,305				
6		Commissions	274,153				
7	Total Sales Expenses		363,458				
8							
9		Salaries	267,543				
10		Communications	20,320				
11		Insurance	25,400				
12		Advertising	76,622				
13		Depreciation	33,443				
14	Total Administrative Expenses		423,328				
15							
16	Total Operating Expenses		786,786				
17	Operating Income		761,969				
18	Interest Expense		130,805				
19	Income before taxes		631,164				
20	Taxes		165,357				
21	Net Income		$ 465,806				
22							
23							

Ⅰ◀ ▶ ▶Ⅰ\ Income Statement / | ◀ |

Figure 3-1: A standard, condensed income statement, denominated in dollars.

To convert the statement shown in Figure 3-1 to a common sized statement, using Net Sales, take these steps:

1. If your workbook has a blank worksheet in it, go on to Step 2. Otherwise, choose Insert → Worksheet.

2. If necessary, activate a blank worksheet and select cell C1. (In this case C1 is the cell that contains the first of the numeric values in the original income statement.)

3. Type an equal sign, switch to the worksheet with the income statement, and click in cell C1.

4. Type a slash (that is, the *divided by sign* or the *division operator*).

5. Click in cell C1 (or wherever the income statement has stored the net sales value).

6. Press Enter. Excel returns you to the blank worksheet. If necessary, select cell C1 again. The formula in the formula bar should look something like this:

='Income Statement'!C1/'Income Statement'!C1

> depending on the name of the worksheet that contains the original income statement.

7. Hold down the mouse button and drag the mouse pointer across the reference that's to the right of the division operator in the formula bar, to highlight it. In this case, that's the second instance of C1 in the formula.

8. Press the F4 key once, and then press Enter. This will convert the highlighted portion of the formula from a relative reference to an absolute reference. (You could also just type the dollar signs directly into the reference, but the F4 key is easier, especially when you're using a laptop on a bumpy flight.) The formula in the formula bar will now look like this:

='Income Statement'!C1/'Income Statement'!$C$1

9. If necessary, activate cell C1 again. Click the Percent Style button on the Formatting toolbar. Cell C1 will now be formatted as a percent, and it is the percentage of net sales. If cell C1 on the original income statement itself contained net sales, then C1 in the new worksheet shows 100%.

10. Move your mouse pointer over the fill handle on cell C1. (The fill handle is the dark square found on the cell's lower right corner; it is visible only on the active cell, or on the lower right cell of a multi-cell selection.) Click the fill handle, hold down the mouse button and drag down through cell C21.

11. Switch back to the original income statement and select the labels in cells A1:B21. Choose Edit → Copy.

12. Switch back to the new worksheet, select cell A1, and choose Edit → Paste.

13. Select columns A, B and C by clicking on the A at the top of the first column, holding down the mouse button, and dragging right into Column C.

14. Double-click the boundary between the A and the B, or between the B and the C. This auto-sizes each column width to match the maximum width of the column's entries.

15. Choose Tools → Options and click the View tab. Clear the Zero Values checkbox.

TIP: *That final step prevents cells that were blank in the original income statement from showing as 0% in the new income statement. The option applies only to the worksheet that's active when you clear the checkbox.*

You now have a common sized income statement in what had been a blank sheet; the result appears in Figure 3-2.

	A	B	C	D	E	F	G
1	Net Sales		100%				
2	Cost of Goods Sold		55%				
3	Gross Profit		45%				
4	Operating Expenses						
5		Travel & Entertainment	3%				
6		Commissions	8%				
7	Total Sales Expenses		11%				
8							
9		Salaries	8%				
10		Communications	1%				
11		Insurance	1%				
12		Advertising	2%				
13		Depreciation	1%				
14	Total Administrative Expenses		12%				
15							
16	Total Operating Expenses		23%				
17	Operating Income		22%				
18	Interest Expense		4%				
19	Income before taxes		18%				
20	Taxes		5%				
21	Net Income		14%				
22							
23							

Common Sized Income Statement

Figure 3-2: A common sized income statement, standardized on net sales.

TIP: *You can change what Excel does when you press Enter. By default, Excel selects the next cell down. To change that behavior, choose Tools → Options and click the Edit tab. If you want to leave the active cell selected when you press Enter, clear the Move Selection After Enter checkbox. Or, leave it selected and choose Up, Left, Right or Down from the Direction drop-down.*

A Comparative Income Statement

Although the percentages can be informative directly, they're seldom really useful to anyone who is not closely familiar with the company's line of business — and therefore who isn't in a position to judge whether the relative amount spent on commissions or salaries is out of line. That's why a *comparative income statement* can be helpful (see Figure 3-3).

	A	B	C	D	E	F	G
1							
2			**2006**	**2007**			
3	Net Sales		$ 3,414,926	$ 4,197,911			
4	Cost of Goods Sold		1,866,171	2,354,930			
5	Gross Profit		1,548,755	1,842,981			
6	Operating Expenses						
7		Travel & Entertainment	89,305	116,873			
8		Commissions	274,153	343,322			
9	Total Sales Expenses		363,458	460,195			
10							
11		Salaries	267,543	364,953			
12		Communications	20,320	22,459			
13		Insurance	25,400	39,303			
14		Advertising	76,622	89,835			
15		Depreciation	33,443	44,917			
16	Total Administrative Expenses		423,328	561,467			
17							
18	Total Operating Expenses		786,786	1,021,662			
19	Operating Income		761,969	821,320			
20	Interest Expense		130,805	104,644			
21	Income before taxes		631,164	716,675			
22	Taxes		165,357	118,264			
23	Net Income		$ 465,806	$ 598,411			
24							
25							

H ◀ ▶ H \Comparative Income Statement , ◀

Figure 3-3: Two years of data is better than one, but it's still difficult to interpret them at a glance.

The income statements shown in Figure 3-3 are for two consecutive fiscal years of the same company. That's convenient: the company tends to group its costs into the same categories from year to year, making comparisons easier.

Of course, if you wanted to structure a comparative income statement that compares one company's annuals with another's, or with a sector's, you'd probably have some re-arrangement to do to bring the statements into alignment with one another. But if the categories are well defined, this seldom poses any real problem.

Because the two years of data shown in Figure 3-3 differ moderately, it's a little tough to tell what's been going on if you focus simply on the dollar amounts. So, convert them to percentages, as shown earlier in Figure 3-2. The steps are more complicated, but trivially so, and you can simplify the process by putting the percentages on the original income statement's worksheet. Take these steps:

1. With a worksheet laid out as in Figure 3-3, select cell F3.

2. In cell F3, enter this formula:

=(D3-C3)/C3

   which divides the difference between the net sales for the two years by the net sales for the first year.

3. With cell F3 active, click the Percent Style button. Adjust the number of decimals to display by using the Increase Decimal or Decrease Decimal buttons on the Formatting toolbar.

4. Using the fill handle on cell F3, drag through F4:F23. You will wind up with #DIV/0! error values in cells F6, F10 and F17. Remove them by selecting each cell in turn and pressing Delete.

5. Select cell H3. Enter this formula:

=C3/$C$3

6. Using the fill handle in cell H3, fill H3 into I3. Notice that I3 now contains this formula:

=D3/D$3

   Both cell references in the formula adjusted in response to the copy-and-paste, because the only dollar sign in the formula anchors the divisor to row 3 and the fill did not copy the formula to a different row.

7. Select H3:I3. Use the fill handle in cell I3 to drag through row 23. You will now have figures that show costs as a percent of net sales in cells H3:I23. Notice what's happened to the formula by the time you get to row 23. For example, the formula in cell I23 is:

=D23/D$3

   The divisor, D$3, is exactly as it started out in cell H3. The row is anchored by the dollar sign; so, no matter which row it's pasted into, the 3 is fixed. The column is not anchored, so in step 6, when you filled the formula from cell H3 into cell I3, the divisor changed from C$3 to D$3. However, the numerator adjusts, first to column D in step 6, then from row 4 to row 23 in step 7.

8. You'll have 0% values in columns H and I, rows 6, 10 and 17. You can eliminate them by selecting the cells and pressing Delete, or by choosing not to show zero values (see step 15 in the prior list of steps).

9. Enter the labels as shown in Figure 3-3 for columns F and H. To get the labels to span columns H and I in rows 1 and 2, select H1:I2. Choose Format → Cells and click the Alignment tab. In the Horizontal drop-down, choose Center Across Selection, and click OK. Select H1 and enter **Percentage**. Select H2 and enter **of Net Sales**.

10. If you want to use single or double underlines, select the cells where you want to use an underline. Choose Format → Cells and click the Font tab. Choose Single Accounting or Double Accounting from the Underline drop-down.

The result is shown in Figure 3-4.

	A	B	C	D	E	F	G	H	I
1						Increase		Percentage	
2			2006	2007		(Decrease)		of Net Sales	
3	Net Sales		$ 3,414,926	$ 4,197,911		22.9%		100.0%	100.0%
4	Cost of Goods Sold		1,866,171	2,354,930		26.2%		54.6%	56.1%
5	Gross Profit		1,548,755	1,842,981		19.0%		45.4%	43.9%
6	Operating Expenses								
7		Travel & Entertainment	89,305	116,873		30.9%		2.6%	2.8%
8		Commissions	274,153	343,322		25.2%		8.0%	8.2%
9	Total Sales Expenses		363,458	460,195		26.6%		10.6%	11.0%
10									
11		Salaries	267,543	364,953		36.4%		7.8%	8.7%
12		Communications	20,320	22,459		10.5%		0.6%	0.5%
13		Insurance	25,400	39,303		54.7%		0.7%	0.9%
14		Advertising	76,622	89,835		17.2%		2.2%	2.1%
15		Depreciation	33,443	44,917		34.3%		1.0%	1.1%
16	Total Administrative Expenses		423,328	561,467		32.6%		12.4%	13.4%
17									
18	Total Operating Expenses		786,786	1,021,662		29.9%		23.0%	24.3%
19	Operating Income		761,969	821,320		7.8%		22.3%	19.6%
20	Interest Expense		130,805	104,644		(20.0%)		3.8%	2.5%
21	Income before taxes		631,164	716,675		13.5%		18.5%	17.1%
22	Taxes		165,357	118,264		(28.5%)		4.8%	2.8%
23	Net Income		$ 465,806	$ 598,411		28.5%		13.6%	14.3%
24									
25									

H ◄ ► H \Comparative Income Statement /| ◄|

Figure 3-4: The common sized comparative income statement makes it easier to see what's happening to a company's cost structure over time.

Points to Remember

In the following sections I'll go over some of the points you should bear in mind for future reference.

Formulas Recalculate

Using formulas, you can change any number in the original income statement; its companion cell on the common size income statement will adjust accordingly. The formulas in the common size statement recalculate when their precedents change.

Formats Are Copied Too

In Steps 6 and 7 of the instructions presented in the preceding section, when you fill into other cells, the Percent Style format follows along with the formula. This is typical behavior in Excel. When you copy-and-paste the contents of a cell (and in effect that's what you do when you use a cell's fill handle) you also copy-and-paste the cell's formats.

Absolute References Don't Change

In Step 7, when you fill the formula from H3:I3 into H4:I23, the references to C$3 and D$3 remain unchanged. The dollar signs indicate that the row reference is absolute, and should not adjust when you copy-and-paste its formula into another cell.

Relative (and Mixed) References Change

In contrast, when you fill the formula from H3 into I3, the reference to C$3 does adjust, to D$3. The absence of a dollar sign indicates that the column reference is relative, and should adjust when you copy-and-paste its formula. These are examples of *mixed references*, where either the column (e.g., $C3) or the row (e.g., C$3) is fixed; the element that's preceded by the dollar sign does not adjust when the formula is copied-and-pasted.

Consider Combining Absolute with Relative References

It is this aspect of the formula — a cell whose reference adjusts as the formula moves, paired with a cell whose reference remains fixed — that makes it so easy to replicate a formula across many different precedent cells. You might use this technique to get a cumulative total. An example is =SUM($A$1:A1). Enter that formula into, say, B1 and then use the fill handle to drag it through B2:B5 — notice what happens to the relative reference A1. (Chapter 5 discusses this feature in more detail.)

The Mechanics: Using Values

The common sized statements built in the prior sections change if any of the precedent cells change — that is, if the pertinent accounting period has not yet ended and the books aren't yet closed, it's normal for, say, COGS to change, or for net sales to change. So you can get a preliminary look at costs as a function of net sales, but retain the capability of recalculation as precedent cells change.

If you're ready to build a final common sized statement for a given period, you might prefer it to contain static values instead of formulas. In that case, you'd take slightly different steps than are shown earlier in this chapter. (There are actually several ways to do this, but these steps get you there fastest.)

1. Activate a blank worksheet, or use Insert → Worksheet to get one.
2. Switch to the current income statement.
3. Click the Select All button (this is the gray rectangular button just above the worksheet's row headers and just left of its column headers). All the cells in the income statement — in fact, all the cells in the worksheet — are selected.
4. Choose Edit → Copy.
5. Switch to the new, blank worksheet.
6. Choose Edit → Paste. All the values (and formulas) from the original income statement are pasted into the new worksheet.
7. Switch back to the original income statement.
8. Select the cell that contains the net sales.
9. Choose Edit → Copy.
10. Switch back to the new worksheet.
11. Select the cells that contain the original income statement.
12. Choose Edit → Paste Special (see Figure 3-5). Click the Divide option, and then click OK.
13. While the income statement range is still selected, click the Percent Style button on the Formatting toolbar.

Figure 3-5: The Paste Special dialog box gives you a laundry list of
actions to accompany the actual paste operation.

WARNING: *In Step 11, do not use the Select All button. If you
do, Step 12 will cause Excel to divide every one of the
16,777,216 (depending on the version you're using) cells in the
worksheet by the net sales value.*

If you've followed all the steps to get this common sized statement, with its
fixed values, as well as the steps to get the common sized statement with its formulas, the two statements should look exactly alike. (Refer back to Figure 3-2.) The
difference between the two versions is not visible — it's hidden inside the cells,
which have either formulas or values, but not both.

Bear in mind that you can select all the cells in a worksheet using the Select All
button. If there is an object — such as a figure or a chart — on the worksheet, it will
also be selected. (This capability can be very convenient, but it can also select a lot
more than you might want.)

The sections that follow present some other points to remember from the second exercise.

Using Paste Special

In Step 12, you used Paste Special instead of just Paste. This option gives you access to a variety of operations that take place as the paste occurs. To common size a financial report, you would use the Divide option, as just illustrated.

More specifically, here's what the Divide option does: it divides any numeric values that it finds in the target range by the number that was copied. Suppose that you have copied the number 2. You intend to paste-special into cells D2 and E2, which contain the numbers 6 and 9, and specify the Divide operation. When you paste, Excel divides 6 by 2 and enters the result, 3, in D2. Note: Excel does not enter the formula =6/2 in the cell, but the value 3. Similarly, Excel enters the result of 9/2, or 4.5, into cell E2.

Notice in Figure 3-5 that you have other numeric options available during the paste operation, and they work in ways that are similar to the Divide option: if you choose Add, for example, the copied value is added to any values in the target range.

The other options show that you can paste formats as well as other aspects of a copied cell (or range). Those options are mutually exclusive: that is, you cannot choose both the Formats option and the Validation option in the same Paste Special operation. However, you can use Paste Special repeatedly, each time selecting a different option.

TIP: Microsoft Office applications, including Excel, use this convention: you can select only one of a group of options that are represented by radio buttons (for example, the various Operation options in the Paste Special dialog box). But you can select any or all of a group of options that are represented by checkboxes (for example, the Skip Blanks and the Transpose options grouped in the dialog box).

Paste Special Options

I think it's important to discuss more about the Paste Special options (references to "range" also pertain to "cell"), and the following sections contain addition information you should find helpful.

Formulas vs. Values

If the copied range contains values only, it does not matter which option you choose — only values are pasted. If the copied range contains formulas, or a mix of formulas and values, formulas are pasted as formulas if you choose Formulas. If you choose Values, formulas are first converted to their results and are then pasted as values.

Converting Text Values to Numeric

In operations work, I often find that I need to convert text values to numeric values. For example, here are the names of two fire-resistant doors as shown in a hospital's equipment inventory:

7REF229
7REF23

In fact, I'm usually dealing with 50 or more such values. As shown, the two names are sorted in text order: "22" in "229" precedes "23" in "23". But my client's requirement involves sorting them in numeric order according to whatever numerals follow the "REF" string. I can strip off those numerals with a formula like this one:

=RIGHT(A1,LEN(A1)-(FIND("REF",A1)+2))

The formula finds where REF begins in 7REF229, adds 2 to it to find where REF stops, subtracts that position from the length of 7REF229, and returns the remaining characters at the right end of the string -- that is, 229. The number of characters would be different if the starting value were 7REF23, and the starting position would differ if the starting value were 17REF229.

If A1 contains 7REF229, the formula returns 229. If A1 contains 7REF23, it returns 23. That's all well and good, but the results of the formula are themselves text, and 229 will still sort before 23.

The solution is to use Paste Special on the formulas. I enter zero in a blank cell, copy it, select the range containing the formulas, and paste special, choosing to add. Adding zero to the text-results of the formulas converts them to numbers.

Now, I can sort the range that contains the original values and the stripped-off numbers, using the numbers as the sort key, and the resulting order for the two sample doors given above is:

7REF23
7REF229

Formats vs. Values and Number Formats

When you paste Formats with Paste Special, you paste all formats that apply to the range you copied. So, if the copied range uses a bold font, has a border drawn around it and shows numbers as percents, then the target range gets the same format characteristics.

On the other hand, when you paste Values and Number Formats, you are pasting *only* formats that pertain to how a number appears, which is a subset of the formats that determine how a range appears. So, pasting number formats means that you paste whether the number is shown as currency, as a date, as a phone number, as a social security number, and so on. You do *not* paste other formatting aspects, such as borders, shading, font size or style, and so on. (The same distinction applies to the choice of Formulas and Number Formats.)

You might find it quicker to avoid Paste Special entirely if the copied source contains a value instead of a formula, or if you want the formula to adjust any cell references it contains. In that case, you can use Edit → Copy and Edit → Paste — so doing copies and pastes both the range's contents and its formats.

Skip Blanks

This option is the source of some anguish among users who haven't yet found that the term "skip blanks" is ambiguous: does it mean that Paste Special will skip blanks in the copied range, or in the pasted range?

Neither, really. The Skip Blanks option can't avoid copying blank cells from the copied range, because the copying occurs before you choose the Skip Blanks option. Nor does it skip blanks in the pasted range: if it did, you could use the option only to overwrite existing data.

No, what this option does is fail to overwrite data in the pasted range with a blank from the copied range. Suppose that you copy a blank cell, then select another cell that already has data in it, then choose Edit → Paste Special and choose the Skip Blanks option. When you click OK, you'll see that the data in the pasted cell is still in place, with the formatting it had before you pasted.

> **TIP**: *If you want to be really obsessive about testing this, start with a cell that has a cell comment — no data, just the comment. Copy that cell and use Paste Special, with Skip Blanks, to paste it into a cell that already has data. You'll see that the comment is pasted, but the original data in the cell you pasted to remains intact.*

I use the Skip Blanks option principally when I'm copying a range of numbers and pasting it to another range in combination with Multiply or Divide in Paste Special. Using Skip Blanks prevents Excel from multiplying an existing number in the paste range by a blank (which is interpreted as a zero) from the copied range.

Transpose

This option turns the copied range 90 degrees to the right. Figure 3-6 shows two ranges: the original in A1:B12, and in A15:L16 the result of copying A1:B12 and then using Paste Special with the Transpose option checked.

	A	B	C	D	E	F	G	H	I	J	K	L	M
1	Jan	$43,815											
2	Feb	$11,572											
3	Mar	$26,533											
4	Apr	$63,442											
5	May	$42,960											
6	Jun	$73,650											
7	Jul	$29,126											
8	Aug	$51,440											
9	Sep	$77,191											
10	Oct	$80,903											
11	Nov	$76,111											
12	Dec	$30,763											
13													
14													
15	Jan	Feb	Mar	Apr	May	Jun	Jul	Aug	Sep	Oct	Nov	Dec	
16	$43,815	$11,572	$26,533	$63,442	$42,960	$73,650	$29,126	$51,440	$77,191	$80,903	$76,111	$30,763	
17													

Transposed Range

Figure 3-6: Notice that the second column of the original range becomes the second row of the transposed range.

It's easy enough to use the Transpose option: just select the original range, copy it, select another cell, choose Edit → Paste Special, check Transpose, and click OK.

This can be a handy way to turn a report on its side. Suppose you have a print file of a report that is formatted in landscape mode (each page is wider than it is tall). You'd like to change that orientation to portrait mode (each page is taller than it is wide) — perhaps it makes your analysis easier that way, or you might want to print the report with comments that are themselves in portrait mode. Figure 3-7 displays an example.

	A	B	C	D	E	F	G	H	I	J	K	L	M	N
1	Parts		Widget A											
2														
3	Date			01/01/2007	01/06/2007	01/11/2007	01/14/2007	01/16/2007	01/17/2007	02/02/2007	02/07/2007	02/09/2007	02/13/2007	02/14/2007
4														
5	Num			769	774	776	778	780	782	794	797	799	803	805
6														
7	Qty			1.00	1.00	1.00	1.00	1.00	1.00	1.00	1.00	1.00	1.00	1.00
8														
9	Sales Price			34.95	34.95	34.95	34.95	34.95	34.95	34.95	34.95	34.95	34.95	34.95
10														
11	Amount			34.95	34.95	34.95	34.95	34.95	34.95	34.95	34.95	34.95	34.95	34.95
12														
13	Balance			34.95	69.90	104.85	139.80	174.75	209.70	244.65	279.60	314.55	349.50	384.45
14														
15														
16		Parts		Date		Num		Qty		Sales Price		Amount		Balance
17														
18		Widget A												
19				01/01/2007		769		1.00		34.95		34.95		34.95
20				01/06/2007		774		1.00		34.95		34.95		69.90
21				01/11/2007		776		1.00		34.95		34.95		104.85
22				01/14/2007		778		1.00		34.95		34.95		139.80
23				01/16/2007		780		1.00		34.95		34.95		174.75
24				01/17/2007		782		1.00		34.95		34.95		209.70
25				02/02/2007		794		1.00		34.95		34.95		244.65
26				02/07/2007		797		1.00		34.95		34.95		279.60
27				02/09/2007		799		1.00		34.95		34.95		314.55
28				02/13/2007		803		1.00		34.95		34.95		349.50
29				02/14/2007		805		1.00		34.95		34.95		384.45

H ◄ ► H \ Sales by Items / ◄

Figure 3-7: The report may be easier to read when it's laid out top to bottom instead of left to right.

There is another way of transposing data, by way of the TRANSPOSE() worksheet function. This has the advantage that the transposed data stay "live," and will update if the underlying data changes. But it has two drawbacks: you have to begin by selecting the dimensions of the range as transposed, which is often a pain; and you have to enter the function as an array formula using Ctrl+Shift+Enter instead of just Enter.

TIP: I just implied that using Ctrl+Shift+Enter is a pain, but it's the basis for Excel's array formulas, which are capable of many surprising and elegant results. If you move on to expert status with Excel, it's essential that you become familiar with array formulas. (Because of the topics it covers, this book has little to say about array formulas.)

A Lengthy Tip

I've spent a lot of time here counseling you to copy things and then paste them. To use Excel effectively — to spend less time doing mechanical stuff and more time in planning and analysis — you should turn some shortcuts into second nature. Here are three tips that have to do with copying and pasting, and over the years they've saved me a lot of time and tooth enamel. (These tips are not restricted to Microsoft Excel, or even to Office — they have to do with just about any application you might run on Microsoft Windows.)

Copying with the Keyboard

Select something in Excel — a cell, a range of cells, or a worksheet object such as a chart. Hold down the Ctrl key and simultaneously press **C** (it's not case sensitive — it could just as well be **c** and usually is). You have just copied your selection. You don't need to use Edit → Copy, and you don't need to right-click a selection and choose Copy from the context menu.

Just hold down Ctrl and press **c**. After not too long a time, you'll find yourself doing it by touch. I hold down the Ctrl key with my left pinkie and press **c** with my left forefinger — we're not talking a Liszt sonata here.

By the way, you can cut something instead of copying it by using Ctrl + **x** instead of Ctrl + **c**. When you cut it, it's still available for you to paste — it's just that it will disappear from its source location, either immediately, as in Word, or when you paste it elsewhere, as in Excel. I find that I have nowhere near as much use for cutting as I do for copying.

Now you can select something else — another cell, another worksheet, a Word document, anything that can accept a paste operation — and paste it there. See the next section to learn how to do that.

Pasting with the Keyboard

Once you have something copied, you can paste it just as easily as you copied it. Simply select the target location — a worksheet cell, a Word document, the search box in your Web browser — and then hold down Ctrl as you press **v**.

Notice how useful this can be. There are plenty of places where you might want to paste something that can accept a paste but that don't offer you a paste option, such as a button's label or a new menu item. Paste it anyway by using Ctrl + **v**.

Using the Mouse

If you've never experimented with pressing the right button (not the "correct" button but the button on the right) on your mouse or other pointing device, try it out. The typical behavior is that when you point at something on your screen and click the right mouse button (also known as "right-clicking") a context menu appears. That context menu displays a list of most of the things you can do with whatever you've selected. (You might sometimes see the term *shortcut menu* instead of *context menu* -- they're the same thing.)

Here's an example. Suppose that you're using Excel and you've copied something — say, a worksheet cell — and now your mouse pointer has targeted another cell. If you right-click that cell, a new context menu appears adjacent to your mouse pointer, and it has these items in it:

- Cut
- Copy
- Paste
- Paste Special
- Insert Copied Cells (just Insert if you haven't started by copying something)
- Delete
- Clear Contents
- Insert Comment (Delete Comment if the cell already contains a comment)
- Format Cells
- Pick from Drop-down List
- Add Watch
- Create List (See Chapter 1)
- Hyperlink
- Look Up (supports searches on Microsoft engines and sources, such as Encarta and MSN)

Clearly, there are plenty of things you can do at this point. In particular, you can click Paste, or Paste Special, to put whatever you've copied into the cell you're pointing at.

TIP: *Suppose you begin by copying a range of cells and choose just one cell to start the paste operation. Excel knows enough to paste the entire copied range to the right of and below the active cell.*

Believe me: a little practice with Ctrl + **c**, Ctrl + **v**, and right-clicking on things will pay large dividends in the long run, in terms of getting you through the work at your customers' sites And the fewer minutes you spend at their workstations, the more you have available for face time.

And by the way, you get a context menu with many objects other than a work-sheet cell. For example, try right-clicking on the various elements of an Excel chart: the gridlines, the axes, the data markers, and so on.

Other Uses of Common Sizing

You can, of course, adapt the techniques you've seen earlier in this chapter to other financial reports. It's just as typical, for instance, to common size balance sheets as it is to common size income statements.

If you want to common size a balance sheet, you would apply the same techniques described earlier in this chapter for income statements. You can choose to use live formulas or static values, whichever you prefer. About the only difference between the two kinds of common size reports is that you normally use net sales as the percentage basis for income statements, and total assets as the percentage basis for balance sheets.

Particularly with income statements, there's another basis that this chapter hasn't yet mentioned: headcount. That is, one divides costs and revenues by headcount over time — often, quarter or even month (in sectors where sales are highly seasonal).

When you do common size by number of employees, you can focus on how costs vary in response to larger and smaller staff and line headcount. You normally expect fixed, and relatively fixed, costs to vary when corrected for headcount — that is, total office lease expenses are normally pretty stable, but on a per employee basis would usually fluctuate.

Similarly, non-fixed costs such as total salaries and payroll taxes usually fluctuate with headcount, and tend to flatten out over time on a per employee basis.

So, one use for common sizing on headcount is to determine if any cost centers are behaving in an unexpected fashion — a fixed cost that looks stable over time, when corrected for number of employees, as headcount rises and falls, or variable costs that remain stable on a per employee basis. Isolating that sort of unusual outcome can help you target unexpected or undesired variables in the company's operations.

Chapter 4

Charting

Why charts?

Time series

Budget variances over time

Pivot charts vs. standard charts

E xcel offers a large variety of charts — line charts, column charts, scatter charts, area charts and so on — but there are two broad classifications: standard charts and pivot charts. Although they often look similar, even identical, they differ as to how you create and fine-tune them.

Why Charts?

Reports and analyses are all well and good, and usually there's just no substitute for them. But for displaying numbers visually, especially when there's a sequence of numbers to view, you can't beat a chart. Excel gives you such strong, visually compelling charts that some accountants use Excel mainly for the charting capability.

About Standard Charts

You start creating a standard chart with a list, just as described in Chapter 1; that is, you lay out your figures in adjacent columns that contain different fields (dates, budget dollars, costs, etc.), and within those columns you have rows that represent different records (monthly costs, for example, or quarterly revenues).

> **NOTE**: *You can also create a standard chart if you turn a list ninety degrees, with fields in rows and records in columns. But then creating a chart is more tedious, and you don't get some of the niceties that Excel offers when you work with a real list.*

Once you have that list, you can create a chart that displays the figures graphically. (As a review, the next section lays out the steps for creating a chart.) The chart has a number of elements that you can subsequently tweak to get just the appearance you're after. All you need to do is click on the chart element to select it; then the Format menu will offer an item that enables you to format the selected element. For example, after you've clicked on a chart's axis, you can select Format → Selected Axis.

The chart elements include:

- Axes, of course. Most chart types, such as line charts or column charts, have a horizontal and a vertical axis (a few types, such as pie charts, have one axis only). Sometimes you add another axis that uses a different scale, such as when you show in the same chart one set of data measured in millions, and another set measured in hundreds.
- Titles. These include a title for the chart itself and for each axis.
- Plot area. This is the section of the chart defined by the chart's axes: the area to the right of the vertical axis and above the horizontal axis.
- Data series. This is the representation, in the chart itself, of the values on the worksheet. For example, if you've created a line chart, the data series is a set of points that represent the values, with lines that connect those points. When you click a data series to select it, the formula bar shows the worksheet range address of the charted data points. A chart can have more than one data series, so that it can show, for example, monthly revenues in one data series and number of units sold in another data series.

- Data points. The data series is displayed by means of data points, with one point for each number that's charted. In a line chart the data points are symbols such as squares, circles and triangles. In a column chart, the data points are columns, and in a bar chart they are bars. You can choose the individual data points' color and shape. You can also choose to attach a label to each data point, which by default shows numerically the value that the point represents (but you can change that to something else, such as a comment).
- Legend. The legend is useful if you have charted more than one data series, so that you need to be able to tell which series is which.

You can choose to place the chart on its own sheet or to embed it as an object in a worksheet. Your choice usually depends on whether you want to see the chart along with the values it's based on: if so, you embed the chart in a worksheet.

When you've finished creating a chart, a new Chart menu appears in the main Excel menu bar, replacing the Data menu. The chart menu enables you to set various chart options, to add data to the chart, to change the chart's location, and to change the chart type (for example, from a column chart to a bar chart).

If you've worked your way through the material on pivot tables in Chapter 2, you'll recall that I suggested you base your pivot tables on a dynamic range. (If you haven't yet looked at Chapter 2, you won't recall that. A dynamic range is a named range whose definition is sensitive to the number of records it contains, so the named range grows as new records are added.) A chart is a great use for a dynamic range: the chart grows automatically as you add new data to the worksheet.

To use a dynamic range as a data source for a chart, start by creating the chart. Then, click on a data series to select it; you'll see the cell addresses of the data points in the Formula Bar, after =SERIES. Just replace the cell addresses with the name of the dynamic range. (Also, you usually need to change a reference to a worksheet to the name of the workbook.) For example, this reference:

```
=SERIES(Sheet1!$B$1,Sheet1!$A$2:$A$25,Sheet1!$B$2:$B$25,1)
```

might become this reference:

=SERIES(Sheet1!$B$1,Book1!XAxisValues,Book1!YAxisValues,1)

If XAxisValues and YAxisValues are dynamic range names in columns A and B, then when new records arrive in, say, A26 and B26 the range definitions expand to capture the new data, and the chart automatically redraws to display the added data.

In a series formula such as the two described here, the first argument (Sheet1!$B$1) gives the location of the data series' name; the second argument (Book1!XAxisValues) gives the location of the x-axis values; the third argument (Book1!YAxisValues) gives the location of the y-axis values.

Most common chart types — column, bar, line, stock, surface and area — have one category axis and one value axis. This enables you to create a chart that shows, for example, the names of car models on the category axis and the number of cars sold on the value axis. Without getting too deeply into the matter, the distinction is that a category axis can show text (e.g., "HUM-V", "Suburban", "Mini-Coop") while a value axis shows numbers. Column, line, stock and area charts use the horizontal axis for categories and the vertical axis for numbers; bar charts use the vertical axis for categories and the horizontal axis for numbers. XY(Scatter) charts and bubble charts use both axes for numeric values, and pie and doughnut charts have one numeric axis only.

About Pivot Charts

A pivot chart is directly connected to a pivot table, so to create a pivot chart you must go through the same steps you do to create a pivot table. An example of creating a pivot chart is given later in this chapter, in the section Pivot Charts vs. Standard Charts.

A pivot chart has much in common with a standard chart. It has the same elements — axes, titles, a plot area, and so on — that a standard chart does, and there are certain circumstances in which you might prefer to create a pivot chart than a standard chart.

For example, pivot tables are ideal for summarizing detail records such as individual transactions into periodic summaries, such as the total debits and credits for an account over a defined period. Pivot charts mirror those capabilities exactly: when you group a date field in a pivot table so that it shows, say, months instead of days, that grouping immediately appears in the associated pivot chart.

But pivot charts are — and I'm trying to be kind here — less flexible than standard charts. Here's one homely example: A legend is included automatically when you create either a standard chart or a pivot chart, and by default Excel puts it to the right of the plot area, halfway between the top and bottom chart borders.

If you don't happen to like the legend there, and modestly wish to improve the chart's appearance by moving the legend to the chart's lower left corner, all's well if you're working with a standard chart. You can move (and resize) a standard chart's legend to your heart's content.

But if you're working with a pivot chart and try to mess with its legend, Excel just ignores you. You can't resize it, and you can't drag it elsewhere. You can right-click it and choose to format it — that gives you some placement options, but they're inflexible. And if you try to edit the address of the data series in the formula bar, Excel whacks your knuckles with the spreadsheet equivalent of a ruler. You can't touch the address.

There are things you can do to the pivot chart's appearance, such as altering the number of decimals displayed on a numeric axis. But there is no crisp, definitive way to state the sort of thing you can do and the sort of thing you can't. It's just a matter of experience, of trial and error.

See the section Pivot Charts vs. Standard Charts for a way to base a standard chart, with all its flexibility, on a pivot table, with all its summary and analytic power.

Charts that Show Time Series

A *time series* is a sequence of values that are laid out in date or time order: that is, the value that occurred earliest heads the list, and the one that occurred most recently is at the end of the list. Usually, the actual date or time associated with the figure accompanies it in an adjacent worksheet column. Although this is a logical and convenient way to arrange the data, there's no requirement to order your numbers in this way. Excel lists work perfectly well if the data isn't in chronological order, and if you build a pivot table based on an un-ordered list, the table orders the data on your behalf.

Charts, it turns out, behave in much the same way. See Figure 4-1 for an example.

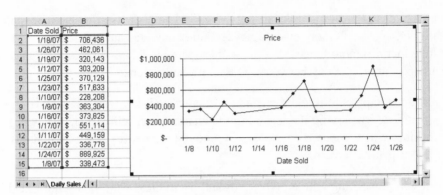

Figure 4-1: When you select a chart, Excel draws a "range finder" around the cells that hold the source data.

This is automatic behavior in Excel. That is, if you build a list so that a date (not time, though) field is to the left of another field such as dollar amounts, then Excel automatically structures a chart so that you can interpret it easily. Most eyes and brains are accustomed to reading time series from left to right on charts, and that's how Excel arranges the values on the chart's category axis.

In fact, you get a special way of formatting the axis, which Excel terms a *time scale*, when you're using it to plot dates. Notice in Figure 4-1, for example, how the spacing between the data markers conforms to their separation in time.

In contrast, Figure 4-2 shows a line chart with a horizontal axis that is *not* a time scale axis — the data markers are all equidistant.

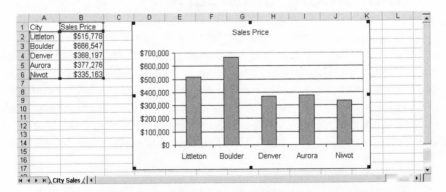

Figure 4-2: As scaled on the horizontal axis, categories aren't measured quantitatively.

NOTE: *Despite its name, you get the time scale axis only if the values are dates: days, months and years. You won't get a time scale axis if the values are shorter intervals such as minutes or hours.*

To see how you can control aspects of the time scale axis, have a look at Figure 4-3.

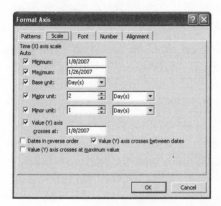

Figure 4-3: The Scale tab on the Format Axis dialog box shows that this is a Time Axis Scale. This tab has different options if the categories aren't dates.

What chart type should you use if you want to chart how dollar amounts vary over time? There are two equally good choices: a line chart and a stock chart. Figure 4-1 shows a line chart; one possible stock chart appears in Figure 4-4.

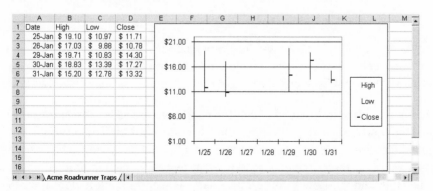

Figure 4-4: Notice there is no key symbol in the legend for High and Low.

You need at least three series of data for a stock chart like the one in Figure 4-4; in this case, the series are values for the daily high, low and close. To get a chart like the one in Figure 4-4, take these steps:

1. With your figures laid out as shown in Figure 4-4, select a cell in the underlying data list. This step is not required but it makes things easier.

2. Click the Chart Wizard button on the main Excel toolbar, or choose Insert → Chart. Either action starts the Chart Wizard.

3. In Step 1 of the Chart Wizard, select Stock in the Chart Type listbox. The default Stock chart sub-type is the High-Low-Close chart, shown in the upper left corner of the Chart Sub-type area. Accept that default and click Next.

4. In Step 2 of the Chart Wizard, verify that the Data Range address is correct and modify it if necessary. (It won't be necessary unless the list has many blank cells.) This is the reason for starting by selecting a cell in the list of data: if you do so, Excel locates the full region automatically. Click Next.

5. In Step 3 of the Chart Wizard, supply any chart or axis titles that you want to use. I believe you'll find, in most cases, that you don't yet want to change options available on the other tabs (Axes, Gridlines, Legend, Data Labels and Data Table); you can get at them later with Chart → Options. Click Next.

6. In Step 4 of the Chart Wizard, indicate where you want the new chart to appear — on its own sheet, or as an object embedded in an existing sheet. Click Finish.

About the legend in a High-Low-Close Stock chart: I suggest that you delete it (click it so that it gets a square black handle on each corner and then press Delete). Because it's a High-Low-Close chart, it's easy to tell which is which visually.

Furthermore, notice in Figure 4-4 that the chart legend has no key corresponding to the High and Low data points, just the Close data points. The reason is that a Stock chart in Excel is actually a Line chart, one that Excel has modified by goofing its formats. Excel suppresses the data markers that represent each individual data point for the High and the Low series on the chart (as well as the left-right lines that connect the consecutive data points), and inserts high-low lines that connect same-day data points. Figure 4-5 shows what the chart looks like with the markers restored.

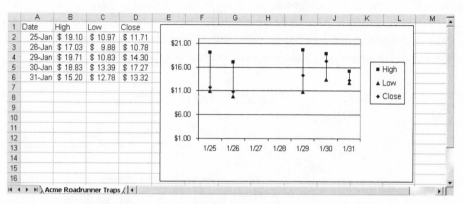

Figure 4-5: This chart legend shows a different key for each of the three data series: High, Low and Close.

You insert or suppress high-low lines by selecting a data series in the chart, choosing Format → Selected Data Series, clicking the Options tab, and either filling or clearing the High-Low Lines checkbox. You can suppress the data markers by selecting the data series, choosing Format → Selected Data Series, clicking the Patterns tab, and choosing the None option in the Marker area.

When you set the data series Marker pattern to None (or when you let Excel do so on your behalf by choosing a Stock chart), the markers disappear not only from the chart, *but also as keys in the chart's legend.* So you wind up with a legend that looks like the one in Figure 4-4: no key for either High or Low, because their markers have been suppressed. It's a little silly to have a legend that displays a name for all three series but a key for one only, so my preference is to just delete the legend from Stock charts.

By default, Excel puts a gray background behind the plotted data in its charts. If you want to change that background, select the plot area by clicking it and choose Format → Selected Plot Area, or right click inside the plot area and choose Format Plot Area from the shortcut menu. In the Area box, either choose the None option or click color that you prefer. (Some of my own clients complain that the default gray background makes it hard for their "aging eyes" to see the plotted data series.)

Pivot Charts vs. Standard Charts

If you've worked your way through the material on pivot tables in Chapter 2, you're aware that Excel offers something called a *pivot chart*. I waited until this chapter to discuss pivot charts because they make a lot more sense in the context of standard Excel charts than in the context of pivot tables. Figure 4-6 shows a pivot chart and the pivot table that it's based on.

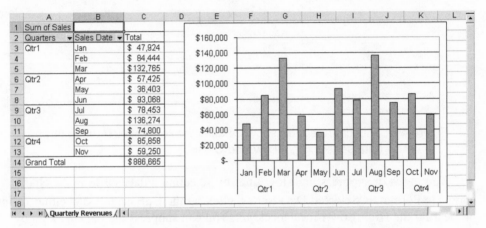

Figure 4-6: A pivot chart always has an accompanying pivot table.

In Figure 4-6, the user has built a pivot table using the methods discussed in Chapter 2. In particular, he has grouped his row field, Sales Date, by quarter and by month within quarter (see the section in Chapter 2 named Grouping Row Values). The only difference between getting a pivot table only, and getting a pivot table with a pivot chart, is that you choose PivotChart Report (with PivotTable Report) in Step 1 of the PivotTable Wizard. To get a pivot table only, you normally accept the default option, PivotTable.

You then proceed as though you were building a pivot table, identifying the location of the underlying data and indicating whether you want to put the pivot table on the active worksheet or on a new worksheet. When you click Finish, you see a new chart sheet with a chart of the data in the pivot table.

> *TIP*: *When you create a pivot chart, you can call for the associated pivot table to appear on the active worksheet, which might well be the one with the underlying data set. But the chart itself always appears on a new chart sheet. If you want the pivot chart to appear as an object in a worksheet, activate the chart sheet, choose Chart → Location, fill the As Object In option button, select from the drop-down the sheet you want, and click OK.*

This feature — pivot charts, that is — can be very convenient if you don't want to get too fancy — or if the time and effort of learning and applying fancy chart stuff aren't worth the payoff. For example, Figure 4-7 shows a data list, a pivot table based on the list, and a pivot chart based on the pivot table.

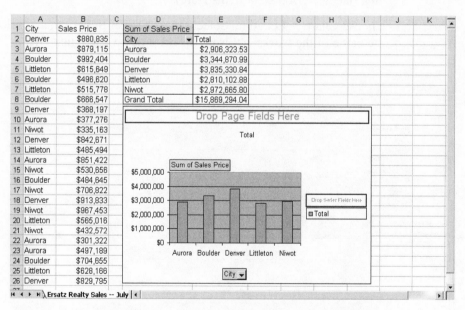

Figure 4-7: The grand total in the pivot table does not appear in the pivot chart.

Figure 4-7 shows a simple pivot chart. Here are the steps to get it (assuming that your list is already in place).

1. Click any cell in the list in A1:B26.

2. Choose Data → PivotTable and PivotChart Report.

3. In Step 1 of the wizard, choose the PivotChart Report (with PivotTable Report) option, and click Next.

4. In Step 2 of the wizard, verify that the address Excel proposes for the source data is correct. Modify it if necessary and click Next.

5. In Step 3 of the wizard, choose where you want to put the pivot table and click Finish. You'll see the pivot chart appear as shown in Figure 4-8.

6. Drag the City button from the Field List box into the Drop Category Fields Here area. Drag the Sales Price button into the chart's plot area (labeled Drop Data Items Here).

7. Choose Chart → Location. Select the As Object In option, and select the name of the worksheet from the drop-down list. Click OK.

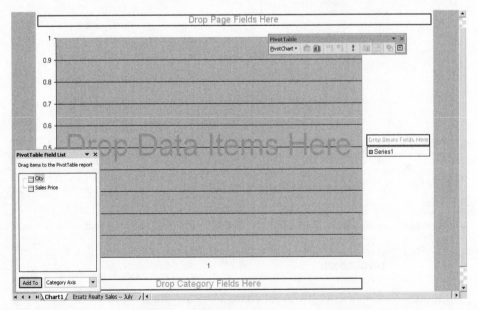

Figure 4-8: You can structure the pivot chart (and therefore the pivot table) on the chart itself.

TIP: To remove the design elements like the Drop Series Fields Here box from the pivot chart, click the Pivot Chart drop-down on the Pivot Table toolbar and then click the Hide PivotChart Field Buttons menu item.

Some points to consider about the pivot chart:

- The pivot table and the pivot chart are *linked*, not only as to the data summaries but also as to the structure. If you make a structural change to one of them, the other one reflects the change. For example, if you change the City from a row field in the pivot table to a column field, it immediately becomes a series field in the chart.
- Going in the other direction, by moving something on the pivot chart: if you drag the City button on the chart into the Drop Page Fields Here area, the pivot table immediately grows a page field and the row field vanishes.
- Similarly, if you change the format of the Sales Price field in the pivot table to something such as Currency, the format on the axis of the pivot chart also changes to currency. (By the way, time scale axes, discussed earlier in this chapter, are not available in pivot charts. More inflexibility.)
- Sadly, though, as soon as you refresh the data cache (see Chapter 2 for more information about the data cache) certain changes that you've made to the pivot chart's format are lost. Suppose you've changed the color of the data markers or added a secondary axis, error bars or data labels. As soon as you refresh the pivot table's data cache, the formatting changes you made are lost. Not all format settings are susceptible to this behavior, but enough are that it's a problem, and one that Microsoft has acknowledged and will doubtless eventually fix.

So pivot charts are a mixed blessing. They are a handy way to visualize the data summaries that you create in a pivot table. And they are undeniably useful when you want to turn the data this way and that, looking for the orientation and format that best depicts the numbers.

But you just can't do as many things with pivot charts as you can with standard Excel charts — for example, there are three standard chart types that you can't get with pivot charts, XY(Scatter) charts, Stock charts and Bubble charts.

And of course there's the problem with losing formats when you refresh the chart. It's amazing that this drawback has lasted through three versions of Excel, but it has. And the best solution available has been to record a macro when you change the pivot chart's format, and then play the macro back when you refresh the cache. Chapter 5 discusses how to use the macro recorder to handle similar tasks.

> *NOTE: You'd think that you could build a standard chart that's based on a pivot table, and once upon a time you could. But since pivot charts were introduced in Excel 2000, Excel has overridden your preference and has insisted on building a pivot chart if you try to base a chart directly on data in a pivot table.*

Charting a Pivot Table's Clone

A possible solution that you might want to keep in mind is to link other worksheet cells to the pivot table and build a standard chart on those linked cells. Figure 4-9 shows an example of how this can work.

In Figure 4-9, the original list data appears in A1:B26 and a pivot table based on that list is in D1:E8. In D10:E14 are "links" to cells in the pivot table: you can see, for example, the formula =D3 appears in the formula bar as the contents of cell D10. This formula is copied and pasted into cell E10, and then into D11:E14. Finally, the chart in Figure 4-9 is based on cells D10:E14, not directly on the pivot table.

This approach allows you to enjoy the benefits of a standard chart along with most of the benefits of the pivot chart. Format changes that you apply to the chart will stay in place if you refresh the pivot table's data cache.

This solution has its own drawback. If you modify the *structure* of the pivot table — such as making the row field a column field, or adding a new item to a row field — the linked worksheet cells do not adapt to the change. For example, in Figure 4-9, if you pivoted the table to make City a column field, then most of the linked cells would show zeros instead of city names and dollar amounts. The next section addresses this drawback.

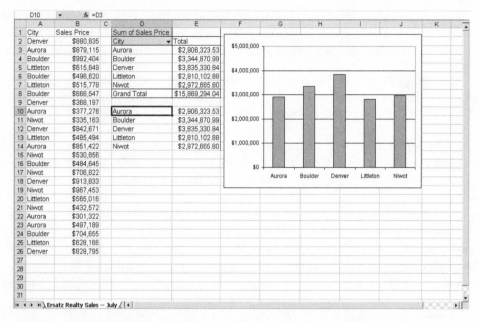

Figure 4-9: A standard chart, built on a clone of the pivot table.

Using the GetPivotData function

Yet another possibility is to use the GetPivotData worksheet function. Using this function is a lot easier than it might seem if you go by Excel's Help documentation — you can make it a simple matter of point and click.

For example, in Figure 4-9, suppose that you select cell E10 and click in cell E3. Here's what might result in the formula bar for cell E10:

=GETPIVOTDATA("Sales Price",$D$1,"City","Aurora")

That is, you can cause Excel to fill in the GetPivotData function's arguments for you, just by selecting the cell where you want to replicate the data, typing an equal sign, and then clicking in a pivot table cell.

So there's no special reason to learn the syntax of the GetPivotData function, but it's useful to know the following. In the example I used:

- The "Sales Price" argument identifies the pivot table's data field (necessary because the pivot table might have more than one data field).

- $D$1 just tells Excel where to find the pivot table you're interested in.
- The "City" argument tells Excel to look at the field named City.
- The "Aurora" argument specifies that item in the City field.

So, the function tells Excel to look at the Sales Price value associated with Aurora in the pivot table that includes cell D1. And in this case, the function returns $2,906,323.53 (see cell E10 in Figure 4-9).

Why is that helpful? Because now you can rearrange the pivot table and as long as it keeps the Sales Price field, the City field, and the Aurora item, the function will continue to return $2,906,323.53. It isn't dependent on a particular cell address; instead, it depends on what's in the pivot table.

Recall that all you needed to do was select a cell outside the pivot table, type an equal sign, and then click in a cell inside the pivot table. You also need to know that this works only with a cell that contains a data field value. In Figure 4-9, if you clicked in cell D3 instead of E3, all you'd get is =D3, with no GetPivotData function.

Finally, the point-and-click capability for GetPivotData must be activated. It's a toggle, so if it's off, clicking in a pivot table cell does nothing but select that cell. Here's how to turn it on and off:

1. Have the pivot table toolbar active.
2. Choose View → Toolbars → Customize.
3. In the Customize dialog box, click the Commands tab.
4. In the Categories listbox, click Data.
5. In the Commands listbox, scroll down until you see Generate GetPivotData. Click its button, just to the left of the Generate GetPivotData label, and drag the button onto the pivot table toolbar. Click Close.

The pivot table toolbar should now look something like the one in Figure 4-10.

Figure 4-10: The button on the far right end of the toolbar toggles the point-and-click option for GetPivotData on and off.

Now, you can toggle Generate GetPivotData. There's no particular reason to turn it off, but if it *is* off, this is the only way to turn it on, other than resorting to VBA code. Unless you do turn it off, it stays on indefinitely.

Budget Variances Over Time

Analyzing budget variances is a useful technique in management accounting, if only because it help focus on how well a department head is managing to a budget. Underspending can be as damaging as overspending, of course, so you have to look at all variances, not just shortfalls.

Naturally, it can be completely unfair to blame a manager for a single, or even a few, major variances. It's only when you spot a longer term pattern of serious mismatches between budgeted amounts and actual expenditures that you can feel confident that there's a management problem.

Excel is a perfect tool for analyzing budget variances, because you have an easy way to calculate the variance, and because its charts display the variances so clearly. Figure 4-11 has an example.

In Figure 4-11, you see the basic data necessary for a variance analysis in columns A, B and C: the date on which invoices were paid, the budgeted amount for the month and the sum of invoices paid for that date.

Problems with a Two-dimensional User Interface

Notice, in Figure 4-11, that the same budget amount is shown for each record that is associated with a particular month-and-year. The reason is that the data was pulled into the Excel worksheet from its point of origin, a true database (in this particular instance, SQL Server is used, but it could equally well be Oracle or Access or just about any other standards-based database management system).

Excel uses a two-dimensional design for is user interface: rows and columns. (Yes, in a sense there's a third dimension consisting of worksheets, but while that can be handy the capabilities are relatively limited.) So to properly associate a monthly budget figure with daily invoice totals, it's necessary to repeat the monthly figure in each day's record.

Row	Invoice Paid	Budget	Sum Of Invoice Amount
2	1/1/05	$559,324.65	$1,726.00
3	1/1/05	$559,324.65	$11,248.74
4	1/4/05	$559,324.65	$91,452.76
5	1/11/05	$559,324.65	$1,425.92
6	1/15/05	$559,324.65	$70,266.70
7	2/1/05	$215,038.48	$56,206.05
8	2/7/05	$215,038.48	$29,962.95
9	2/16/05	$215,038.48	$314.44
10	2/23/05	$215,038.48	$811.88
11	2/28/05	$215,038.48	$5,726.00
12	3/1/05	$1,387,304.73	$655.00
13	3/13/05	$1,387,304.73	$212.76
14	3/15/05	$1,387,304.73	$165,429.90
15	3/15/05	$1,387,304.73	$189,999.90
16	3/31/05	$1,387,304.73	$364.26
17	5/1/05	$32,710.03	$330.00
18	5/1/05	$32,710.03	$630.00
19	5/18/05	$32,710.03	$90.00
20	6/6/05	$36,550.48	$2,168.75
21	6/15/05	$36,550.48	$580.00
22	6/21/05	$36,550.48	$199.00
23	7/1/05	$64,690.00	$2,880.00
24	7/3/05	$64,690.00	$10,600.00
25	8/11/05	$68,414.00	$31,432.55
26	8/14/05	$68,414.00	$2,111.28
27	8/14/05	$68,414.00	$7,715.60
28	9/1/05	$25,922.87	$1,624.32
29	9/15/05	$25,922.87	$486.83
30	9/20/05	$25,922.87	$5,854.76
31	9/20/05	$25,922.87	$30,258.46
32	10/16/05	$57,265.60	$157.26
33	10/17/05	$57,265.60	$220.00
34	10/18/05	$57,265.60	$180.00

Data

Years	Invoice Paid	Budget	Sum Of Invoice Amounts
2005	Jan	$559,324.65	$176,120.12
	Feb	$215,038.48	$93,021.32
	Mar	$1,387,304.73	$356,661.82
	May	$32,710.03	$1,050.00
	Jun	$36,550.48	$2,947.75
	Jul	$64,690.00	$13,480.00
	Aug	$68,414.00	$41,259.43
	Sep	$25,922.87	$38,224.37
	Oct	$57,265.60	$26,331.34
	Nov	$56,209.84	$23,082.88
	Dec	$22,847.10	$10,796.77
2006	Jan	$786,497.13	$669,656.70
	Feb	$360,835.36	$406,828.45
	Mar	$1,385,064.51	$898,896.87
	Apr	$233,243.88	$283,931.49
	May	$680,659.23	$548,549.70
	Jun	$420,786.10	$518,352.92
	Jul	$303,981.28	$319,103.80
	Aug	$490,296.15	$545,115.50
	Sep	$222,178.19	$301,962.49
	Oct	$272,203.51	$364,309.99
	Nov	$267,989.57	$278,697.14
	Dec	$775,543.41	$1,220,401.10
2007	Jan	$260,641.92	$522,324.35
	Feb	$232,992.56	$2,558,607.87
	Mar	$632,253.62	$387,945.34
	Apr	$372,594.08	$354,230.46
	May	$181,751.90	$216,518.98
	Jun	$311,305.40	$250,234.12
	Jul	$328,384.41	$255,375.13
	Aug	$182,072.05	$86,328.66

Variance Analysis

Figure 4-11: The pivot table in F1:I33 associates total invoices for each month with the budget for that month.

True database management systems are designed to handle this sort of thing more effectively: they have parent records and associated child records. In this example, the parent record would be monthly data such as which month within which year, the monthly budget amount, the monthly FTEs, and so on.

The child record would be the invoices paid on a given date within a given month. The database manages the relationship between the daily records and the monthly records, so that it associates a budgeted amount for the month with the invoices paid on a given date. The result is that it's easy to total the invoices for a given month and compare the total with the monthly budget.

This is one reason that, given the rationale and the opportunity, I much prefer to base pivot tables directly on a true database (which is one of the "external data sources" that Excel makes reference to in the pivot table wizard's first step, which you can find in Figure 2-14 in Chapter 2).

Managing the connection between an Excel pivot table and a source database is beyond the scope of this book, but if you have that sort of situation you'll find guidance in Excel 2002: The Complete Reference, McGraw-Hill, by Ivens and Carlberg, and in Managing Data with Microsoft Excel, Que Publishing, by Carlberg.

Designing the Pivot Table and Pivot Chart

In Chapter 2 of this book, you'll find specific steps for constructing the pivot table shown earlier in this chapter in Figure 4-11. Some matters to bear in mind:

- The Invoice Paid field shown in Column A is the date on which invoices were paid; this helps tie particular invoices to particular budget months.
- In the pivot table, the budget amount is the *average* of the list's budget amounts for a particular month. Because the monthly budgeted amount is constant in the underlying list, using Field Settings (discussed in Chapter 2 and displayed in Figure 2-4) to call for an average rather than a sum accurately reports the monthly budget in the pivot table.
- The two dollar fields, budget amounts and invoice amounts, appear in two columns in the pivot table. This is accomplished by first calling for a pivot chart: start the chart wizard by clicking its button on either the main toolbar or the pivot table toolbar. The pivot chart appears immediately in its own sheet. Then, drag the button labeled "Data" to the Series area on the chart.

Figure 4-12 shows the resulting pivot chart.

Notice how sharply the budget variances jump out at you from the chart. Going over this chart with a department manager, you'd want to know more about the apparent under-spending, or over-budgeting, in March 2005, and the wild spree the department went on during February 2007. Apart from that, the manager seems to be doing pretty well. (By the way, apart from changing the years, Figures 4-11 and 4-12 display actual figures from a hospital's engineering department.)

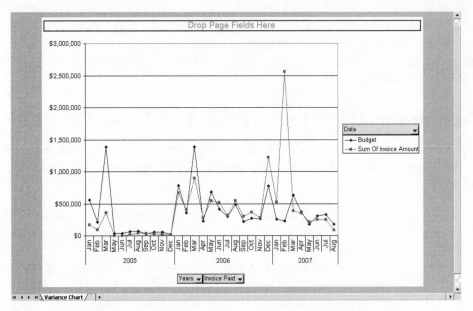

Figure 4-12 The drop-down arrows on the buttons enable you to select which categories or data series to show in the chart.

Chapter 5

Tools for Accountants

What tools do accountants need?

Built-in lists

Building custom lists

Using the Macro Recorder

Keyboard shortcuts

I'm driving south on the 405 in Southern California, through Fountain Valley, where Michelle Pfeiffer once worked as a supermarket checker. This may account for the fact that I'm doing 75 mph and also talking with my accountant Frank, who's in Denver.

What Tools do Accountants Need?

Frank is expressing some opinions about Excel. He uses it frequently at his clients' sites, where he pulls data together from various sources to construct cost and income analyses. Sometimes he does this as part of an audit, sometimes simply as a matter of making a point that he wants to make sure that the client's managers really get.

That, says Frank, is why he uses Excel. The formatting that he can get into the reports, and the charts that he can create, are so good that his clients aren't distracted by lousy appearance, but concentrate on the message that Frank's trying to get across.

Frank tells me that he's faithfully taken courses in Excel every time a new version comes out. He feels duty bound to do that, but by now he's really questioning how much benefit he's getting from those courses. They teach him how to format a working capital analysis, how to create a chart of budget variances, and where to go for a page-break preview of a worksheet.

But the courses never seem to get to tools that would really make his on-site time more effective. It's stupid, Frank says, but he seems to have to type the names of the months and quarters into worksheets every time he visits a client. Same thing with a chart of accounts. Ditto repetitive formulas and statement footings.

By now I'm in Irvine and I can feel the sense of entitlement emanate from the malls as I speed past. I ignore it and explain to Frank that he can get Excel to do those things automatically. I also ignore him muttering, "This is so cool," as I walk him through automatically getting month names onto a worksheet. Frank wants more, but it occurs to me that I'm not absolutely certain he's off the clock, so I say goodbye and concentrate on avoiding a swarm of SUVs as I merge onto the 5. I try not to dwell on a news story that California has more drivers with guns in their vehicles than drivers with auto insurance.

And I resolve to start writing a chapter when I get home. The chapter will discuss some tools that those Excel courses never seem to get around to.

Built-in Lists

Since way back, at least as far as Excel 97 and maybe even Excel 95, Excel has come with some pre-defined lists. I'm a little surprised to find that a decade later, Microsoft hasn't thought of anything else that its users might want to list on their worksheets (state names and abbreviations, for example? or the names and ticker symbols of the Dow 30 Industrials?). But it hasn't, so it's a good thing that you can define your own custom lists.

The two built-in lists that come with Excel are days of the week and months of the year. If you count their abbreviations, that's really four lists.

Suppose you want a list of the names of the twelve months, spelled out. Do this:

1. In, say, cell A2 type the word **January** and press Enter.

2. Re-select cell A2. Notice that the active cell, A2 here, has a square black block at its lower right corner. That's called the Fill Handle. Move your mouse pointer over it until the pointer turns into a crosshairs.

3. Hold down the mouse button and keep holding it down while you drag across several cells either to the right or down. Notice that each successive cell shows the name of the next month: February, March, April, etc.

4. When you've had enough, release the mouse button.

You now have the names of several months in consecutive cells. It's quicker than typing them yourself. And they're spelled correctly. A few more items to know about:

- If you drag on past twelve cells, the list starts repeating: November, December, January, February …
- If you start by dragging up or left, the end of the list appears next: January, December, November …
- This capability is called *drag-and-drop*. If it doesn't work, or if it stops working, the first thing to check is whether it's been turned off. Choose Tools → Options, click the Edit tab, and make sure that the checkbox labeled Allow Cell Drag and Drop is filled. If drag-and-drop still doesn't work, make sure you've begun by entering an actual value from the list. If your initial entry was accurate and it still doesn't work, reboot.
- You can start with an item within the list, such as April or October.

The other built-in lists are abbreviated month names (Jan, Feb, Mar, etc.), days of the week (Monday, Tuesday, Wednesday, etc.) and abbreviated days of the week (Mon, Tue, Wed, etc.).

Building Custom Lists

There are probably plenty of related items that you or an assistant need to enter on a worksheet from time to time: the names of employees, their social security numbers, payroll deductions, and so on. You can just about eliminate the need to enter and re-enter this information on new worksheets by putting it in custom lists.

The simplest sort of list has just one column. Figure 5-1 shows a list of customers. Once entered on a worksheet, you can convert this temporary list to a permanent list.

	A	B	C	D	E	F	G
1	Customer Name						
2	B2 Window Cleaning						
3	Specialty Uniforms						
4	TIRCO Industries						
5	MrTel Voice and Data						
6	Wedeln Slats						
7	Property Innovations						
8	John Kepler Models						
9	Hoyle's Steady States						
10							
11							

Customers

Figure 5-1: You can get Excel to store this list so that it's always available.

Take these steps to create a custom list:

1. Choose Tools → Options.

2. Click the Custom Lists tab.

3. Click in the Import List from Cells box. (See Figure 5-2.)

4. Drag through the list in the worksheet (in Figure 5-1, cells A2:A9).

5. Click the Import button, and then click OK.

The list is now stored in Excel itself, not just in a workbook. As a result, the list is available any time you start this installation of Excel. You don't have to open any particular workbook.

You can also put the list in any workbook by entering any item in the list into a worksheet cell and then using drag-and-drop as described in the prior section. And when you do so, you can be confident that no misspellings have crept into the list: it's the same as the one you saved.

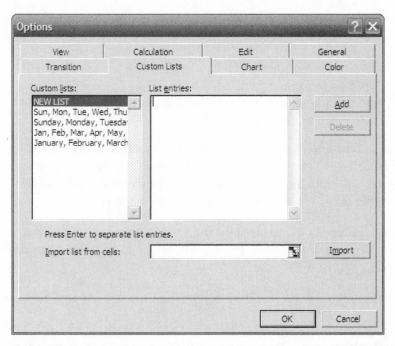

Figure 5-2: Use this dialog box to edit a list after you've established it.

If you've read Chapter 1 on Excel lists, you might have noticed that there's a difference between a typical worksheet list and a custom list: the custom list is not maintained with a column header (see, for example, Figure 1-2 for a true Excel list). In Figure 5-1, on the other hand, you would ignore the column header in cell A1 when you save it as a custom list — notice in Step 4, you use cell A2 as the start of the list.

This is an annoying distinction if you're writing about Excel, and it's emblematic of the cavalier approach that Microsoft brings to defining structures used in its applications. But if you're not writing about Excel, it's not that big a deal. It quickly becomes second nature to add a column header to a worksheet list and to omit it in a saved custom list.

Managing Custom Lists

In the prior section I described how to save a custom list using data that's already on a worksheet. I believe that's the way to do it because then you have all kinds of tools to bring to bear. For example, before converting a worksheet list to a saved, custom list, you can:

- Use Excel's spellchecker on it.
- Sort it using Data → Sort.
- Start by pulling the list into the worksheet from an external data source such as a web site or a database.

However, if you want to, you can create the list from scratch using the dialog box shown in Figure 5-2. Click NEW LIST in the Custom Lists box, if necessary, and start adding list entries in the List Entries box. As the dialog box admonishes you, press Enter after every list entry to get a new line for another item.

You can do some editing of a custom list from the Custom Lists dialog box (although you're prevented from editing the lists of day and month names and from deleting either those lists or their entries).

For example, select a list that you have built in the Custom Lists box. Now, in the List Entries box, you can:

- Delete an entry. Drag across it with your mouse pointer and press your keyboard's Delete key (the Delete button in the dialog box deletes complete lists only).
- Edit an entry. For example, drag across the "u" in "honour" and press your Delete key.
- Add an entry to the end of the list. Click immediately to the right of what is now the final entry in the list, press Enter, and then type another entry.

Minor edits like these are best done directly in the dialog box. That's a lot quicker than putting the list on the worksheet with drag-and-drop, editing it there, deleting it from the set of custom lists, and then importing the newly edited version.

Creating Complex Lists

The example customer list that was built earlier was described as simple, and it's hard to imagine a simpler one. Many lists occupy two columns, or more, on a worksheet. Excel's custom lists aren't built to accommodate more than one column, so you're forced to use a workaround.

For example, Figure 5-3 shows a simple, partial chart of accounts, one that you might find it necessary to use repeatedly in Excel worksheets. Two aspects of the data in columns A and B are that the data occupy two columns, and that the data in column A is apparently numeric.

	A	B	C	D	E
1	Account Number	Account Name			
2	1000	Petty Cash			
3	1010	Checking Account -- First National			
4	1020	Checking Account -- Security Trust			
5	1030	Savings Account -- Security Trust			
6	1050	Money Market Fund			
7	1060	Certificates of Deposit			
8	1100	Accounts Receivable			
9	1140	Other Receivables			
10	1160	Doubtful Accounts			
11	1200	Raw Materials			
12	1205	Supplies			
13	1210	Work in Progress			
14	1215	Finished Goods Inventory - USB ports			
15	1220	Finished Goods Inventory - Ethernet ports			
16	1230	Finished Goods Inventory - Video ports			
17	1400	Prepaid Expenses			
18	1410	Notes Receivable - Current			
19	1420	Prepaid Interest			
20	1430	Other Current Assets			
21					
22					

Current Asset Accounts

Figure 5-3: Two-column lists are just a little harder to manage than one-column lists.

One rule about custom lists is that their entries can't start with a number (and they can't be a formula). But the account numbers in Figure 5-3 are, well, numbers. Here's how to finesse that:

1. Enter the numbers and account names as shown in Figure 5-3, or enter any values in two columns that you want to convert to a custom list.

2. Suppose that you started the list of numbers in cell A2. In that case, enter this formula in cell C2:

```
=A2 & " " & B2
```

The formula combines the numeric value in A2 with the text in B2, sticking a blank space between the two. The formula results in a text value.

3. Drag-and-drop the formula in C2 down into C3:C20.

4. Select C2:C20 and choose Edit → Copy.

5. Choose Edit → Paste Special. In the Paste area, click Values and then click OK.

By taking these steps, you have:

- Entered numbers in column A and text values in column B.
- Represented them as text, via formulas in C2:C20.
- Copied the formulas in column C and pasted them as values on top of the original formulas.

TIP: What appears to be a number might actually be stored as a text value, and the five steps just above converted numbers to text. A quick way to tell if a cell contains a number or a text value is to check the justification. If the value is right justified, it's probably a number. If it's left justified, it's probably text. I say "probably" because that's Excel's default behavior, and you can change it by formatting cells differently.

When, in a formula, you combine a numeric value with a text value, as in step 2 above, the value returned by the formula is itself a text value. That takes care of the first problem, having numeric values in list entries. When you use Paste Special Values, you convert the formula to the value it returns, and that takes care of the second problem, trying to use formulas as list entries.

Your worksheet now looks something like the one shown in Figure 5-4.

Now, follow the same steps outlined earlier to establish a new custom list, importing the values from column C. Then, to use the custom list, just type in any worksheet cell an entry in the list (such as **1000 Petty Cash**) and then drag-and-drop to extend the list.

	A	B	C
1	Account Number	Account Name	
2	1000	Petty Cash	1000 Petty Cash
3	1010	Checking Account -- First National	1010 Checking Account -- First National
4	1020	Checking Account -- Security Trust	1020 Checking Account -- Security Trust
5	1030	Savings Account -- Security Trust	1030 Savings Account -- Security Trust
6	1050	Money Market Fund	1050 Money Market Fund
7	1060	Certificates of Deposit	1060 Certificates of Deposit
8	1100	Accounts Receivable	1100 Accounts Receivable
9	1140	Other Receivables	1140 Other Receivables
10	1160	Doubtful Accounts	1160 Doubtful Accounts
11	1200	Raw Materials	1200 Raw Materials
12	1205	Supplies	1205 Supplies
13	1210	Work in Progress	1210 Work in Progress
14	1215	Finished Goods Inventory - USB ports	1215 Finished Goods Inventory - USB ports
15	1220	Finished Goods Inventory - Ethernet ports	1220 Finished Goods Inventory - Ethernet ports
16	1230	Finished Goods Inventory - Video ports	1230 Finished Goods Inventory - Video ports
17	1400	Prepaid Expenses	1400 Prepaid Expenses
18	1410	Notes Receivable - Current	1410 Notes Receivable - Current
19	1420	Prepaid Interest	1420 Prepaid Interest
20	1430	Other Current Assets	1430 Other Current Assets
21			
22			

Current Asset Accounts

Figure 5-4: The values in column C are ready for import into Excel's Custom Lists

Note that because of the way the formula that defines the combined number-and-name was written, you separate the number from the name by a space. To review, this is the initial formula:

=A2 & " " & B2

Plugging in values for the cell references results in:

=1000 & " " & "Petty Cash"

and, evaluating further:

="1000 Petty Cash"

TIP: The ampersand (&) is the text equivalent of a numeric plus sign. It tells Excel to jam two values together. So "X" & "Y" & "Z" evaluates to XYZ.

Using the Macro Recorder

I know what you're thinking. "I didn't get a degree in accounting just to become a programming geek. Next!" And I don't blame you. In the user's manual for the very first commercial release of Lotus 1-2-3, a section was headed in big bold letters: **Advanced Topic: Do You Sincerely Want To Be a Programmer?** I thought to myself, "No, I sincerely want to get this stupid chart to print," and I moved on.

But that section, which talked about programming in Lotus, turned out to be prescient. Lots of people did want to learn how to program in 1-2-3, to get it to do things that its developers never anticipated. One result was a flood of malicious macros that people would hide in 1-2-3 files, and later in Excel workbooks, that would do things like erase files from hard disks when you opened them. I wrote one myself. I didn't stop at erasing files. The nasty macro I wrote conned the user into reformatting her C: drive.

(A *macro*, in the context of an application like Excel or Word, is a program that's usually written by a user and that we all hope is a benign way to extend the program's reach.)

That sort of thing caused companies like Microsoft to check for the presence of a macro or macros — and warn you — before it permits a file to fully open. Nevertheless, if you're alerted that a file you're opening contains macros, the best advice is not to open it unless you're certain of where it came from and that you trust the source.

Of course, you're a potential source, and I assume that you have good reason to trust yourself. So, why not write your own macros? It is true that they can save you time and make your life easier.

One reason not to write macros is that you sincerely *don't* want to be a programmer. Okay: you can get Excel to write them for you. Then, your role is limited to running them and saving time. Here's how:

Recording a Macro

Suppose that whenever you arrive at a particular customer's site, you open several Excel files — an income statement, a balance sheet, a current version of journals and one of ledgers, and a working capital analysis. These files are always in the same folders they were the last time you visited, but they're not all in the *same* folder. So you have to start Excel, locate and open one of the files, locate and open another file, locate and open another file, and so on until they're all open.

You can get Excel to do this for you automatically, if you record and save a macro. If you do that, you can play the macro back at a later time and it will do exactly what you did when you recorded it. More specifically, take these steps to set the scene:

1. Start Excel by clicking the Excel icon, not by clicking an icon for an existing Excel workbook. The name of the default workbook that opens when you start Excel is probably Book1; you'll want to activate it in Step 6.

2. Choose Tools → Macros → Record New Macro. A new, small toolbar that says Stop appears. Ignore it for now.

3. One by one, open the workbooks.

4. If you usually start by examining one workbook in particular — the income statement, say — activate it.

5. Stop the macro recorder by clicking the square box on the Stop toolbar.

6. Switch back to the Book1. Save it, and while you're doing so you might rename it to something like *Start Here.xls*.

Here's what you've just done: you have told Excel that you want it to make a record of some typical actions — in this case, opening some workbooks. Then you took the actions and, behind the scenes, Excel made the record you asked for. Finally, you told Excel to stop making its record. Here's what the record looks like (the only parts that would differ materially are the names and locations of the workbooks):

```
Sub Macro1()
'
' Macro1 Macro
' Macro recorded 11/3/2007 by Conrad Carlberg
'

'
Workbooks.Open Filename:= _
    "H:\Financials\2007\Income Statements\Income07.xls"
    Workbooks.Open Filename:= _
```

```
            "H:\Financials\2007\Balance Sheets\Balance07.xls"
        Workbooks.Open Filename:= _
            "H:\Financials\2007\Capital Analysis\Working07.xls"
        Workbooks.Open Filename:= _
            "H:\Financials\2007\Journals\Journals07.xls"
        Workbooks.Open Filename:= _
            "H:\Financials\2007\Ledgers\Ledgers07.xls"
        Windows("Book1.xls").Activate
End Sub
```

The code you see here is written in a language called Visual Basic for Applications, usually referred to for short as VBA. It's Basic because it is derived from the BASIC programming language. It's Visual largely because it was originally designed to make it easy to program using forms that users would fill in. And it's for Applications because it includes "objects" that belong to applications like Excel and Word.

For example, notice that the example macro refers to Workbooks — that's because VBA for Excel knows what Excel workbooks are and lets you refer to them and manipulate them.

Running a Macro

What good is all this? Well, now that you have the macro recorded, in the future all you have to do to open the five workbooks is to open the book named Book1.xls and run the macro. Excel executes each of the statements in the macro, leaving you with six open workbooks (including Book1.xls). To do that, you'd take these steps:

1. Start Excel and open Book1.xls.

2. Choose Tools → Macro → Macros.

3. The Macro dialog box shown in Figure 5-5 appears. In this case the Book1.xls workbook contains only one macro, so it's automatically highlighted in the listbox. If there were more than one macro listed, you'd click on the one you want to run.

4. Click the Run button. Excel executes all the statements in the macro you chose to run.

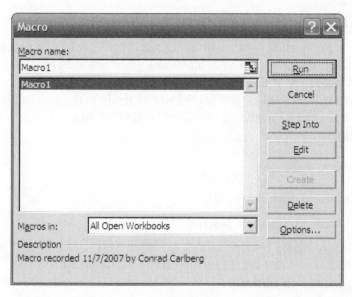

Figure 5-5: You can run a macro one statement at a time by clicking
Step Into.

And that's all there is to it. Instead of opening a workbook, then browsing around to find another workbook, opening it, browsing and opening, browsing and opening — you just open one workbook and run its macro. Excel takes care of the rest of the repetitive, time-consuming pointing and clicking.

Yes, there are other ways to get five workbooks open. For example, you could drop five shortcuts onto the desktop and click each one in turn. That approach has drawbacks, though — it takes up real estate on your screen, and you would probably have to minimize Excel after each workbook was opened in order to find the next shortcut. I'd rather run a macro.

Editing a Macro

What I've described so far is easy to put into place. It's quick and it's effective. It's also bare-bones. There's no crying need to spiff it up, but here are some things I do to make things a little cleaner:

Rename the Macro

Excel's macro recorder is pretty slick — it's *way* better than Word's macro recorder — but it's not omniscient. It doesn't know your intentions when you start recording, so it names the macro Macro1 (or, if there's already a Macro1 in the active workbook, it names it Macro2, or Macro3, and so on.) When I'm ready to run a macro, I want it to tell me what it does. So I'd rename the macro something like OpenFinancialWorkbooks.

You'd do that by taking these steps:

1. Start Excel and open Book1.xls.

2. Choose Tools → Macro → Macros.

3. In the Macro dialog box (refer back to Figure 5-5), select Macro1 in the listbox and click Edit. The Visual Basic Editor opens and you see the code given earlier.

4. Replace this:

Sub Macro1()

with this:

Sub OpenFinancialWorkbooks()

5. Choose File → Save. (Your choice might appear as File → Save Book1.xls.)

You have now renamed the macro, and when you run it next you'll look for OpenFinancialWorkbooks in the Macro window's listbox, instead of Macro1.

While I'm on the topic of editing macros, I'll mention that:

- A line of code that begins with an apostrophe is a comment. Excel does not try to execute it, and if you find it annoying you can delete it with no functional loss at all. The original code from the macro recorder, given earlier in this chapter, has five comment lines.
- The line of code (or *statement*) that you could edit to rename the macro began with the word *Sub*. That's short for *subroutine*. The word Sub plus the name you assign together define the start of a

group of statements that stand alone, like a paragraph. The words End Sub define the end of the group.

- You might have noticed that the macro code uses a colon followed by an equals sign in several places. Together, they say, "Let what's to the left equal what's to the right." I'm not going to get within shouting distance of the nuances of VBA code here, but it helps to know that in some situations you need to use := instead of just =.
- Notice the underscores following the := symbols. The underscores are line continuation characters. They tell Excel that the next line belongs with the current one. That is, this:

```
Workbooks.Open Filename:= _
"H:\Financials\2007\Income Statements\Income07.xls"
```

is exactly equivalent to this:

```
Workbooks.Open Filename:= "H:\Financials\2007\Income Statements\Income07.xls"
```

You use those underscores so that you can break a statement in two, to keep it from running off the right edge of the screen.

Rename the Workbook

Besides renaming the macro, I'd save the workbook with a different name than Book1.xls. I'd save it with a name like File Handler.xls.

Add Another Macro

I suppose there's a limit to the number of macros that you can put in an Excel workbook, but I don't know what it is and I've never run into it. For practical purposes you can assume it's possible to put as many macros in a workbook as you want. In this particular case, I'd certainly put another one in: one that closes and saves all five workbooks.

If you rely on yourself to close the workbooks one by one, you'll have to tell Excel whether you want to save any changes you might have made (or that calculations and links might have made on your behalf). You'll nearly always want to save changes, so to save time I like to have a macro that will save and close all my workbooks.

You would do this in much the same way you recorded the macro that opens the workbooks. Begin by making a small change in each workbook, and then reverse that change; this is so Excel will prompt you if you want to save the workbook when you close it.

Then, follow the steps given in the section titled Recording a Macro, above, except that you should close the files one by one. When all the files have been closed except the one where you're recording the macro, click the Stop Recording button. Then rename the newly recorded macro to something like CloseFinancialWorkbooks and save the workbook (in order to save the new macro).

Advanced Macro Modifications

This is a chapter on Excel tools that are of special interest to accountants, not a treatise on VBA and what Microsoft terms the Integrated Development Environment. So I'm not going to tell you how to do what's mentioned in this section, but I want you to know these things are possible and straightforward — so you'll know to look for them if you're interested.

- Over the long haul, I wouldn't want to jump through a hoop to get my file-handling macros (the one that opens files and the one that closes files) to run. I'd want OpenFinancialWorkbooks to run automatically when I open one of them, and CloseFinancialWorkbooks when I close one of them. *Associate them with the Workbook Open and the Workbook OnClose events.*
- If I wanted a little more control over when the macros run, I'd put two buttons on a toolbar — perhaps a custom toolbar — and associate the macros with those buttons. *Get the process started with View → Toolbars → Customize.*
- In the sample macro shown earlier, you probably noticed that the path to and name of each file were provided — after all, you have to tell Excel where to find the file and what its name. There are other things you might want to tell it, including whether or not to update any links it has to other files. *You can do this either by editing the macro or by re-recording it.*

Using Keyboard Shortcuts

Full disclosure: Years ago, Microsoft gave me a wristwatch. It was called a DataLink, and it worked with Schedule +, which was Office 95's PIM (Personal

Information Manager). You entered information about phone numbers, appointments, mailing addresses and so on into the PIM. Later, when you pressed a simple keyboard sequence, Schedule + did a screen dump of all that information in a barcode format. While that was going on, you dangled the wristwatch in front of the screen and it read all that data into its memory.

It was a great idea, I thought — and I still do. The problem was with the buttons on the watch. You had to memorize all these arcane sequences, or carry the manual around with you. Of course I lost the manual, so I was stuck. Twice a year I wanted to change the time between Standard and Daylight, and I couldn't remember how to do that. So every six months I found myself dangling that stupid watch in front of the computer screen just to change the time.

(I wore that watch for almost ten years. It tickled me that the world's richest man had flown me and my wife from Denver to Seattle and back, put us up for two nights, served us Copper River salmon — and gave me a wristwatch made by Timex.)

So it was a long time before I could persuade myself to use the similarly arcane keyboard sequences in Windows applications. I still know only a few of them — and Excel has, literally, hundreds. But I've never had a compelling reason to memorize *Ctrl + Shift +)* as the sequence to unhide columns.

I have had good reason to learn a few of them, the more so because they work not only in Excel but also in Word and Access, and some work in just about every Windows application I've found, including Windows itself.

Copying, Cutting and Pasting

I frequently find myself in a situation where I want to copy (less frequently, to cut) something, but I'm somewhere that doesn't give me a Copy button or menu item. I can usually copy it anyway using Ctrl + C (that is, I hold down the Ctrl key and simultaneously press the C key, either upper or lower case).

Doing that puts whatever I've selected onto the clipboard, a usually invisible location where Windows stores copied objects temporarily. Later, I can paste it elsewhere, using Ctrl + V.

Suppose that I'm doing some work for a veterinary supply company, and that one of their inventory worksheets makes multiple references to a tongue depressor for large animals — say, "Elephant Tongue Depressor #1". That particular model has been discontinued and replaced with #2. I don't want to do a global replace of #1 with #2 because that would alter other product descriptions that contained #1 or #2.

So I select one of the cells that contains "Elephant Tongue Depressor #1" and drag across that value in the formula bar. I press Ctrl + C, and then Esc to leave the cell as is. (Yes, I could also use Edit → Copy.) Now I choose Edit → Replace, and with the Find What box active I press Ctrl + V. This pastes the product description into the box.

Now I click in the Replace With box, change #1 to #2, and click Replace All. Notice that the Replace dialog box doesn't give you a Paste button or command; and when the Replace dialog box is open, Edit → Paste in the main Excel menu is either inactive or pastes only to the worksheet, depending on your version.

TIP: *Bear in mind that the clipboard crosses applications. For example, you can copy something in your Web browser, switch to something like Excel or Word, and paste it there. This may seem obvious, but I've worked with plenty of people who went through some remarkable and inspired contortions because they didn't know it.*

Selecting Cells in Excel

Suppose that you have a long list of values in a worksheet: they occupy contiguous cells such as A1:A1500. But you don't know where the list stops. It could be at cell A750, A2000, A3000 — anywhere in Column A. You want to find the last cell that contains a value.

Begin by selecting a cell in that list: A1, A10, whatever. Then press Ctrl and the keyboard's down arrow. Excel takes you to the final contiguous cell that contains a value. If you start in A1, and there are values (including blank spaces) in every cell from A1:A515, and A516 is empty, then pressing Ctrl + Down takes you to A515. If the list goes left to right instead of top to bottom, use the right arrow instead of the down arrow.

What if you want to select that list instead of just going to its last cell? Then use Ctrl + Shift + Down (or Right, or Up, or Left). That captures all contiguous cells with values.

But if the cell you start with is empty, the effect is the reverse. Ctrl + Down, for example, takes you to the first non-empty cell below the active one. Ctrl + Shift + Down selects the contiguous empty cells, *and* the non-empty cell that terminates the range of empty ones. More specifically, if A1:A500 are empty and A501 contains "E" then selecting A1 and using Ctrl + Shift + Down selects A1:A501.

What if the range of cells you want to select has the occasional empty cell or cells scattered throughout? Perhaps the full range you want to select starts in A1 and ends somewhere between A1500 and A2000, and some unknown number of cells in between are empty.

Start by getting to the bottom row of the worksheet. In versions prior to Excel 12, you could click in the Name Box, enter A65536, and press Enter. Those versions end the worksheet at row 65,536. (The last row in Excel 12 is 1,048,576.) Now use Ctrl + Up to get to the lowermost used cell in column A. With that cell active, use the *scroll bar* to make cell A1 visible. Hold down the Shift key and click in cell A1. This activates the full range from A1 to the final used cell in column A.

Changing Reference Types

If you've had a look at the material on cell references in Chapter 3, you probably know something about the difference between a cell reference that looks like $A$1 and one that looks like A1. The dollar signs make the references behave differently, because they *anchor* the reference.

Suppose that in cell B1 you have entered the formula =**A1**. That is, B1 contains a formula that references the cell one column to its left and in the same row. If you copy the formula and paste it into, say, Q1, the formula in Q1 will be =**P1**. It still points at a cell one column to the left and in the same row. Copied and pasted into D5, it would be =**C5** -- again, one column to the left and in the same row. Excel terms a reference with no dollar signs a *relative reference*. The location of the cell it names is relative to the location of the cell where it's entered.

Now suppose that you have entered =**$A$1** in cell B1. Copy the formula in B1 and paste it in some other cell. It will still be =**$A$1**. The dollar signs anchor the reference to cell A1. Excel terms this an *absolute reference*. The location of the cell it names is absolute, independent of the location of the cell where it's entered.

One more type of reference is the *mixed reference*. It uses a dollar sign to anchor either the column or the row. So, both **$A1** and **A$1** are mixed references. No matter which column you paste a reference to $A1 into, the reference continues to be to column A (but the row can change). No matter which row you paste a reference to A$1 into, the reference continues to be to row 1 (but the column can change).

The preceding three paragraphs are accurate so far as they go. The informed use of reference types has major implications for the effectiveness of a worksheet with any complexity at all. Again, Chapter 3 gives you a hint of this power.

But the present topic is keyboard shortcuts. Suppose you're using your laptop at 35,000 feet on a plane that you wish would climb above the chop. You're bouncing up and down, left and right, and you're trying to manage your laptop's touch pad with enough dexterity that you can slip a dollar sign between the A and the 1. After a few tries, you decide to give up until the plane gets to smoother air.

But you wouldn't have to give up if you knew about the F4 key. Try this:

1. Enter a formula like =**A1** in a cell. Re-select the cell so that you can see the formula in the formula bar.

2. Drag across the formula to highlight it.

3. With that address highlighted, press F4. **A1** changes to **$A$1** -- that is, the relative reference becomes an absolute reference.

4. Press F4 again. **$A$1** becomes **A$1**, a mixed reference with the row anchored.

5. Press F4 again. **A$1** becomes **$A1**, a mixed reference with the column fixed.

6. Press F4 again. **$A1** becomes **A1**, completing the cycle.

Here's another example of how you can put reference typing to work for you. You start with the data shown in columns A and B. You'd like to get a running total of the revenues in column B over the months shown in column A. That running total is in column B.

	A	B	C	D	E	F	G
1	Month	Revenue	Running Total				
2	January	$ 191,681	$ 191,681				
3	February	$ 714,049	$ 905,730				
4	March	$ 895,750	$ 1,801,480				
5	April	$ 376,162	$ 2,177,642				
6	May	$ 502,024	$ 2,679,666				
7	June	$ 597,565	$ 3,277,231				
8	July	$ 901,236	$ 4,178,467				
9	August	$ 251,578	$ 4,430,045				
10	September	$ 965,908	$ 5,395,953				
11	October						
12	November						
13	December						
14							
15							

Monthly Revenues

Figure 5-6: The running totals in column C depend on formulas with mixed references.

You get the running total by entering this formula in cell C2:

=SUM(B2:B2)

That formula uses the SUM function to get the total of the cells in parenthesis, so in C2 it simply returns the value in B2. Now select C2, drag across the first instance of B2 in the formula bar, press F4 and then press Enter. The formula in C2 is now:

=SUM($B$2:B2)

It's still returning the total of the value in B2, so what you see in C2 doesn't change. But now re-select C2, click on its fill handle, and drag down into C10. You'll see the running totals shown in Figure 5-6, but select C3 and look at its formula:

=SUM($B$2:B3)

As you drag the formula down through the rows, the relative reference adjusts to include more rows, until in C10 it refers to B10. But the absolute reference, $B$2, stays the same, so the range that is summed continues to start with the second row. And the final formula, in C10, is:

=SUM($B$2:B10)

There are many other ways you can use a combination of reference types in one formula to make your worksheets easier to set up. If you haven't yet looked through it, see Chapter 3 for some examples.

Chapter 6

Scenarios In Excel

About Scenarios

Creating Scenarios

Managing Scenarios

Protecting Scenarios

Creating Scenarios with the Solver

In 1996, PBS broadcast a documentary titled Triumph of the Nerds. It told the story of how personal computers and the World Wide Web changed the world. The documentary took some pains to emphasize that from time to time this ongoing revolution required a "killer app," an application so desirable that people would buy a computer to run it.

At one point in the revolution, the killer app was VisiCalc. VisiCalc was the first electronic spreadsheet, and it was written to run on the Apple II. It offered something that folks in b-school found irresistible: the ability to recalculate the results of formulas when the user changed a value that the formulas used, whether directly or indirectly.

On the documentary, you could actually watch the values in the spreadsheet change as the effect of a new value rippled through the spreadsheet. The changes were not instantaneous as they are now, but took place one after another, like the galloping hooves of Muybridge's thoroughbreds hitting the camera tripwires.

About Scenarios

For one who has pulled the crank on a Burroughs adding machine every time an adjusting entry was made to a trial balance, it was fascinating to watch the recalculations happen automatically, both in the documentary and in the real-time world of the late 1970s. And that's the heart of the electronic spreadsheet (or, if you prefer, the electronic worksheet): automatic recalculation. Inputs change so fast and so frequently that timely accounting has become just about impossible without that degree of automation.

But even automatic recalculation can't solve the problem of multiple inputs all by itself. Suppose you're building a business case and want to examine discounted cash flows over a several year period. The location of the breakeven point depends on a variety of factors, and you'll want to test the effects of changing them: discount factors, tax rates, depreciation methods, and so on. (You might be familiar with this sort of thing as a *sensitivity analysis*.)

Scenarios and Multiple Inputs

Managing those factors can be a little complicated. You want to keep track of what happens to your business case's payback period as you vary those inputs. At a minimum you'll want to look at a base case, a best case and a worst case. And you'll want to determine how sensitive your measures of profit are to changing those inputs: some inputs will have only a minor effect, others will be critical to a go vs. no-go decision.

Fairly early in its development cycle, Excel started to provide tools to help manage all those analyses — particularly the Scenario Manager. The Scenario Manager enables you to group a set of worksheet cells together and save their values with a scenario name.

Usually, you define several such scenarios. You might have one named Optimistic, with fairly low values for the discount rate and the corporate tax rate. Another scenario, perhaps named Pessimistic, uses relatively high rates. Yet another might be named Variable Rates, which uses discount and tax rates that change during the business case's planning horizon. You can define as many different scenarios as you want, subject to your computer's amount of available memory. (Just as a test, I used a macro to successfully define the ludicrous number of 10,000 scenarios in an Excel 2000 workbook.)

The values that you put in these scenarios are stored in an out-of-the-way location, so they're not cluttering up your worksheet when you don't want to see them. When you do want to see them, you just tell the Scenario Manager to show one of them by choosing from a list of available scenario names.

When you make that choice, Excel retrieves the values and puts them in the cells where they belong. At this point the formulas that you've put into the workbook recalculate, and you see new results, based on the scenario's values, for rate of return, payback periods, profitability indexes, and so on.

As soon as you select another scenario, Excel puts its values in place and all those formulas recalculate — but now that we're in the new millennium, they recalculate too fast for you to actually watch the changes ripple through the cells.

Excel terms the cells that are associated with a scenario its *changing cells*. Each changing cell has a particular value in a scenario. Commonly, the scenarios that belong to a worksheet use the same changing cells but assign different values to them. With a worksheet's scenarios set up in this way, you can switch from scenario to scenario and see the results of making repeated changes to one subset of cells. That's the typical setup, but nothing other than the logic of your situation would prevent you from having, say, five different scenarios that supply values to five different sets of cells.

Scenarios and Worksheets

Compared to other publishers of electronic spreadsheets, Excel was a little late in getting around to so-called 3-D workbooks — that is, workbooks that contain more than one worksheet. It's difficult now to envision a workbook with just one worksheet, but multiple worksheets became the standard only after Excel got on board in the mid-1990s. Did multiple worksheets make scenarios unnecessary?

Figure 6-1 shows a worksheet with a scenario that supports a simple breakeven analysis:

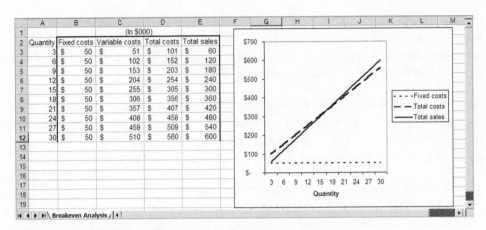

Figure 6-1: The scenario provides the values for variable costs in
        C3:C12.

With the values shown in Figure 6-1, the breakeven point occurs between the
15th and the 18th item sold. Calling for another scenario yields different results,
shown in Figure 6-2.

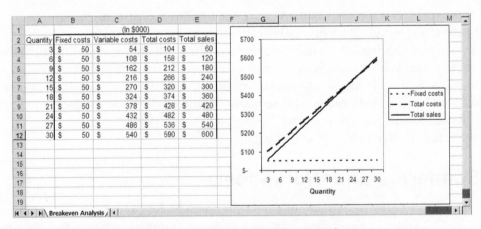

Figure 6-2: The variable costs are higher in this scenario.

In Figures 6-1 and 6-2, you can see the difference between the two sets of values supplied by the scenario manager. The values get plugged into cells C3:C12, the
formulas in D3:D12 recalculate, and the chart updates in response.

You might be asking yourself, "Why would I want to bother with that? I could put the same analyses and charts on two different worksheets, now that Microsoft has seen fit to offer multiple worksheets in the same workbook."

And you ask a good question. There's no reason you couldn't do that. Figure 6-3 shows a workbook with two windows, one for each of two worksheets, with the same analyses as shown in Figures 6-1 and 6-2.

	A	B	C	D	E			A	B	C	D	E	F
1			(In $000)				1			(In $000)			
2	Quantity	Fixed costs	Variable costs	Total costs	Total sales		2	Quantity	Fixed costs	Variable costs	Total costs	Total sales	
3	3	$ 50	$ 51	$ 101	$ 60		3	3	$ 50	$ 54	$ 104	$ 60	
4	6	$ 50	$ 102	$ 152	$ 120		4	6	$ 50	$ 108	$ 158	$ 120	
5	9	$ 50	$ 153	$ 203	$ 180		5	9	$ 50	$ 162	$ 212	$ 180	
6	12	$ 50	$ 204	$ 254	$ 240		6	12	$ 50	$ 216	$ 266	$ 240	
7	15	$ 50	$ 255	$ 305	$ 300		7	15	$ 50	$ 270	$ 320	$ 300	
8	18	$ 50	$ 306	$ 356	$ 360		8	18	$ 50	$ 324	$ 374	$ 360	
9	21	$ 50	$ 357	$ 407	$ 420		9	21	$ 50	$ 378	$ 428	$ 420	
10	24	$ 50	$ 408	$ 458	$ 480		10	24	$ 50	$ 432	$ 482	$ 480	
11	27	$ 50	$ 459	$ 509	$ 540		11	27	$ 50	$ 486	$ 536	$ 540	
12	30	$ 50	$ 510	$ 560	$ 600		12	30	$ 50	$ 540	$ 590	$ 600	
13							13						
14							14						
15							15						
16							16						
17							17						

Low Variable Costs / High Variable Costs ‖ Low Variable Costs \ High Variable Costs

Figure 6-3: The two worksheets replace the scenarios.

So, strictly from the standpoint of doing and viewing the analysis, there's no meaningful difference between the two approaches. (And perhaps, if Microsoft had put multiple worksheets into workbooks much earlier, it wouldn't have needed to develop a Scenario Manager.)

But there are some aspects of the Scenario Manager that turn out to be pretty useful. I'll discuss them here, and then you decide whether they're worth the trouble.

NOTE: You can't create, edit or show scenarios in a shared workbook. Whether this is an argument against scenarios or against shared workbooks is up to you. I already mentioned in Chapter 5 that I steer my own clients away from shared workbooks, so my thoughts on the topic should be pretty clear.

Creating Scenarios

First, you need to know how to create a scenario. Figure 6-4 shows a pro forma income statement that projects various cost categories according to estimates of quarterly net sales. (It's not strictly relevant to this discussion, but I'm defining *net sales* as total sales less discounts and returns.)

	A	B	C	D	E	F
1		Quarter 1	Quarter 2	Quarter 3	Quarter 4	
2	Net Sales	$ 150,000	$ 250,000	$ 360,000	$ 470,000	
3	COGS	$ 67,500	$ 112,500	$ 162,000	$ 211,500	
4	Gross Profit	$ 82,500	$ 137,500	$ 198,000	$ 258,500	
5	Operating Expenses					
6	Production					
7	Variable Costs	$ 15,000	$ 25,000	$ 36,000	$ 47,000	
8	Fixed Costs	$ 24,000	$ 24,000	$ 24,000	$ 24,000	
9	Sales and Administrative					
10	Advertising	$ 20,000	$ 20,000	$ 20,000	$ 20,000	
11	Salaries	$ 100,000	$ 100,000	$ 100,000	$ 100,000	
12	Other fixed costs	$ 30,000	$ 30,000	$ 30,000	$ 30,000	
13	Total Expenses	$ 189,000	$ 199,000	$ 210,000	$ 221,000	
14	Operating Income	$ (106,500)	$ (61,500)	$ (12,000)	$ 37,500	
15						
16	COGS percent	45%				
17	Variable costs percent	10%				
18	Fixed production costs	$ 24,000				
19	Advertising	$ 20,000				
20	Salaries	$ 100,000				
21	Other fixed costs	$ 30,000				
22						

Pro Forma

Figure 6-4: The sales-sensitive cost projections are based on prior year's cost-to-sales ratios.

It's useful to classify the figures shown in Figure 6-4 into three categories:

- Constants. These are in cells B16:B21, and do not change over time. For example, the Advertising value in B19 is used in cells B10:E10 as the same quarterly value.
- Changing cells, found in B2:E2. These net sales figures change when you change from one scenario to another.
- Formulas. These are in cells B3:E3 (COGS) and B7:E7 (Variable costs). They depend on the constants and the changing cells. For

example, cell B3 is the product of the COGS Percent, or 45%, and the first quarter's net sales, $150,000.

There are other formulas in Figure 6-4, but they depend only indirectly on the changing cells. For example, cell B4 is the result of subtracting the first quarter's COGS from the first quarter's net sales.

You might think of the constants as fixed — that is, costs that will not change, or will change only slightly, with net sales. You expect that $100,000 in salaries will be paid in each quarter regardless of whether the net sales are as shown, or are much higher or lower.

Like the one shown in Figure 6-4, the typical Excel scenario consists of constants, changing cells and formulas whose values depend on the constants and the changing cells. The purpose of the Scenario Manager is to help you handle the values of the changing cells, and to help you compare the results of various scenarios. Using the Scenario Manager, you can add, show, edit, delete, merge and summarize scenarios.

To access the Scenario Manager, choose Tools → Scenarios. The dialog box shown in Figure 6-5 appears.

Figure 6-5: If there were scenarios defined already, their names would appear in the box, on the upper left.

From the Scenario Manager you begin the process of creating scenarios. One reasonable place to start is with a scenario based on the most likely inputs. In this case, your client might think of the values in cells B2:E2 as realistic values, a sales forecast that is based on reasonable assumptions about the market's acceptance of a new product. After building the worksheet shown in Figure 6-4, you'd take these steps to make a formal Excel scenario from the values as shown.

NOTE: *The worksheet that contains the changing cells should be active before you take Step 1. This is because scenarios belong directly to the worksheet that's active when you create them. If you enter the scenario on Sheet1, you can't use the Scenario Manager to display it on Sheet2, without first merging it.*

---

1. For the worksheet shown in Figure 6-4, select cells B2:E2. These will be the *changing cells*. Choose Tools → Scenarios to get the dialog box in Figure 6-5.

2. As yet there is no scenario on the active worksheet. When you click the Add button, the Add Scenario dialog box shown in Figure 6-6 appears.

3. Because you started by selecting B2:E2 in Step 1, that range appears in the Changing Cells box. Type a name for the scenario, such as **Best Guess**, in the Scenario Name box, and click OK.

4. The Scenario Values dialog box appears, as shown in Figure 6-7. You can use this as an opportunity to edit any of the values now in the scenario, or you can leave them in place. You can always decide to edit them later, via the Scenario Manager's Edit button.

5. When you're through editing values for the changing cells, click OK to return to the Scenario Manager, and Close to return to the worksheet.

TIP: *It's a good idea to save the workbook at this point, to make sure that it will retain the new scenario.*

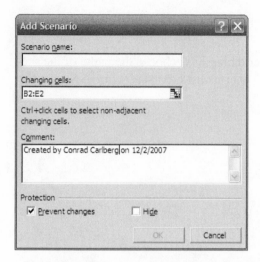

Figure 6-6: The OK button is enabled as soon as you start to enter a name for the scenario.

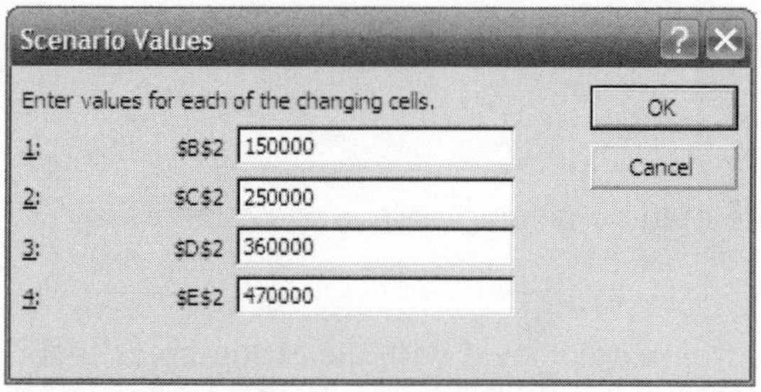

Figure 6-7: With more changing cells than used here, you'll get a scroll bar to access the others.

TIP: *If you have already given the range B2:E2 a name, such as Net_Sales, you can type that name into the Changing Cells box instead of the range address.*

That's all there is to it. Now you can enter anything you want in the Net_Sales range, B2:E2, and then bring back the scenario you just created. Bring it back with these steps:

1. With the worksheet contain the scenario active, choose Tools → Scenarios.

2. In the Scenario Manager dialog box, choose the name of the scenario you want in the Scenarios list box (see Figure 6-8).

3. Click Show.

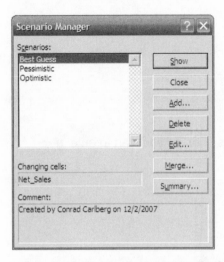

Figure 6-8: Notice that the name of the changing cells range appears in the dialog box.

When you click Show, the values you associated with the changing cells for the scenario you chose appear in the proper range and the Scenario Manager dialog box disappears.

Of course, you don't realize much benefit from defining only one scenario. To get real value from this tool, you should be defining two or more scenarios, so that you can study the effect of different inputs — that is, changing cells — on your projected results. For example, in addition to defining a Best Guess scenario, you might want to define another with conservative guesses for the net sales, and yet another with aggressive guesses.

So far I've skipped over a number of bells and whistles that scenarios offer. Before I get to them, it's helpful to take a look at something called the *implicit inter-*

section. This device can make your life easier, not only in scenarios but in other sorts of situations that call for the use of named ranges.

Defining an Implicit Intersection

To make this discussion easier to follow, look at Figure 6-9, which shows a subset of the information in Figure 6-4.

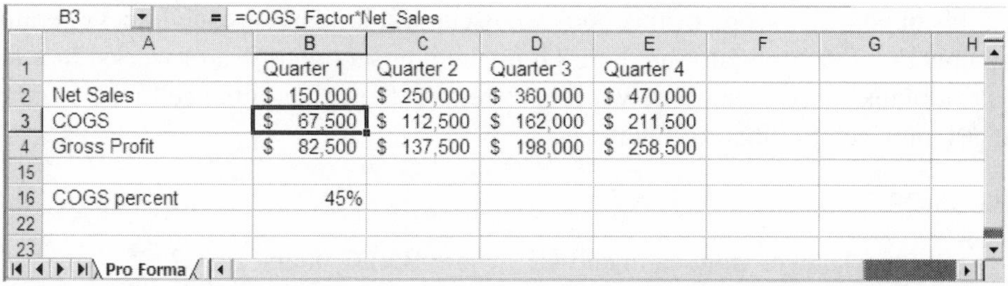

	B3	▼	=	=COGS_Factor*Net_Sales				
	A	B	C	D	E	F	G	H
1		Quarter 1	Quarter 2	Quarter 3	Quarter 4			
2	Net Sales	$ 150,000	$ 250,000	$ 360,000	$ 470,000			
3	COGS	$ 67,500	$ 112,500	$ 162,000	$ 211,500			
4	Gross Profit	$ 82,500	$ 137,500	$ 198,000	$ 258,500			
15								
16	COGS percent	45%						
22								
23								

Figure 6-9: The formula that's shown intersects Net_Sales at column B.

Figure 6-9 repeats two named ranges from Figure 6-4, COGS_Factor in cell B16 and Net_Sales in cells B2:E2. It also repeats the COGS estimates in cells B3:E3, which are the products of the COGS_Factor value of 45% and the Net_Sales values of $150,000, $250,000, $360,000, and $470,000.

I said earlier that the value in cell B3 is the product of 45% and $150,000, and that's true, but here's the actual formula that's used in B3:

=COGS_Factor*Net_Sales

NOTE: *If you're not familiar with range names, see the material in Chapter 2 under the heading Using Named Ranges as Data Sources.*

The formula's use of COGS_Factor is straightforward: its value is 45%, the value in the cell named by COGS_Factor. But what's the value of Net_Sales in the formula? Net_Sales is the name of the range B2:E2, which contains four different values.

In a case like this, Excel chooses which value in a range to use by noting the location of the formula that points at the range. In this particular case, the formula COGS_Factor*Net_Sales is found in column B, so the formula uses the value in Net_Sales that is *also* in column B.

That's the *implicit intersection*. The formula's column, B, intersects Net_Sales where its value is $150,000. The intersection is implicit because Excel's intersection operator, a blank space, is not used.

It's outside the scope of this book to discuss all kinds of arcane Excel operators. But now that I've brought it up, here's how the intersection operator works. In a formula, a blank space separating two ranges returns the value in the cell where the two ranges intersect. So, this formula:

=B3:D3 C2:C5

returns whatever value is in cell C3, where B3:D3 intersects C2:C5.

And so, each cell in the range B3:E3 can contain this formula:

=COGS_Factor*Net_Sales

and each instance of the formula returns a different result. For example, in C3, the formula intersects Net_Sales in column C, uses the value $250,000 instead of $150,000, and returns 45% of $250,000 or $112,500.

The implicit intersection is a powerful tool, particularly when combined with scenarios. If you keep it in mind you'll not only save yourself time in the long run, you'll find your own formulas easer to understand. Six months after you structure it, you'll find it easier to understand this:

=COGS_Factor*Net_Sales

than this:

=B16*B2

More Help from the Scenario Manager

Figure 6-6 showed the Add Scenario dialog box. There are a couple of items on that box that deserve more attention.

The Comments Box

The Comments box is a good place to put additional information about a scenario. By default, Excel enters the user name and the date when you create the scenario. The comment information is saved in the scenario along with the values of the changing cells.

If the scenario is edited, Excel adds another default comment, which says "Modified by Jane Doe on 11/30/2007" instead of "Created by John Doe on 11/29/2007." The name of the person creating or modifying the scenario is the user name associated with the particular installation of Excel that's in use.

TIP: You can change the user name by choosing Tools →
Options, clicking the General tab and editing whatever value
is in the User Name box.

It turns out that the Comments box is most useful in a networked environment, where the workbook that has the scenarios is stored in a shared network folder. That way, multiple users can, at different times, examine the scenario and make changes to it — presumably in their areas of expertise. The Comments box stores information about who made a particular change and on what date; however, it does not track what specific change might have been made. So, it's helpful for the user to document his or her own changes in the Comments box, along with the name and date of the modification.

Protecting Scenarios

With complicated scenarios — those that have many changing cells — you may want to protect a scenario from changes. This is especially true when you're nearing the end of a development cycle, and you want to make it harder to make wholesale changes to a scenario without your okay.

In that case, fill the Protect Scenario checkbox before you leave the Scenario Manager. But doing so is only half the process. You also need to protect the worksheet where the scenario is used. To protect the scenario and its worksheet, take these steps:

1. Fill the Protect Scenario checkbox.

2. Click OK to dismiss the Add Scenario dialog box.

3. Click Close to dismiss the Scenario Manager.

4. Choose Tools → Protection → Protect Sheet.

5. The Protect Sheet dialog box appears (see Figure 6-10). Make sure the Scenarios checkbox is filled.

6. Supply a password if you want. If you do, you'll be prompted to confirm the password when you click OK.

7. Click OK after confirming the password and OK again to dismiss the Protect Sheet dialog box.

8. Save the workbook to preserve the worksheet's protected status.

Figure 6-10: Leave the password blank if you just want a reminder not to make a change without first thinking about it.

WARNING*: Excel's password protection for worksheets is very weak. Anyone can download a short VBA macro from a newsgroup for free, and then run it to "crack" a worksheet password. If your clients have users who are reasonably sophisticated regarding Excel, you should consider password protection for worksheets like the lock on your front door: effective against casual intruders but useless against a determined burglar.*

Once you protect your work, no one can change the values of any of the changing cells in the scenario unless they know they password you supplied. Users must also know that they need to unprotect the worksheet first.

To unprotect the worksheet, first activate it, then choose Tools → Unprotect Worksheet. Supply the password when you're prompted to do so, and click OK. Now you can modify or delete the scenario.

In Step 5 above, you can also choose to protect the worksheet's contents and objects. (*Contents* refers to the formulas and values in the worksheet's cells; *objects* refers to items such as charts that might be embedded on the worksheet.) Leaving the checkboxes filled means that those items will be protected.

In turn, that means that leaving the checkboxes filled prevents any changes to worksheet cells. And if changes can't be made to worksheet cells, you have a problem with showing different scenarios, because showing a scenario depends on changing the value of a worksheet cell. The next section discusses some background information you'll need to decide how to solve this problem.

Protected and Locked Cells

There are two issues involved in the protected status of a worksheet cell:

- Is the cell locked?
- Is the worksheet protected?

If a cell is locked and the contents of the worksheet are protected, then the user cannot enter, change or delete information in the cell.

By default, worksheet cells are locked. You can check this by opening a new or unused worksheet, selecting any cell, and choosing Format → Cells. Click the Protection tab. You'll see the dialog box shown in Figure 6-11.

Notice that the Locked checkbox is filled. That means that if you protect the worksheet, no one will be able to modify the cell's contents without first unprotecting the sheet. It makes sense for the cell's default status to be locked: You'll normally want to prevent changes to cells when you protect a worksheet.

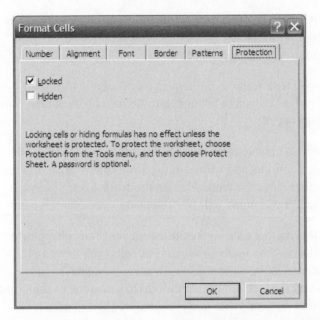

Figure 6-11: If you fill the Hidden checkbox, any formula in the cell is invisible when the sheet is protected and the cell is selected.

If there are some cells that you want to be able to modify on a protected worksheet, unlock those cells before you protect the worksheet — you do that, of course, by clearing the Locked checkbox.

So, the four possible combinations of locking cells and protecting worksheets are:

- Worksheet unprotected, cell unlocked. Any cell can be modified.
- Worksheet unprotected, cell locked. Any cell can be modified.
- Worksheet protected, cell unlocked. Any unlocked cell can be modified.
- Worksheet protected, cell locked. No locked cell can be modified.

Preventing Changes to Scenarios

Conceptually, what the previous section had to say about worksheet cells applies to scenarios, too. If you want to prevent someone from changing the values in a scenario, or deleting it, you need to prevent changes to the scenario *and* protect the worksheet's scenarios.

You prevent changes to a scenario by means of the Scenario Manager. If you refer back to Figure 6-6, you see that it shows the Add Scenario dialog box. Both it and the Edit Scenario dialog box have a Prevent Changes checkbox. Fill it to protect the values in the changing cells that are stored by the scenario that you're adding or editing.

You prevent changes to the worksheet's scenarios by choosing Tools → Protection → Protect Sheet, making sure that the Scenarios checkbox is filled, and clicking OK.

When you fill both those checkboxes (and then save the workbook), a user who brings up the Scenario Manager finds that two buttons are disabled: Edit and Delete. The user can't change or dispose of the scenario. However, if you only prevent changes to the scenario or if you only protect the worksheet's scenarios, anyone will be able to change or delete the scenario.

When you consider protecting a scenario, your thoughts should run along these lines:

"I don't want anyone other than me to change the values saved in this scenario. To make sure of that, I need to protect the scenario. To do so, first I need to use the Scenario Manager to prevent changes to the scenario.

"Then I need to protect the worksheet. If I do that, I need to allow the Scenario Manager to write values to the worksheet — otherwise I won't be able to look at the effects of different sets of values in the changing cells.

"So, I need to start by preventing changes to the scenario. After I've done that, I need to protect the worksheet, and that forces me to make a couple of choices.

"One choice is whether to protect scenarios on the worksheet. I definitely want to do that. Otherwise, preventing changes to the scenario in the Scenario Manager will have no effect. So I'll fill the Scenarios checkbox in the Protect Worksheet dialog box.

"The other choice is how I'll allow changes to the worksheet cells when I switch between scenarios. I can do this either by unlocking the changing cells —

using Format → Cells and clicking the Protection tab — or by clearing the Contents checkbox on the Protect Worksheet dialog box."

At any rate, that's the conversation tend to have with myself. And I usually resolve that last question — how to allow changes to the worksheet cells — according to what else is on the worksheet and how much time I have:

- If there's nothing elsewhere on the worksheet that I can't bear to lose, and if I'm really pressed for time, I clear the Contents checkbox on the Protect Sheet dialog box. This allows all cells — changing cells, cells with formulas, locked cells, unlocked cells — to be changed as the user sees fit.
- If I need to protect other cells on the worksheet, and if I have a little more time, I unlock the changing cells so that the Scenario Manager can change them. Then I protect the worksheet, making sure that both the Contents and the Scenarios boxes are filled.

I know this all seems complicated, and I admit that it is, at first. You do get used to it, though. It helps to keep the following in mind:

Preventing changes to a scenario and locking worksheet cells are two different things. When you prevent changes to a scenario, you keep users from changing the values that the Scenario Manager puts in the changing cells when you show a given scenario. When you lock worksheet cells, you keep users from altering their contents, whether the contents are formulas or values.

The two kinds of prevention — of changes to scenarios and of changes to worksheet cells — at first seem to be related because you do the same thing to enforce them both: protect the worksheet. When you protect the worksheet with Tools → Protection, you're saying that you really mean it about preventing changes to scenarios and about the locked cells. If the worksheet isn't protected in that way, your prevention of scenario changes and the locked status of cells *have no effect*.

Miscellaneous Actions with Scenarios

There are three actions that you take with scenarios that are quite straightforward: Editing, deleting and merging them. I'll go over these actions in this section.

Editing Scenarios

Editing a scenario is about as complicated as creating one. You activate the worksheet where the scenario is found and choose Tools → Scenarios. Select the scenario that you want to edit from the Scenarios list box and click Edit on the Scenario Manager.

The Edit Scenario dialog box appears. In terms of both function and appearance it is identical to the Add Scenario dialog box, except that it's labeled "Edit" instead of "Add."

Use the dialog box (its Add Scenario version was shown in Figure 6-6) to change the scenario's name, the addresses of its changing cells, or its comments. Excel adds a new default comment when the combination of user name and edit date changes — that is, if John Doe edits the scenario more than once on the same date, only the first instance is commented. If he edits it once on Monday and once again on Tuesday, both instances are commented.

Click OK to get to the Scenario Values dialog box, which was shown in Figure 6-7. You have an alternative if you want to edit the values for the changing cells. If you want to make a change to just a couple of values, then the Scenario Values dialog box is probably the place to do it.

If you want to edit many values, or even just several, consider doing it on the worksheet. There are a couple of reasons to start from the worksheet. One is that you can immediately see the effect of the changes on the formulas that depend on the changing cells. You might find out right away that a change to a value or values results in an absurd outcome. The other is that by looking at the worksheet context for the values, you know which value goes in which cell. That's a lot more difficult to do in the Scenario Values dialog box, where all you have to guide you is cell addresses (or range names, if you've thought ahead and defined them).

If you do make your changes on the worksheet, the first step is to use the Scenario Manager to show the scenario; this way, you have the existing values on the worksheet, ready for editing. The next step is to use the Scenario Manager to delete the existing scenario — the one that you are editing. Finally, add the edited values to a new scenario, presumably one with a name that's the same as the one you just deleted.

The drawback to this approach is that you lose the comments that are part of the scenario's development history. But you could, if you wanted to, copy and paste them from the Comment box onto the worksheet before you delete the scenario; then, copy them from the worksheet and into the Comment box of the new scenario.

To copy the comments from the Comment box, take these steps:

1. Choose Tools → Scenarios and then click Edit on the Scenario Manager.

2. On the Edit Scenario dialog box, click in the Comment box at the end of the final comment.

3. Hold down your mouse button, and drag up and left to highlight all the comments.

3. On your keyboard, press Ctrl-C to copy the comments.

4. Click OK twice to get back to the Scenario Manager. Then click Close to get back to the worksheet.

5. Choose Edit → Paste to paste the comments into blank cells.

Once the new scenario is added, finish with these steps:

1. Switch to the worksheet and select the cells containing the old comments.

2. Press Ctrl-X to cut the cells' contents.

3. Use the Scenario Manager to select the new scenario and click Edit to get back to the Comment box.

4. Click in the Comment box. Press Ctrl-V to paste the comments back into the box.

5. Click OK twice to get back to the Scenario Manager, and then click Close to return to the worksheet.

6. Save the workbook to preserve your changes.

I know that this looks like a lot of steps just to retain the comments from a scenario that you've deleted, but after you've done it a couple of times it takes just a few seconds. Besides, it's good practice with the keyboard shortcuts, which I guarantee you will save you hours over the course of a year.

NOTE: Chapter 5 has material on using keyboard shortcuts to do things like copying and pasting when there are no menu commands that carry them out. In this case, for example, if you want to copy something into the Comment box, you have to use Ctrl-V. This is because Excel's worksheet menu is disabled while the Scenario Manager's dialog boxes are active.

Deleting Scenarios

After all that about editing scenarios, deleting them is going to seem just too easy. Start the Scenario Manager, choose a scenario from the Scenarios list box, and click the Delete button.

Maybe it is too easy. Excel does not ask you to confirm that you really want to delete the scenario, and when the deed is done you can't use Edit → Undo to undo the deletion. If you change your mind, you need to hope that you didn't save the workbook after deleting the scenario, because then only a recent backup will save you from having to rebuild the scenario.

Merging Scenarios

Think of the act of merging scenarios as that of importing scenarios — that term is a clearer description of what's going on. Suppose that you have scenarios that belong to another worksheet (say, "Sheet 2007") and you want to use them on the active worksheet (say, "Sheet 2008").

Just start the Scenario Manager (the menu sequence Tools → Scenarios should be familiar by now) and click the Merge button. You get a new dialog box that looks like the one in Figure 6-12.

In the Merge Scenarios dialog box, choose a worksheet from the Sheet list box — choose the worksheet with the scenario or scenarios you want to import into the active worksheet. Then click OK.

Notice in Figure 6-12 that the OK button is dimmed, which means it's not enabled. Before you can click it, you must choose a worksheet that has at least one scenario on it, and that cannot be the active worksheet (that is, the one that was active when you started the Scenario Manager).

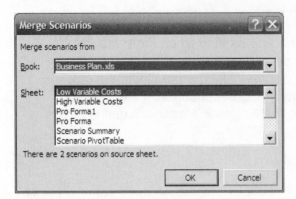

Figure 6-12: The "source sheet" is the one currently selected in the Sheet list box.

Once you've chosen such a worksheet, the OK button is enabled. When you click it, all the scenarios on the worksheet you chose are imported into the active worksheet: their names, their changing cell addresses, and the values associated with the changing cells.

As you can tell from Figure 6-12, you can also import scenarios from other workbooks. Just have a source workbook open when you start the Scenario Manager from the target workbook. Click the Merge button, and then choose the source workbook in the Book drop-down. Select the worksheet that you want to import from in the Sheet list box.

If you happen to select a scenario to import that has the same name as one already on the target worksheet, Excel gives the imported version a new name, based on the date and, if necessary, a numeric increment.

Summarizing Scenarios

Summarizing scenarios is only a trifle more complex than editing, deleting or merging them. Actually, summarizing them is very easy — it's understanding the summaries that can get a little complicated, but only a little.

The idea behind a scenario summary is to clear away any underbrush that might be obscuring what goes on when you create two or more scenarios, and to focus on the changing cells and the results of changing their values. Clearly, there's very little point to summarizing only one scenario. You already have all the information at hand, so there's nothing to be learned by summarizing it.

Suppose you have three scenarios on the worksheet: Pessimistic, Best Guess and Optimistic. When you click the Summarize button on the Scenario Manager, you see the dialog box shown in Figure 6-13.

Figure 6-13: Excel makes its best guess as to the result cells' address; you can override it.

Choose the Scenario Summary button on the dialog box, and the result cells that you want to see, and click OK. The summary report shown in Figure 6-14 appears.

In Figure 6-14 you see information about the three scenarios in columns E, F and G. As the note says, the Current Values in column B are the values of the changing cells at the time that the report was created. The current values are not necessarily part of an existing scenario, but in practice they usually are. The scenario names in row 3 are the names given to the Scenario Manager.

The changing cell values for each scenario appear in the range E6:G9. The results of using the values in the changing cells for each scenario are shown in E11:G14. Notice that the result cells have been given range names on the worksheet, and those names appear in cells C11:C14. Although the range Net_Sales, B2:E2 on the worksheet, has a name, the individual cells do not and so are identified by their cell addresses.

The worksheet in Figure 6-14 has some symbols that you might not have seen before. They are outline symbols, and you can click on a square with a plus sign to show one or more hidden rows or columns, and a square with a minus sign to hide them. For example, if you click the square with the minus sign that's just to the left of the header for row 5, Excel hides rows 6 through 9.

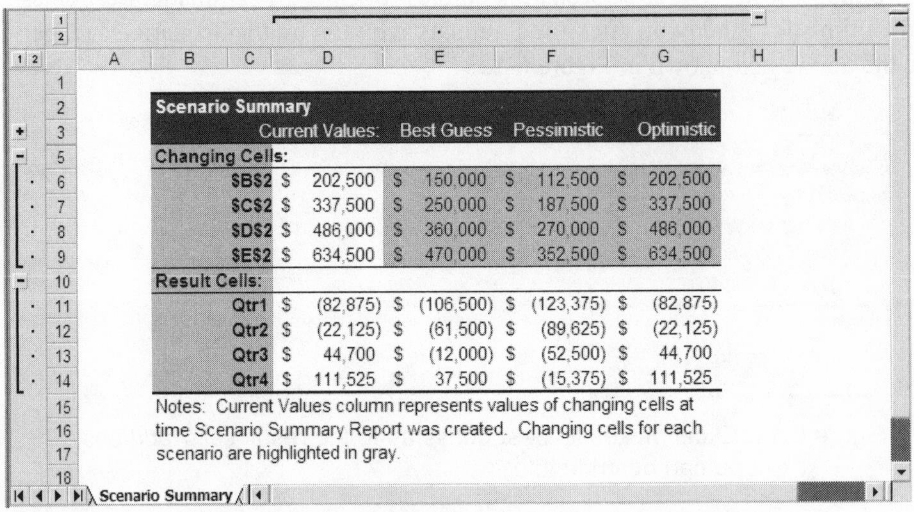

Scenario Summary				
	Current Values:	Best Guess	Pessimistic	Optimistic
Changing Cells:				
$B$2	$ 202,500	$ 150,000	$ 112,500	$ 202,500
$C$2	$ 337,500	$ 250,000	$ 187,500	$ 337,500
$D$2	$ 486,000	$ 360,000	$ 270,000	$ 486,000
$E$2	$ 634,500	$ 470,000	$ 352,500	$ 634,500
Result Cells:				
Qtr1	$ (82,875)	$ (106,500)	$ (123,375)	$ (82,875)
Qtr2	$ (22,125)	$ (61,500)	$ (89,625)	$ (22,125)
Qtr3	$ 44,700	$ (12,000)	$ (52,500)	$ 44,700
Qtr4	$ 111,525	$ 37,500	$ (15,375)	$ 111,525

Notes: Current Values column represents values of changing cells at time Scenario Summary Report was created. Changing cells for each scenario are highlighted in gray.

Figure 6-14: A glance at the result cells across the different scenarios gives you a quick-and-dirty take on their differential effects.

Outlines were an early feature in Excel, appearing well before pivot tables showed up. They were intended as a way to help the user create data summaries. Compared to pivot tables, though, they are clumsy and underpowered. It is likely that Excel continues to offer them mainly for backward compatibility, and I don't recommend that you spend any significant amount of time learning about them.

Outlines do continue to show up as scenario summaries, though, and you should know what you're looking at if you encounter one.

Referring back to Figure 6-13, notice that you can choose a Scenario PivotTable instead of a Scenario Summary. Figure 6-15 shows a scenario pivot table based on the scenarios summarized in Figure 6-14. (If you're unfamiliar with pivot tables, even this very simple one won't make a lot of sense — see Chapter 2 for more information about pivot tables).

In a scenario pivot table, the scenarios are shown as different rows (in Figure 6-15, rows 5 through 7). The result cells are shown in columns B through E. Notice in Figure 6-15 that the pivot table has a page field in A1:B1. This is very useful when you have multiple users contributing to scenarios. You can use the page field to select the results from a particular user, or you can choose All to show all the defined scenarios in different rows of the pivot table.

	A	B	C	D	E	F
1	Net_Sales by	Conrad Carlberg ▼				
2						
3		Result Cells ▼				
4	Net_Sales ▼	Qtr1	Qtr2	Qtr3	Qtr4	
5	Best Guess	-106500	-61500	-12000	37500	
6	Optimistic	-82875	-22125	44700	111525	
7	Pessimistic	-123375	-89625	-52500	-15375	
8						

Scenario PivotTable

Figure 6-15: All the extensive capabilities of pivot tables are available to you in a scenario pivot table, including basing a pivot chart on it.

Grinding It Out with Goal Seek and Solver

This is going to seem like a real lurch, but I promise you there's a good reason for it. Excel has for years offered various worksheet functions that take care of a lot of work for you. These worksheet functions are, in effect, pre-written formulas: you supply the numbers and Excel supplies the results. As one simple example, this formula:

=AVERAGE(B2:B50)

adds all the numeric values in the range B2:B50, divides by the number of such values, and displays the result in the cell where you enter it. The addition, counting and division are taken care of for you.

There are over three hundred such functions available to you in Excel (and chapters 7 and 8 of this book discuss two function families, amortization and depreciation, in some detail). But some problems don't lend themselves neatly to solution with functions.

In theory you could solve them algebraically or by using something more sophisticated such as analytic geometry, trigonometry or calculus. But you're usually a lot more interested in getting an accurate numeric answer quickly than in deploying your high school and college textbooks. So you should consider using a couple of Excel tools that are designed to do the heavy lifting for you: Goal Seek and Solver.

Using Goal Seek

Suppose your client anticipates that the fixed costs for the production of his product will increase by $125,000 next quarter, when a new labor contract kicks in with higher health insurance premiums. Before he makes any decisions about reducing variable and other costs to counter the fixed cost increase, he wants to know what effect the increase in fixed costs will have on his breakeven point. Figure 6-16 summarizes the situation.

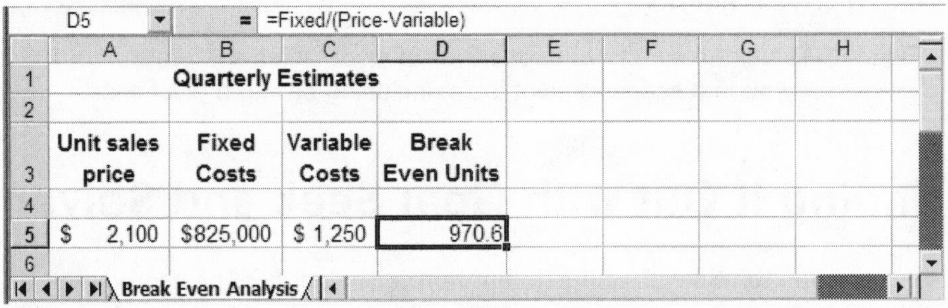

Figure 6-16: Range names have been defined for the input factors.

The breakeven analysis in Figure 6-16 makes use of this relationship:

Break Even = Fixed Costs / (Sales Price - Variable Costs)

where the usual definitions apply:

- Break Even is the minimum number of units that must be sold to cover all fixed and variable costs
- Fixed Costs is the amount of periodic costs that accrue regardless of the number of units produced
- Sales Price is the amount that each unit sells for
- Variable Costs is the cost of production of each unit sold

The formula in cell D5 of Figure 6-16 is based on that relationship:

=Fixed/(Price-Variable)

(The formula uses range names instead of cell addresses: *Fixed* refers to B5, *Price* refers to A5 and *Variable* refers to C5.)

Because things are set up to recalculate breakeven when inputs change, it's easy to figure a new breakeven assuming a $125,000 increase in fixed costs. One good way is to use Paste Special to increase the fixed cost figure. Take these steps:

1. In some blank cell — say, B15 — enter the number 125000.

2. Select B15 and choose Edit → Copy.

3. Select B5, which contains the Fixed Costs figure, and choose Edit → Paste Special.

4. In the Operation area of the Paste Special dialog box, choose the Add option and click OK.

(Now clear B15 if you want to.) The original figure of $825,000 for Fixed Costs is increased by $125,000 to $950,000. In response, the formula for the breakeven units increases to 1,117.6 (see Figure 6-17).

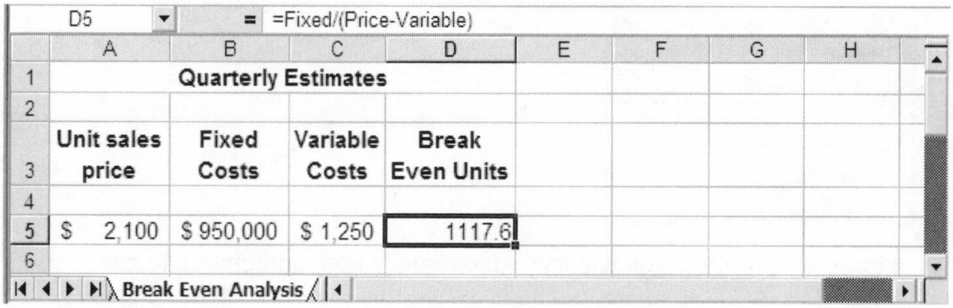

	D5	▼	=	=Fixed/(Price-Variable)					
	A	B	C	D	E	F	G	H	
1		Quarterly Estimates							
2									
3	Unit sales price	Fixed Costs	Variable Costs	Break Even Units					
4									
5	$ 2,100	$ 950,000	$ 1,250	1117.6					
6									

◄ ◄ ► ►◄ Break Even Analysis ◄ ◄

Figure 6-17: A simple linear relationship. Reality is messier.

So, given that the fixed costs are to increase by $125,000, your client must sell an additional 147 units to cover the increase, or take some other action. The first alternative that occurs to him is to increase the sales price. If he doesn't think that he can move another 147 units per quarter, perhaps charging more on a unit basis is feasible. Holding the variable costs and the breakeven point constant, what sales price will he have to charge to cover the increase in fixed costs?

One good way to answer that is to rearrange the formula to solve for sales price instead of breakeven:

Sales Price = (Fixed Costs / Break Even) + Variable Costs

But if you don't want to go to that trouble, use the existing formula setup with Goal Seek. Goal Seek is an Excel tool that uses a simple algorithm to search for a value that satisfies a condition you define. Here's how you'd use it in the current case:

1. Using Figure 6-17 as a starting point, select cell D5. At present, the formula for breakeven returns 1117.6.

2. Choose Tools → Goal Seek. The dialog box shown in Figure 6-18 appears.

3. Accept D5, the active cell, as the Set Cell.

4. In the To Value box, enter **970.6**. This is the previous breakeven point that was shown in Figure 6-16.

5. In the By Changing Cell box, enter A5 (or just click in cell A5 on the worksheet). Click OK.

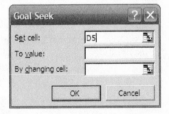

Figure 6-18: Goal Seek allows you to identify only one changing cell.

Now Excel tries different values for A5, Unit Sales Price, to satisfy the condition you set in the To Value box: that is, it looks for the sales price that will bring about a breakeven of 970.6, given the current values for Fixed and Variable costs. It's a simple problem, one that's well within Goal Seek's capabilities, and Excel returns the value $2,229.

There are a couple of requirements to use Goal Seek:

• The Set Cell must contain a formula. This is because it must be capable of changing in response to a changing value elsewhere.

- The Changing Cell must contain a value, not a formula.

These are "hard" requirements, and Excel won't execute Goal Seek if you don't meet them. A "soft" requirement is that the Set Cell's formula must depend, either directly or indirectly, on the Changing Cell's value. If it doesn't, Excel will stop trying new values for the Set Cell and will tell you it can't find a solution.

Excel tries an initial value for the Changing Cell, and then moves away from that value to see if the Set Cell's formula gets closer to or farther from the To Value that you supply. Goal Seek can go through hundreds or thousands of iterations looking for a value that satisfies your condition. In a linear problem that has a solution, Goal Seek usually finds it.

> **NOTE**: You can change the iteration specifications for Goal Seek by choosing Tools → Options, clicking the Calculation tab, and altering Maximum Iterations, Maximum Change, or both.

As I implied earlier, Goal Seek is not a sophisticated tool. It works best with linear problems, and with linear problems you can usually derive or rearrange a formula that gives you the answer directly, without grinding out hundreds or even thousands of possible solutions. With nonlinear problems, Goal Seek is less likely to be able to arrive at a solution, due to the simplicity of its algorithm. But those are precisely the situations in which it might be more difficult (and more fun, by the way, but that's not the point) to derive a formula that solves the problem.

And when you have multiple inputs that might change, things can get really complicated. I introduced Goal Seek partly so you'll know that it's there and why it's there, but also to introduce the basic approach used by Excel's Solver (which will get us back to this chapter's main topic, scenarios).

More Complicated Problems: Using the Solver

You'll need a different tool if you have a problem to solve that uses multiple inputs, or that relies on nonlinear relationships for its solution. In Excel, that tool is the Solver. This section walks you through its use, but first you have to be able to get at it.

Installing the Solver

Unlike tools such as Goal Seek and the Scenario Manager, the Solver is not built into Excel. It's what is termed an *add-in*, something similar to what other applications refer to as *plug-ins*. The Solver is included on your Excel installation disk and you either choose to install it with Excel, or you can install it later on.

Because you might have installed the Solver with the rest of Excel, it's a good idea to look for it first before you go looking for your Excel disk. Start Excel and look in the Tools menu. If you see Solver there, you're all set: it's installed and you're ready to start using it.

If you don't see Solver in the Tools menu, look just a little further. Choose Tools → Add-Ins. An Add-Ins dialog box appears, with a list box named Add-Ins Available. If you see Solver Add-in as one of the available add-ins, fill its checkbox and click OK. Excel will process for a couple of seconds, after which you should find Solver as an item in Excel's Tools menu. (I say "should" because there are a couple of problems that can arise, but they're rare and you'd have to go out of your way to set them up. If that happens, start from scratch as described below.)

If you don't find Solver in Excel's Tools menu, and also can't find it in the Add-Ins Available list box, you'll have to go back to your installation disk. The specific installation instructions and wording vary from version to version, so here I'll just note that to get the ball rolling you need to put the disk in the drive and either wait for AutoRun to start the installation wizard, or select the CD drive in My Computer and double-click the Setup icon.

As the installation wizard drags you along, you'll come to a point where you can choose among a typical installation, a complete installation and a custom installation. Choose the custom installation and continue. If you have an opportunity to indicate that you want to choose the detailed options yourself, do so.

Under Excel, you'll find an Add-ins option — since 2000, you get to it by clicking the plus sign next to Excel in the features list. The Add-ins option has its own plus sign. Click it to reveal a Solver item. Click the drop-down next to the Solver's icon, choose Run From My Computer, and complete the installation wizard. When you are through, Excel will have installed the Solver add-in in the default location on your internal disk.

You still have to tell Excel that you want it to put the Solver into the Tools menu, where you can get at it. As described above, start Excel, choose Tools → Add-Ins, fill the Solver checkbox, and click OK.

Running the Solver

As you'll see, getting a useful answer from the Solver is every bit as much a matter of structuring the problem as selecting the right options in the Solver. So consider the setup shown in Figure 6-19.

	A	B	C	D	E	F	G
1	Product Life Cycle: Rollout to Breakeven						
2	Year:	1	2	3	4	5	
3	*Benefits*						
4	Units sold	220	253	291	335	385	
5	Unit sales price	$ 10,000	$ 10,000	$ 10,000	$ 10,000	$ 10,000	
6	Gross sales	$ 2,200,000	$ 2,530,000	$ 2,910,000	$ 3,350,000	$ 3,850,000	
7	Incremental net sales	$1,282,863	$1,454,817	$1,650,075	$1,873,011	$2,122,827	
8						Diminishing returns:	0.9
9	*Costs*						
10	Lost product revenues	$700,000	$0	$0	$0	$0	
11	Advertising	$350,000	$315,000	$283,500	$255,150	$229,635	$229,635
12	New staff	$450,000	$481,500	$515,205	$551,269	$589,858	$450,000
13	Product rollout	$250,000	$0	$0	$0	$0	$0
14	Warranty costs	$0	$50,000	$56,711	$64,373	$72,959	
15							
16	Total costs	$1,750,000	$846,500	$855,416	$870,792	$892,452	
17							
18	EBITDA	($467,137)	$608,317	$794,659	$1,002,219	$1,230,376	
19	Less: Equipment Depreciation	$200,000	$200,000	$200,000	$200,000	$200,000	
20	Income before taxes	($667,137)	$408,317	$594,659	$802,219	$1,030,376	
21	Less: Taxes @ 36%	($240,169)	$146,994	$214,077	$288,799	$370,935	
22	Net income	($426,967)	$261,323	$380,582	$513,420	$659,440	
23	Plus: Depreciation	$200,000	$200,000	$200,000	$200,000	$200,000	
24	Minus: Investment	$2,000,000	$0	$0	$0	$0	
25	Net Cash Flow	($2,226,967)	$461,323	$580,582	$713,420	$859,440	
26							
27	Cumulative Net Cash Flow	($2,226,967)	($1,765,644)	($1,185,062)	($471,642)	$387,798	
28	Undiscounted payback period:	4.55					

New Product Pro Forma

Figure 6-19: You could extend this analysis to discounted cash flow by incorporating a discount factor.

Figure 6-19 shows a partial pro forma for a new product offering. It focuses on the first five years of the product's life cycle, during which the company wishes to reach the breakeven point when measured by cumulative net cash flow (but not discounted cumulative cash flow; that would take the example beyond its intended purpose).

The cost and benefit categories in the pro forma are largely self-explanatory, but there are a few things to note:

- The diminishing returns figure in cell G8 is used to quantify the difficulty of filling a distribution channel. The incremental net sales figures in row 7 make use of this figure. For example, the figure of \$1,282,863 in cell B7 is the result of raising the units sold of 220 to the .9th power, and then multiplying by the unit sales price: B4^\$G\$8*B5. Obviously, this renders the situation non-linear.
- The lost product revenues of \$700,000 in cell B10 represents the fact that the product under consideration will replace an existing product, one that was scheduled for retirement a year later.
- The EBITDA in row 18 is the estimated incremental net sales less the year's total cost estimates.
- The depreciation shown in row 19 is on \$2,000,000 in new equipment, shown as a purchase in cell B24. The depreciation is straight line, using Excel's SLN function with a life of 10 years and a residual value of \$0.
- The undiscounted payback period shown in cell B28, 4.55, means that the cumulative net cash flow turns positive a little more than halfway through year 5. The examples of using the Solver that are given next make use of this figure as a criterion: the Solver will adjust the inputs so as to reduce the calculated payback period from 4.55 to 4.00 — that is, to the end of the fourth year.
- The figures in cells G11:G13 use Excel's MIN function to return the smallest value in a range; for example, the formula in cell G11 is =MIN(B11:F11), and it returns \$229,635, the smallest value in the range B11:F11. In an example given below, the Solver will use cell G12 to constrain the adjustments it makes. No cost in row 12 will be allowed to be less than zero: that could lower costs enough to reduce the breakeven point to 4.00, but you would disallow any negative direct costs by means of the constraint.

So, with the setup as given, the estimates of units sold in row 4 flow through to cell B28: the units sold estimate helps determine the incremental net sales, which in turn helps determine EBITDA. After allowing for taxes, re-introducing depreciation and accounting for the initial equipment investment, the EBITDA figures in to the net and the cumulative net cash flow, which then determine the undiscounted payback period.

There are, then, various ways that the inputs can be manipulated to reduce the payback period (or breakeven point). Normally you would choose to vary inputs that your client can attempt to manipulate in reality, such as unit sales, sales price and direct costs.

Suppose you decide first to see what would happen if you recommend to you client that he focus on increasing units sold, perhaps by tinkering with sales commissions. That means you would alter the units sold estimates in cells B4:F4. To make sure you can get back to the values that are currently shown in Figure 6-19, you should begin be defining a scenario that saves the current values in B4:F4. Use the Scenario Manager to define that range as the changing cells, so that the scenario retains the cells' current values, and name the scenario something such as Base Case Sales.

Save the workbook so that the scenario is also saved, and now you can easily get back to the existing values of units sold by having the Scenario Manager show that base case. This frees you to change the units sold as you see fit, in order to reduce the payback period from its current value of 4.55 to 4.00.

NOTE: *You can obtain the worksheet as shown in Figure 6-19, with all the necessary formulas, from cpa911publishing.com/downloads.htm. The same is true for all workbooks illustrated and discussed in this book.*

Using the Solver's Interface

To solve for a shorter payback period, have the worksheet shown in Figure 6-19 active, and select the target cell — in this case, cell B28. With the Solver installed, as discussed earlier in this chapter, choose Tools → Solver. The dialog box shown in Figure 6-20 appears.

Figure 6-20: It's usually necessary to set only a few of these options.

Now, take these steps:

1. If you began by selecting the target cell, Excel puts its address in the Set Target Cell box. Otherwise, first click in the Set Target Cell box and then click in the target cell on the worksheet.

2. For this example, you would click the Value Of option to the right of the Equal To label. Then, enter the number you want to solve for in the box to the right of Value Of. Since your client wants to reduce the payback period to 4.0 years, you would enter the value 4.0 in the box.

3. Click in the By Changing Cells box. Then, drag through cells B4:F4 on the worksheet. This informs the Solver that it is to modify the values in B4:F4 until the target cell equals your specification.

4. If you have constraints to specify, they will be listed in the Subject to the Constraints list box. In this particular case, where you are directing the Solver to adjust the units sold, there are no such constraints.

5. Click Solve. Excel will try different values in the changing cells you specified and if it can find a combination that sets cell B28 equal to 4.0, it will report to you as shown in Figure 6-21.

6. Click the Save Scenario button in the Solver Results dialog box. Doing so brings up another dialog box where you can name a new

scenario. The new scenario's changing cells will be the same as the changing cells you specified for the Solver in step 3.

7. After naming the new scenario, select the Restore Original Values option and click OK. You're returned to the worksheet with the original values for the changing cells intact.

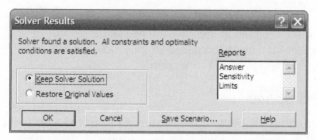

Figure 6-21: The Reports available are technical descriptions of the intermediate steps the Solver took.

By adopting the recommendations in steps 6 and 7 above, your worksheet will show the original values in the changing cells. But you can easily display the values that result in successfully meeting your target cell requirement — the one that you set in step 2. Just use the Scenario Manager to show the scenario you saved in step 6.

TIP: In the prior section, I recommended that you use the Scenario Manager to create a scenario named Base Case Sales. I also recommend that you save the scenario based on the Solver's solution as something such as Base Case Sales Solved. That makes it very easy to switch back and forth between the two scenarios: the one that doesn't meet your target cell requirement, and the one that does.

As set up, there are many different possible solutions, involving unit sales, to the problem of reducing the payback period from 4.55 years to 4.0 years. One possible solution, showing only the benefits section of Figure 6-19, appears in Figure 6-22. With the unit sales as shown there, and no other changes to the pro forma, the payback period is reduced to 4.0 years.

	A	B	C	D	E	F	G
B7		=	=B4^$G$8*B5				
	A	B	C	D	E	F	G
1	**Product Life Cycle: Rollout to Breakeven**						
2	Year:	1	2	3	4	5	
3	*Benefits*						
4	Units sold	256	293	325	368	403	
5	Unit sales price	$ 10,000	$ 10,000	$ 10,000	$ 10,000	$ 10,000	
6	Gross sales	$ 2,562,985	$ 2,927,603	$ 3,250,348	$ 3,682,042	$ 4,030,399	
7	Incremental net sales	$1,471,877	$1,659,056	$1,822,791	$2,039,294	$2,212,143	

New Product Pro Forma

Figure 6-22: Notice that the increases in incremental net sales are not related in a linear fashion to increases in units sold. This is due to the diminishing returns calculation.

Using Constraints in the Solver

Instead of (or perhaps in addition to) changing the unit sales to achieve a particular payback period, you could tell the Solver to alter costs that are under your client's control. For example, if the cost of advertising, new staff or a product rollout (rows 11 through 13 of Figure 6-19) can be reduced, it may be possible to achieve a payback period of 4.0 years without increasing the projected unit sales over the base case.

As before, use the Scenario Manager to establish a base case before invoking the Solver. However, instead of making the changing cells in the new scenario represent unit sales, use the controllable costs — that is, the projected costs of advertising, new staff and product rollout. The easiest way to do that is to select cells B11:F13 and then start the Scenario Manager. This will cause the Scenario Manager to assume that B11:F13 are the changing cells in a new scenario. Name the scenario something such as Base Case Costs.

With some or all the original cost values from the pro forma saved in a scenario, take the following steps. The cell references are as shown in Figure 6-19.

1. Select cell B28. This will cause the Solver to treat that cell as its target cell.

2. Choose Tools → Solver. The Solver Parameters dialog box appears (refer back to Figure 6-20).

3. Suppose you want to start by focusing on new staff costs as a candidate for shortening the payback period. Click in the Solver's By Changing Cells box, and then drag through cells B12:F12 on the

worksheet. This establishes the new staff costs as the values that the Solver will change.

4. The Solver is perfectly willing to assign negative salaries to new staff in its quest for a payback period of 4.0, but your client won't be able to hire them at that rate. Some constraints are needed, so click the Add button. The Add Constraint dialog box, shown in Figure 6-23, appears.

5. With the flashing I-bar in the Cell Reference box, click in cell G12 on the worksheet. This establishes G12 as the location of a constraint.

6. Use the drop-down in the center of the Add Constraint dialog box to choose a comparison operator. Because this constraint is intended to keep values above zero, choose the *Greater Than or Equal To* operator (>=).

7. In the Constraint box, enter **0**. Click OK to return to the Solver Parameters dialog box.

Figure 6-23: You can use the operator drop-down to constrain the value of a cell to an integer, or to equal a particular value.

You now see this constraint in the Subject to the Constraints list box:

$G$12 >= 0

The formula in cell G12 is:

=MIN(B12:F12)

By constraining the value returned by this formula to a positive number, you guarantee that the Solver will not put a negative number into any cell in the range B12:F12. If it did so, the MIN function in G12 would return a negative number and would be in violation of the constraint you applied to cell G12.

The Solver Parameters dialog box should now appear as shown in Figure 6-24.

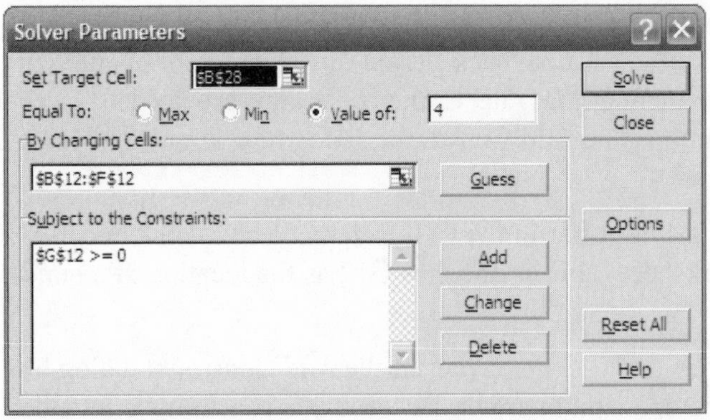

Figure 6-24: You usually set constraints either on the changing cells themselves or, as in this case, on cells that depend on the changing cells' values.

When you click Solve, the Solver tries different values for the changing cells — subject to the constraint that you set — until it arrives at a payback period of 4.0. You'll see the dialog box shown earlier in Figure 6-21.

As before, it's a good idea at this point to click the Save Scenario button. This displays the dialog box shown in Figure 6-25, where you can name the new scenario with a name such as Base Case Costs Solved.

Figure 6-25: All you need to do is supply the name for the scenario. Its changing cells are automatically set to those used by the Solver.

You can now switch back and forth between the scenario that shows the base case costs, and the associated payback period of 4.55, and the costs as adjusted by the Solver, with the associated payback period of 4.0.

Again, there is a large number of possible solutions given the problem as it has been set up. One solution, based on new values for staff costs in row 12, appears in Figure 6-26.

	A	B	C	D	E	F	G	
1	Product Life Cycle: Rollout to Breakeven							
2	Year:	1	2	3	4	5		
3	*Benefits*							
4	Units sold	220	253	291	335	385		
5	Unit sales price	$ 10,000	$ 10,000	$ 10,000	$ 10,000	$ 10,000		
6	Gross sales	$ 2,200,000	$2,530,000	$2,910,000	$ 3,350,000	$ 3,850,000		
7	Incremental net sales	$1,282,863	$1,454,817	$1,650,075	$1,873,011	$2,122,827		
8						Diminishing returns:	0.9	
9	*Costs*							
10	Lost product revenues	$700,000	$0	$0	$0	$0		
11	Advertising	$350,000	$315,000	$283,500	$255,150	$229,635	$229,635	
12	New staff	$265,784	$297,284	$330,989	$367,054	$488,778	$265,784	
13	Product rollout	$250,000	$0	$0	$0	$0	$0	
14	Warranty costs	$0	$50,000	$56,702	$64,302	$72,921		
15								
16	Total costs	$1,565,784	$662,284	$671,191	$686,506	$791,335		
17								

New Product Pro Forma

Figure 6-26: Notice that none of the annual costs for New Staff is less than zero.

Figure 6-26 shows that the annual New Staff costs have been reduced (compare to Figure 6-19), and that cell G12 returns a new minimum value for the range B12:F12.

Wrapping Up Scenarios

This chapter has covered a lot of ground, some of it seemingly unrelated, and it will probably help to finish with a brief review of the material. If it doesn't help you, at least it'll help me.

Most of the chapter has been concerned with scenarios: creating them, managing them and analyzing the relationships between them. At its simplest, a scenario is nothing more than a set of cells that have certain values, and these cells are termed *changing cells*. More usefully, there are other cells that depend on the values of the cells in the scenario; those other cells usually contain formulas that return different results depending on the values of the scenario's cells.

Even more usefully, you can define several different scenarios that have different values for the same set of changing cells. You can then switch back and forth among the scenarios, which might be named something such as Worst Case, Best Case and Best Guess, to see what effect their different values have on the result cells — the ones with the formulas. In situations like these it's helpful to make use of a scenario's comment field, which can make it easier for you to keep track of what each scenario is supposed to represent.

Instead of switching back and forth between different scenarios, you might want to use a scenario summary, which shows in one place the differences among the scenarios. You can choose a tabular form of summary, or you can have Excel put the summary in a pivot table.

If often happens that you have a fairly complicated analysis: complicated because of the math involved, or because there are many inputs to manage, or both. In situations like that, you might want (or you might be forced) to look for a desirable outcome by having Excel seek it out, using an educated trial-and-error approach. Goal Seek is one such, although its approach is so simple that you can probably get a better outcome by manipulating formulas.

In the complex situations, a more sophisticated trial-and-error system is available in the Solver. You can use the Solver to manipulate several inputs, not just one at a time as required by Goal Seek. You can set constraints on how the Solver tries out different solution sets. And when the Solver has reached a solution, you can save the values of the Solver's changing cells as the changing cells in a scenario. Then, if you have several such solutions provided by the Solver, you're in a position to use the Scenario Manager to help you summarize and compare the different solutions, so you can choose the one that you think will work most effectively in reality.

Chapter 7

Payment Functions

Functions are really what make Excel go. Excel is a convenient place to store a few numbers, and it has a good, strong charting capability. It has some tools that are valuable for managing data, such as sorting and filtering. But it's not until you get to the functions that Excel really shines.

About Functions

A function is a pre-written formula that knows how to provide you a result (in Excel terminology, "how to return a result") when you supply the inputs (in Excel terminology, "when you supply the arguments").

Excel has basic math functions that add numbers and find their factorials, financial functions that amortize loans and calculate variable depreciation amounts, trigonometric functions that calculate ratios such as the sine, statistical functions that calculate standard deviations and confidence intervals, and text functions that find one text string inside another. There are others – over three hundred of them that are native to Excel and many more that can be added. You can even write your own functions for use directly on a worksheet.

Here's a brief tour of some aspects of Excel functions. If you already feel comfortable with Excel functions and the function wizard, you might as well skip ahead to the section titled Payment Functions.

Using a Function

All functions are used in formulas, and almost all formulas with functions are entered in the same way. For example, here's a formula:

=5 + 17 + 2 + 8

and you enter it into an Excel cell by selecting the cell, typing the formula, and pressing Enter. When you do that, the cell where you entered the formula displays the result, 32. If cells B1, B2, B3 and B4 contain the numbers 5, 17, 2 and 8, then this formula:

=B1+B2+B3+B4

also returns 32. The formula treats the references to the cells as the contents of the cells themselves.

If you include a function in the formula, you can avoid typing all those cell references:

=SUM(B1:B4)

There are two points of interest about this formula:

- It uses the SUM function.
- It uses the *range operator*, the colon. This operator creates a reference to all the cells between two cell references, in this case B1 and B4, inclusive. As used here, the operator creates a reference to B1, B2, B3 and B4.

The SUM function *returns* the sum of its *arguments* – here, B1, B2, B3 and B4. The cell displays 32, just as it would if you had used plus signs instead of the SUM function and individual cell references instead of the range created by the range operator.

(This use of the term *argument* dates from the 15th century, when astronomers used it to mean "angle".)

NOTE: The Excel documentation states, correctly, that the maximum number of arguments a function can take is 30. What some users do not realize, however, is that an expression such as B1:B4 is not four arguments (one for each cell in the range); it's one argument (the range itself). The 30 argument limit is no real restriction.

You often combine functions in the same formula. One common situation occurs when you want to get one result if some condition is true, and another result if the condition is false. For an example, see Figure 7-1.

You would not normally arrange things as shown in Figure 7-1, but sometimes other programs and other people foist these layouts on us. Let's suppose you wanted to calculate the sum of the salaries for the employees in "CA". One way is to use this formula:

=IF(D1="CA",SUM(B2:B16),SUM(A2:A16))

This is an (admittedly, somewhat strained) example of a formula that uses one function as an argument to another. The basic syntax of Excel's IF function is this:

=IF(Condition,Outcome if Condition is TRUE, Outcome if Condition is FALSE)

There are three arguments here:

- *Condition.* This is a statement that Excel can evaluate as being either TRUE or FALSE. In the example, the condition is *D1 = "CA"* and, in Figure 7-1, the condition is TRUE.
- *Outcome if Condition is TRUE.* This argument is what happens when the condition is TRUE. The outcome can be a value, or a reference to another cell, or another function. In this case, it's another function: the sum of the values in the range B2:B16.
- *Outcome if Condition is FALSE.* This argument is what happens when the condition is FALSE. Again, it can be a value, another cell, or another function, and here it's a function that returns the sum of A2:A16.

	A	B	C	D	E	F	G
				=IF(D1="CA",SUM(B2:B16),SUM(A2:A16))			
1	NV	CA		CA			
2	$ -	$ 36,455		$ 451,812			
3	$ 41,519	$ -					
4	$ -	$ 81,613					
5	$ 42,002	$ -					
6	$ -	$ 24,645					
7	$ 61,382	$ -					
8	$ -	$ 56,331					
9	$ -	$ 43,286					
10	$ -	$ 28,042					
11	$ 18,628	$ -					
12	$ -	$ 65,173					
13	$ -	$ 86,621					
14	$ -	$ 29,647					
15	$ 84,469	$ -					
16	$ 94,212	$ -					
17							

Southwest Salaries

Figure 7-1: Excel chooses which range of cells to sum depending on the result of the IF function.

Earlier, you saw that the SUM function can use (in Excel terminology, *can take*) values such as 5 and 17 as arguments, and it can take cell references as arguments. It can take up to 30 arguments, and it can take them in any order. There are many Excel functions that behave in this way – the number of arguments is up to you, and they can come in any order. Examples are AVERAGE, MEDIAN, MAX and TREND. Some functions take no arguments at all, such as PI and RAND.

Other functions, including the IF function, are pickier. To continue the present example, the IF function can take three arguments only, and the first one must be a condition, also termed a *logical test*. It must be an expression that can be evaluated as either TRUE or FALSE. The other two arguments, only one of which can apply, are less restrictive – they can be values or cell references or other functions, but they must be the second and third arguments, and they must be in the order *Outcome if TRUE* and then *Outcome if FALSE*.

> **NOTE**: Although the IF function can take three arguments only, the second or third argument could be another IF function, which itself can take three arguments … and so on. The number of arguments therefore can cascade.

Using the Function Wizard

With over 300 worksheet functions, and a broad range of arguments that the functions can take, you need an efficient way of getting help with all but the most straightforward functions. Excel offers that help by way of the *function wizard*. (This is also termed *paste function* and *insert function*.)

You get the function wizard going by means of the Paste Function button. That button is found in different places depending on your version of Excel. It is the button with a stylized f and an x: *fx*. When you click it, the dialog box in Figure 7-2 appears.

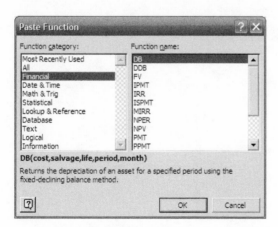

Figure 7-2: The appearance of this dialog box differs by Excel version, but you always select a category and then a function from the category.

The version of the function wizard you see in Figure 7-2 is from Excel 97 and Excel 2000. The newer versions, including Excel 2007, differ only trivially. You use the dialog box by first selecting a function category from among the following choices (each choice is followed by an *extremely* abbreviated list of examples):

- Financial (for example, amortize a loan or depreciate an asset)
- Date & Time (for example, get the day of the week from a date)
- Math & Trig (permutations, logarithms, matrix algebra)
- Statistical (everything from averages to the hypergeometric distribution)
- Lookup & Reference (find values in tables)
- Database (statistical functions for use with an Excel list; no longer of much practical use)
- Text (find one string within another string)
- Logical (IF, AND, OR, etc.)
- Information (properties of values, such as text, numeric and errors)
- Engineering (convert a binary number to hexadecimal)

You can also select All as a category, as well as Most Recently Used to select from up to ten functions that you've recently chosen by way of the function wizard.

Suppose you choose Financial as the category in Figure 7-2. One of your 16 choices is PMT (*payment*). Click it in the Function Name list box; the dialog box changes to show the function's arguments and a brief description of its purpose, as shown in Figure 7-3.

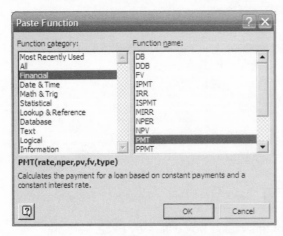

Figure 7-3: If you include the Analysis ToolPak when you install Office, you'll get many more functions in the Financial category.

Once you've selected the PMT function, click OK to get to the dialog box shown in Figure 7-4.

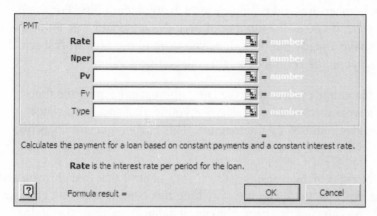

Figure 7-4: The appearance of this dialog box differs depending on the function you chose.

Notice that the dialog box in Figure 7-4 solves the problem of not knowing what a particular function's arguments are, or how many there are, or in what order to enter them. They're listed for you, by name and in order from top to bottom.

You also see the function description, repeated from the dialog box shown in Figure 7-3. And the definition of each argument is spelled out below the function description – the argument defined is the one whose box you click in. When you click in the Nper box, for example, the definition changes from "**Rate** is the interest rate per period for the loan" to "**Nper** is the total number of payments for the loan."

Notice in Figure 7-4 that the names of two arguments, Fv and Type, are shown in a normal font, while the first three are shown in boldface. This highlights a difference among function arguments: some functions have arguments that are required and others that are optional. Optional arguments appear in the function wizard in a normal typeface, at the end of the argument list. In the case of the PMT function, the Fv (future value) and Type (end of period or beginning of period) arguments are optional. The names of required arguments appear in boldface.

Optional arguments usually have default values – figures that Excel assigns if you don't supply any. In the case of the PMT function, the Fv argument has a default value of zero. The Type argument also has a default value of zero, and that is interpreted as meaning that the payment is made at the end of each period (therefore, interest accrues during the period on the principal portion of the payment).

You can enter a number or a cell reference in each argument's box. For example, if you wanted to specify 60 as the number of periods, you could type **60** in the Nper box. Or, if you have already put the values you want to use on a worksheet, you can enter a reference to the cell that contains the pertinent value.

Excel actually encourages you to take the latter approach: keeping the function's arguments on a worksheet makes it easier for you to alter them and watch what happens to the value returned by the function. This encouragement takes two forms:

- At the right of each argument's box is a control that first shrinks, and then expands the dialog box. Clicking this control uncovers cells so that you can click in them; clicking it again re-expands the dialog box so that you have access to the other controls.
- The value contained in the cell appears to the right of the edit box. See Figure 7-5 for an example.

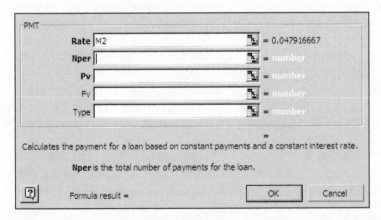

Figure 7-5: Even if cell M2 can't be seen, the dialog box shows you its contents.

Finally, when you have supplied a value or cell reference for each required argument, the current value returned by the function appears at the bottom of the dialog box. When you've supplied all the required arguments and as many optional arguments as you want (see Figure 7-6), click OK to have Excel put the function and argument values into the worksheet, as shown in Figure 7-7.

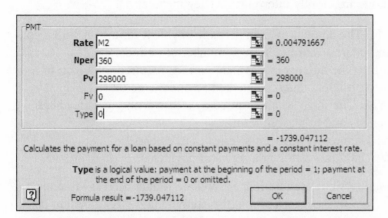

Figure 7-6: The Rate argument is in cell M2; the other arguments are given as numeric values.

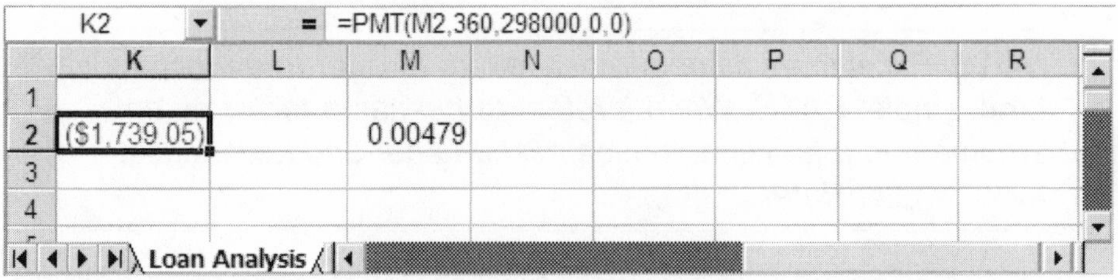

Figure 7-7: Clicking the function wizard's OK button puts the function and its arguments into a formula in the selected worksheet cell.

TIP: If you select a cell that already contains a function and then click the function wizard button, the function wizard dialog box appears with the arguments filled in with their current values.

With that as background, it's time to take a closer look at the payment functions.

Payment Functions

The payment functions are closely interrelated. They include:

- PMT: The amount of each periodic payment for a loan with a constant interest rate and a given number of periods.
- NPER: The number of payment periods required for a loan of a given principal, interest rate and payment amount.
- RATE: The interest rate implied by a loan with given payment amounts and of a given term.
- PV: The present value of a series of payments.
- FV: The future value of a series of payments.

To repeat, these functions are interrelated, and are in fact used as arguments to one another. As you saw in the prior section, for example, the PMT function takes Rate, Nper and Pv as arguments. There are several other functions in this family, including IPMT, PPMT and NPV, which are covered in this section, but aren't used as arguments to other functions.

NOTE: *Excel uses all uppercase letters to refer to a function: for example, RATE. When it refers to the same factor as an argument to a function, it uses mixed upper and lower case: for example, Rate.*

The following formula shows how the functions relate to one another. It's the general formula from which the individual function formulas are derived:

$$Pv*((1+ Rate)^{Nper})+ Pmt*(1+Rate*Type)*(((1+ Rate)^{Nper})-1)/Rate+Fv = 0$$

Type indicates whether the payment is made at the start or the end of the payment period. The default value, zero, indicates that payment is made at the end of the period; if Type equals 1, payment is made at the beginning of the period. If you rearrange the formula given above to solve for the payment amount, you get:

$$PMT = (Rate*(Fv+Pv*(1+ Rate)^{Nper}))/((1+Rate*Type)*(1-(1+ Rate)^{Nper}))$$

If Type is 0, the factor (1+Rate*Type) drops out of the denominator and the result of the formula is slightly greater.

PMT Function

The PMT function, as noted earlier, takes three required and two optional arguments:

- Rate: The interest rate per payment period.
- Nper: The number of periods in the life of the loan or investment.
- Pv: The present value, or principal amount, of the loan at the start of the first period; or, the present value of the investment (often, zero).
- Fv (optional): The future value of the loan (normally, zero, at the time the loan is retired), or the investment, at the end of the final period. Default: 0.
- Type (optional): 0 if the payment is made at the end of each period, 1 if it is made at the beginning of the period. Default: 0.

Suppose your worksheet is set up as in Figure 7-8:

	A	B	C	D	E	F	G
1	Pv	Nper	Pmt	Rate	Fv	Type	
2	$ (298,000.00)	360	$1,739.05	0.48%	$0.00	0	
3							
4							

⊲ ◂ ▸ ▹ ＼ Loan Analysis ／ ◂

Figure 7-8: One of the values in A2:F2 is normally an unknown (the value you're solving for). For clarity later on, the Pmt value is supplied here.

With this arrangement it's very easy to use the PMT function. You should consider naming each cell in the range A2:F2, using the labels in the range A1:F1. To do that quickly, take these steps:

1. Select the range A1:F2 – that is, the labels in the first row and the values in the second row.

2. Choose Insert → Name → Create. The dialog box shown in Figure 7-9 appears.

3. Fill the Top Row checkbox and clear the other checkboxes.

4. Click OK.

Figure 7-9: Create Name is a quick way to name the columns in an Excel list.

You now have six range names defined: Pv, Nper, Pmt, Rate, Fv and Type, each referring to a different cell in row 2. You could have given the cells any name that's legal in Excel; I find it convenient to give them the same names as the names of the function's arguments. If you do that, though, be sure you understand that the fact that the cells' names and the arguments' names are identical is just for convenience and has no meaning or purpose beyond that.

NOTE: *Range names in Excel aren't allowed to use special characters. You can use letters, numbers, periods, and under-score characters. You're not allowed to define a name that looks like a cell reference: for example, Excel won't let you define a range named M2.*

TIP: *A quick way to make sure that Excel has assigned the correct name to each cell is to select that cell and check the Name Box. In this example, if you select cell B2 after using Create Name, the Name Box (directly above the A column header) should show Nper.*

Now you can enter the PMT function directly on the worksheet, like this:

=PMT(Rate,Nper,Pv)

or you can use the function wizard, as shown in Figure 7-10.

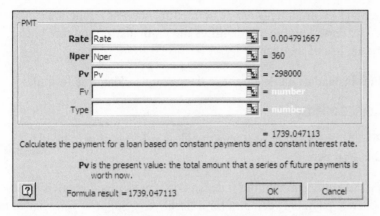

Figure 7-10: Creating range names identical to the function arguments makes it easy to complete this dialog box.

Either way, given the values shown earlier in Figure 7-8 for the arguments, you get the value $1,739.05 as the periodic payment for a periodic interest rate of 0.48% over 360 periods on a loan with a present value of $298,000.

You can also determine the periodic investment amount, given the number of periods, the periodic rate and the future value. On the worksheet, change the Pv value of $298,000 to zero and change the Fv value to, say, $300,000. Then enter this formula:

=PMT(Rate,Nper,Pv,Fv)

to get $313.22 as the periodic investment at 0.48% over 360 periods to get to $300,000.

IPMT Function

Closely related to the PMT function is the IPMT function, which returns the interest portion of a loan payment made during a given period. You might not have much use for that particular figure, but you can easily extend the function's reach so that it returns, for example, the total interest paid during twelve periods.

Here's the basic syntax for the IPMT function (each of the four arguments is required):

=IPMT(Rate,Period,Nper,Pv)

The Rate, Nper and Pv arguments are as defined for the PMT function in the preceding section. The Period argument identifies the particular period that you're interested in during the life of the loan.

So, using values instead of names to make the example clear, this formula:

=IPMT(0.004792,43,360,298000)

returns $(1,358.84). the amount of interest paid on a 360-period loan of $298,000 during the 43rd period.

That's a fun fact to know and tell, but it doesn't do you as much good as knowing what the total interest payments come to for a fiscal year. Suppose you wanted the sum of interest payments on the same loan from the 37th through the 48th periods. You could lay out the data, including the numbers 37 through 48, on a worksheet, and enter the IPMT function 12 times, each time pointing it at a different value for the Period argument: 37, then 38, then 39 and so on. Then you'd total the twelve results.

Here's an easier and (if it makes a difference to you) more elegant way. It's also guaranteed to make at least some of your colleagues say, "I didn't know you could do that." It will send them scuttling back to their workstations to try what you just showed them.

The solution involves an *array formula*. (Array formulas are mentioned briefly in Chapter 3.) An array formula is one that returns an array of values, or that includes a function that normally gets a single value for an argument but is getting an array of values instead. I know that sounds like doubletalk. It turns out that it's extremely difficult to come up with a crisp but complete definition of an array formula. I, and others who write about these things, have been trying and failing to do so for years.

The IPMT function normally expects a single number, such as 43 in the prior example, as its Period argument. The problem is to get IPMT to accept the array of values {37, 38, 39, ... , 48} for Period. First, though, you have to get that array.

A handy way to get Excel to return an array of consecutive integers is to use the ROW function. The ROW function returns the number of a cell's row: ROW(A57) returns 57, because A57 is in row 57. You can also present an array of cells to the ROW function, like this:

=ROW(A37:A48)

Although you can't see it without special handling, that formula returns the array of values {37, 38, 39, ... 48}. Just what you're looking for. So an incomplete solution to the original problem, getting the sum of interest payments for the 37th through the 48th periods, is this:

=IPMT(0.004792,ROW(A37:A48),360,298000)

Notice that the expression ROW(A37:A48) replaces the single number identifying a particular period. The second argument, Period, is now an array of values.

There are two more matters to take care of, and neither of them is a big deal. First, you want the *total* of those interest payments. So enclose the formula just given with the SUM function, which will total the twelve interest amounts:

=SUM(IPMT(0.004792,ROW(A37:A48),360,298000))

Finally, array-enter the formula. This calls for a special keyboard sequence. After you've entered a formula, instead of simply pressing Enter, use Ctrl-Shift-Enter. That is, hold down the Ctrl and Shift keys simultaneously as you press Enter. When you array-enter a formula, Excel shows you that it interprets what you've put in the cell as an array formula: the formula is surrounded by curly brackets, {}, in the Formula Bar. For example, the formula just given will look like this in the Formula Bar if you array-enter it using Ctrl-Shift-Enter:

{=SUM(IPMT(0.004792,ROW(A37:A48),360,298000))}

Notice the curly brackets at the beginning and the end of the formula. Don't type them yourself: if you use Ctrl-Shift-Enter Excel will provide them for you. In fact, if you do type the curly brackets yourself, Excel interprets the formula as nothing more than static text, like the word Fred.

That formula returns the value $(16,316.33), the total interest paid from the 37th through the 48th periods of a 360-period loan of $298,000 at .4792% periodic interest. If you use range names instead of numeric values for the arguments, as was done earlier with the PMT function, the formula might look like this:

{=SUM(IPMT(Rate,ROW(A37:A48),Nper,Pv))}

PPMT Function

The PPMT function is almost exactly the same as the IPMT function, except that it returns the principal amount paid for a given loan period. The syntax is:

PPMT(Rate,Period,Nper,Pv)

For example, this formula:

=PPMT(0.004792,43,360,298000)

returns $(380.28), the amount of principal paid during the 43rd period of a 360-period loan of $298,000 at .4792% periodic interest. Notice that none of the arguments is an array; they are each single values. Therefore, there's no need to array-enter the formula with Ctrl-Shift-Enter.

However, if you wanted to know the sum of the principal paid on the loan from, say, the 13th period through the 24th, you could array-enter this formula:

=SUM(PPMT(0.004792,ROW(A13:A24),360,298000))

or $(4,059.60). As before, if you array-enter the formula with Ctrl-Shift-Enter, Excel supplies curly brackets around the formula as shown in the formula bar.

Positive and Negative Values

Before continuing with the remaining payment functions, it's helpful to understand the relationship between positive and negative values as arguments, and the result of the function. As Excel's developers designed the functions, outflows should be entered as negative numbers and inflows as positive numbers.

If you experimented with the values for the arguments to the PMT function in the prior section, for example, you probably noticed that you got a negative value for the periodic payment. You might want to regard that payment as a negative value, and if so you're already in good shape. If you want it to be a positive value, then you should change the value of Pv (or Fv) to a negative – in the context of the prior examples, $(298,000) or $(300,000).

Similarly, if you're calculating other quantities, adjust the positive or negative status of the arguments accordingly:

- Calculating present value by means of the PV function, you might want to use a negative value for the Pmt argument.
- Calculating number of periods by means of the NPER function, use a negative Pv or a negative Pmt (but not both) to obtain a positive number of periods.

- Calculating the periodic interest rate by means of the RATE function, use a negative Pv or a negative Pmt (but not both) to get a positive interest rate.

NOTE: On the topic of interest rate, whether as a function or as an argument to another function, it's a good idea to keep in mind that it's up to you to make sure that the rate is consistent with the number of periods. If you're assessing a five-year loan with an 8.4% annual rate, you need to remember that analyzing the loan on a monthly basis means 60 periods at .07% per period.

PV Function

If you want to look at taking out a loan or initiating an investment from a different perspective, you might want to determine its present value, given a rate, a number of periods and a payment amount.

Your client might have it in mind to take out a 10-year loan for improvements to the building that houses her retail operation. She can afford $3,800 per month in loan payments, and the improvements will total $400,000. How large a loan can she get at current commercial rates, and how much in additional funds will she have to supply?

With the data laid out as shown in Figure 7-11, and the cells named with the labels in row 1, use this formula:

=PV(Rate,Nper,Pmt)

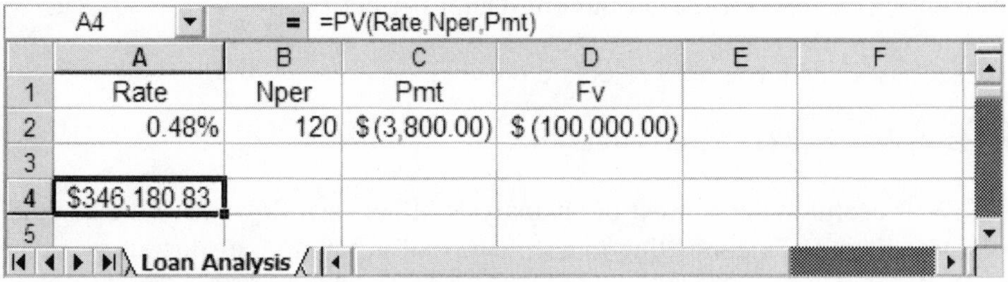

	A	B	C	D	E	F
	A4	▼	= =PV(Rate,Nper,Pmt)			
	A	B	C	D	E	F
1	Rate	Nper	Pmt	Fv		
2	0.48%	120	$(3,800.00)	$(100,000.00)		
3						
4	$346,180.83					
5						

Loan Analysis

Figure 7-11:The Pmt argument is negative, so the PV function returns a positive number.

Of course, you can enter it yourself or have the function wizard do so for you. With these arguments the PV function returns ($346,180.83), so your client would have to front $53,819.17 for the improvements.

Both Fv and Type are optional arguments for the PV function. Suppose your client in the prior example wants the outstanding principal on her loan to be $100,000 after ten years. You can add the Fv argument, with the value shown in cell D2 of Figure 7-11, and then this formula:

=PV(Rate,Nper,Pmt,Fv)

returns $402,528.64, so she can afford an additional $2,528.64 in improvements, without fronting a penny – but she'll still owe $100,000 ten years from now.

NPV Function

Excel also has a NPV function, which is closely related to the PV function. The NPV, or *net present value*, function returns the present value of a series of cash flows, net of a discount factor. Its syntax is:

=NPV(discount rate, value, value, value …)

where each *value* argument is a different amount, positive income values or negative payment values. The value arguments are assumed to be in chronological order, earliest to latest, and to occur at the end of equal length periods. The discount rate is assumed to apply across all the periods. So, the net present value of three annual amounts of $10,000, with a discount rate of 12%, is returned by this formula:

=NPV(.12,10000,10000,10000)

which returns $24,018.31, the value in today's dollars of three periodic $10,000 investments, assuming a 12% discounting factor per period.

Excel uses this formula to calculate NPV:

Σ [j=1 to n] (Values$_j$ / (1+discount rate)^j)

NPV is useful in the context of an analysis of net cash flows. Use the discount rate as an estimate of a competing investment or of inflation to evaluate, say, annual net cash flows. An example of how the data might be laid out is at the end of Chapter 6, in the section titled Running the Solver.

NPER Function

NPER returns the number of periods necessary to retire a loan or reach an investment target, given the Rate and the Pmt. NPER does not necessarily return an integer value, so you'll have to deal with a fractional number of periods as your situation requires.

The function's syntax is:

=NPER(Rate, Pmt, Pv)

Optionally you can include Fv and Type as arguments, just as shown earlier with the PMT function.

RATE Function

The RATE function is a little different from the other functions in the payment family. Excel does not calculate its returned value by means of a direct rearrangement of the general formula, given earlier as:

$$Pv*((1+ Rate)^{\wedge}Nper)+ Pmt*(1+Rate*Type)*(((1+ Rate)^{\wedge}Nper)-1)/Rate+Fv = 0$$

The reason is that the value for RATE depends on powers of the interest rate, of an order defined by the number of periods. Instead of a direct solution, Excel uses an iterative approach (conceptually similar to Excel's Goal Seek tool) to solve for an interest rate. It doesn't take any longer to solve in this way, as long as you don't supply arguments that can't result in a solution.

The RATE function's usual syntax is:

=RATE(Nper,Pmt,Pv)

Either the Pmt or the Pv argument, but not both, must be a negative number, else RATE returns the #NUM! error value.

In addition to the Nper, Pmt and Pv arguments, RATE can also take the optional Fv and Type arguments, discussed above in the section on the PMT function. The RATE function takes another optional argument, Guess, which other functions in this family do not use.

TIP: *When you use the function wizard to help enumerate the RATE function's arguments, if you don't see the Guess argument, notice that the list of arguments might have a vertical scroll bar. Scroll down to find the Guess argument's edit box.*

Although Excel provides the Guess argument, it's unlikely to do you much good; in fact, Guess goes back to the early days of Excel, when personal computers were very much slower than they are now. The idea was that if a user provided a rough guess of what the interest rate should be, given knowledge of number of payments, payment amount and present value, then Excel could use the guess as a starting point and arrive at an accurate result more quickly.

By all means experiment with the Guess argument if you wish, but I think you'll find that it doesn't help much. If you're getting a #NUM! error when you use the RATE function, you'll solve the problem much more reliably if you take another look at the values you've supplied for Nper, Pmt and Pv. Make sure that either Pmt or Pv is a negative value, and that the value you've supplied for Pmt makes sense in terms of the values you've supplied for Nper and Pv. If you encounter a problem with RATE, checking those values is much more likely to solve the problem than fooling around with the Guess argument.

Chapter 8

Excel's Depreciation Functions

The Family of Depreciation Functions

Straight-Line Depreciation

Depreciation Using Sum of Year's Digits

Declining Balance Depreciation

Double Declining Balance Depreciation

Variable Declining Balance Depreciation

xcel's depreciation functions have something in common with the crazy old aunt in gothic fiction; the one that the family keeps locked in the attic. They exist (both the functions and the aunt), they have existed from time immemorial, and nobody ever says anything about them. Not in polite company, anyway.

To prove this to yourself, go to the Microsoft newsgroups such as microsoft.public.excel.worksheet.functions and search for function names such as DB or SLN. I can guarantee that you'll find relatively little material.

This fact – that is, the difficulty of finding material on the functions – can be particularly frustrating in view of the errors in Excel's documentation of the functions, particularly Excel's Help documentation. The material is not always correct, and not just in terms of how depreciation should be calculated: the documentation incorrectly describes how Excel calculates the results.

This chapter is here for a couple of reasons. One, to help you stay on track if you want to use one of these functions and find that you're not getting what you expect. And two, to describe how you can calculate accelerated depreciation accurately in Excel if you decide to avoid using the built-in functions.

Family of Depreciation Functions

The family of depreciation functions includes both the straight-line approach and the accelerated methods, declining balance and sum of years digits. They go so far back in Excel's development history that for several years Microsoft has felt compelled to point out in the documentation that depreciation rates are rounded to three decimal places. Excel has five depreciation functions:

- SLN. Short for "straight line." You know what this one does: it divides the depreciable value of an asset equally across its useful life.
- SYD. Short for "sum of years' digits." The most basic of the accelerated depreciation functions.
- DB. Short for "declining balance." The accounting literature often refers to this as "double declining balance," and the DB function can work in this way.
- DDB. Short for "double declining balance." Again, it is possible to use this function in the usual way, to double the straight-line rate, but you can optionally supply other rates.
- VDB. Short for "variable declining balance." Establish greater control over start and end depreciation periods, and optionally switch to straight-line depreciation.

As is the case with the family of payment functions discussed in Chapter 7, the depreciation functions take just a few arguments, which must be listed in a specific order, and not all the arguments are required. The arguments common to all the depreciation functions include the following:

- Cost. The original book value of the asset you're depreciating. Required by all depreciation functions.

- Salvage. Excel uses the term "salvage" in place of "residual," and to avoid confusion this chapter does the same. The value of the asset at the end of the final depreciation period. Required by all depreciation functions.
- Life. The number of accounting periods, normally years, over which the asset is to be depreciated. Required by all depreciation functions.
- Period. The period for which the depreciation is to be calculated. Required by all the depreciation functions, except SLN (which by definition returns a constant figure regardless of period).

In this context, "required argument" does not mean that you have to supply a value. It does mean that you have to account for it. For example, =SLN(1000,0,5) specifies a Cost of 1000, a Salvage of 0 and a Life of 5. An equivalent usage is =SLN(1000,,5), which does not supply a Salvage value but accounts for it by means of two consecutive commas. The Salvage argument would normally go there, but because it's missing Excel assumes that Salvage is 0.

The following sections describe the other arguments to depreciation functions and how you use them.

SLN Function

The SLN function returns the amount of depreciation to take in each period. It conforms to the usual tax regulations in requiring that you supply a salvage value that is subtracted from the original book value before calculating the depreciation.

The SLN function syntax is:

=SLN(Cost, Salvage, Life)

Figure 8-1 shows how you might lay out a worksheet to give names to cells and make it easier to enter and edit the values of the three arguments, whether you decide to use the function wizard or to enter the function and its arguments directly on the worksheet.

If you want, you can use the instructions in the section titled PMT Function in Chapter 7 to name the cells A2, B2 and C2 as Cost, Salvage and Life. Then, either enter this formula directly:

=SLN(Cost, Salvage, Life)

or use the function wizard to build the formula. The result in this case is $2,000.00, obtained by subtracting the salvage from the cost and dividing the difference by the asset's life, measured in periods.

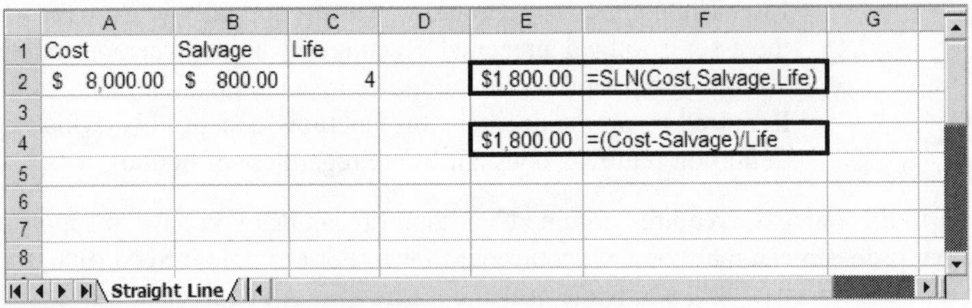

	A	B	C	D	E	F	G
1	Cost	Salvage	Life				
2	$ 8,000.00	$ 800.00	4		$1,800.00	=SLN(Cost,Salvage,Life)	
3							
4					$1,800.00	=(Cost-Salvage)/Life	
5							
6							
7							
8							

I◄ ◄ ► ►I \ Straight Line / I◄

Figure 8-1: Giving cells the same names as arguments makes it easier to supply the arguments to the function.

Of course, you could also enter this formula on the worksheet:

=(A2-B2)/C2

or this one:

=(Cost-Salvage)/Life

assuming that you've given those names to the cells. There's no convincing argument about whether you should use the function or specify the equation.

The cell reference form of the equation is inconvenient if you want to copy-and-paste it elsewhere, unless you first make the cell references absolute. And the equation doesn't insist that you provide for all three arguments, so if you're hurried you might conceivably forget to account for the Salvage value.

On the other hand, an Excel newbie is unlikely to recognize the "SLN" short-hand and will probably be puzzled by it. If you want to copy-and-paste the function form, you'll still need to use absolute cell references or name the cells. So the choice between equation and function is really a matter of personal preference, or your client's policy as to worksheet practices.

Of course, because straight-line depreciation by definition returns a constant periodic value, there's no need to enter it once for each period. The tax regulations have long required that the salvage value be subtracted from the original cost before dividing by the useful life. You can get around this on the worksheet by supplying 0 as a salvage value, but it's not Excel that enforces the tax laws.

Accelerated Depreciation

Besides straight-line depreciation, Excel provides for four methods of accelerated depreciation. Accelerated depreciation front-loads the depreciation in the earlier periods of an asset's useful life. The rationale is part cupidity and part logic.

As to greed: we usually like to depreciate greater amounts earlier.

As to logic: it's just an extension of the matching principle. To the degree possible, costs should appear in the same accounting period as the benefits they bring to a company. Other things being equal, the newer an asset, the greater benefit it offers. Therefore, the greater portion of the asset's cost should also be recognized earlier.

The Excel functions that accelerate depreciation beyond a straight line are SYD, DB, DDB, and VDB.

SYD Function

The most straightforward of the accelerated depreciation methods is SYD, sum of years' digits. Figure 8-2 shows how you might set up the worksheet to take advantage of the SYD function.

F2	▼	= =SYD(Cost,Salvage,Life,Period)							
	A	B	C	D	E	F	G	H	
1	Cost	Salvage	Life	Period		SYD by function		SYD by formula	
2	$8,000.00	$800.00	4	1		$ 2,880.00		$ 2,880.00	
3				2		$ 2,160.00		$ 2,160.00	
4				3		$ 1,440.00		$ 1,440.00	
5				4		$ 720.00		$ 720.00	
6									
7				Total depreciation:		$ 7,200.00		$ 7,200.00	
8									
	◄ ◄ ► ►I \ Sum of Years' Digits / ◄							► I	

Figure 8-2: Note that the depreciation is accelerated early compared to the SLN function.

Like the straight-line approach, the sum of years' digits method requires that you apply the depreciation factor to the asset's depreciable value – the difference between the original cost and the salvage value. The syntax for the SYD function is:

=SYD (Cost, Salvage, Life, Per)

Yes, "Per." That's the name of the Period argument as used in the SYD function. It probably has something to do with Y2K.

SYD is the only form of depreciation in Excel that is easier to get via a function than via a formula. I don't intend to get into the derivation of the following array formula, but for any reader whose interests turn that way, here's the formula that's array-entered, using Ctrl-Shift-Enter, into cells H2:H5 of Figure 8-2:

=LARGE(Period,Period)/SUM(Period)*(Cost-Salvage)

(Period is the name of the range D2:D5 in Figure 8-2.)

Briefly, the sum of years' digits approach sums the ordinal numbers that identify each period of depreciation: if the useful life is four, then the "years' digits" are 1, 2, 3 and 4. Their sum is 10, and it is divided first into 4, then into 3, then into 2, then into 1. So, the normal Excel formulas that would return the depreciation of $7,200 over four periods are:

=4/10*(Cost – Salvage), or $2,880

=3/10*(Cost – Salvage), or $2,160

=2/10*(Cost – Salvage), or $1,440

=1/10*(Cost – Salvage), or $720

If the Life value is 5, then the factors are 5/15, 4/15, 3/15 and so on.

DB Function

In the traditional method of calculating declining balance depreciation, the straight-line rate is doubled. If an asset is judged to have a useful life of four periods, the straight-line method would depreciate it at 25% per period; 25% would be applied to the difference between the cost and the salvage in each period.

The two principal differences between the declining balance method and the straight-line method are these:

- The straight-line depreciation rate is doubled. The declining balance method depreciates an asset with a useful life of four years at 50% per year of the remaining book value. For this reason, the accounting literature has used the terms "declining balance" and "double declining balance" interchangeably.
- The amount that is depreciated during the first period is the asset's original cost, *not* the cost less the salvage, as in the straight line and the sum of years' digits methods. In subsequent periods, the amount depreciated is the original cost less the accumulated depreciation.

Figure 8-3 shows how this works, using formulas.

	E4 ▼	=	=(2/Life)*(Cost-SUM($E$2:E3))				
	A	B	C	D	E	F	G
1	Cost	Life	Period		Depreciation		
2	$11,000.00	4	1		$ 5,500.00		
3			2		$ 2,750.00		
4			3		$ 1,375.00		
5			4		$ 687.50		
6							
7				Total depreciation:	$ 10,312.50		
8				Salvage value:	$ 687.50		
9							

I◄ ◄ ► ►I \ Declining Balance / ◄

Figure 8-3: Each period depreciates the asset at 50% of its undepreciated value.

Notice in Figure 8-3 that the asset's cost and life are given, and the rate of depreciation is obtained from the asset's useful life. The salvage value is then determined by applying the three known figures. The rate using straight-line depreciation would be 1/4, or 25%. The traditional declining balance method doubles that rate, and applies the result to the original cost. So the differences between the two approaches are expressed via formulas as follows:

- Straight line, all periods: 1/Periods * (Cost – Salvage)
- Declining balance, first period: 2/Periods * Cost
- Declining balance, later periods: 2/Periods * (Cost – Accumulated depreciation)

The salvage value is whatever the undepreciated asset value is at the end of its useful life.

But this is not how Excel's DB function works. Using the DB function, you supply Cost, Salvage and Life, and Excel uses those three arguments to determine the rate of depreciation. As a result, it's only in a very specific situation that the DB function returns the periodic depreciation you would expect from the traditional declining balance method.

The syntax of the DB function is:

=DB(Cost, Salvage, Life, Period, Month)

The Month argument is optional. You can use it to indicate that the asset was put in service sometime during the first period, and it assumes that the Life argument is in years.

The Month argument is not only optional, it's badly named. The term "Month" implies that it represents the month during the year when the asset was put in service. A better name, "Months," would imply the truth of the matter, which is that the argument specifies the number of months in the period that the asset was in use. If it were in use from March through December, you'd supply 10 for the Month argument.

Figure 8-4 contrasts Excel's DB function with the traditional formula. The sheet has several points of interest that could use some further explanation, and I'll go over them in the following sections.

Salvage Value Derived

As you see in cell F10 of Figure 8-4, the traditional calculation, using the formula discussed for Figure 8-3, results in a salvage value of $687.50. It is simply the undepreciated value of the asset.

Salvage Value Supplied

In contrast, you supply a Salvage argument to the DB function. The function's result in the present example is affected by the value you supply for the Salvage argument as follows:

If you give the DB function a smaller Salvage argument than $687.50 (that is, the one obtained from the traditional calculation), DB's periodic depreciation in the early periods is smaller than with the standard formulas, and smaller than the standard in the later periods.

	A	B	C	D	E	F	G	H	I
1					Declining balance via formula				
2									
3	Cost		Life	Period		Depreciation			
4	$11,000.00		4	1		$ 5,500.00			
5				2		$ 2,750.00			
6				3		$ 1,375.00			
7				4		$ 687.50			
8									
9					Total depreciation:	$ 10,312.50			
10					Remaining book value:	$ 687.50			
11									
12					Declining balance via DB()				
13									
14	Cost	Salvage	Life	Period		Depreciation			
15	$11,000.00	$1,000.00	4	1		$ 4,961.00			
16				2		$ 2,723.59			
17				3		$ 1,495.25			
18				4		$ 820.89			
19									
20					Total depreciation:	$ 10,000.73			
21					Remaining book value:	$ 999.27			
22									
23					Declining balance via DB()				
24	Cost	Salvage	Life	Period		Depreciation			
25	$11,000.00	$ -	4	1		$11,000.00			
26				2		$0.00			
27				3		$0.00			
28				4		$0.00			
29									
30					Total depreciation:	$ 11,000.00			
31					Remaining book value:	$ -			

Declining Balance

Figure 8-4: The DB results differ depending on how you set the salvage value.

On the other hand, a Salvage argument to DB that's larger than the one you get from traditional formulas results in smaller periodic depreciation in the early periods, and larger in later periods, compared to the traditional approach. In Figure 8-4, compare the range F4:F7 with F15:F18.

Rounding Errors in the DB Function

Notice cell F20 in Figure 8-4. The total depreciation across the four periods is slightly greater than the difference between the original cost in A15 and the declared salvage value in B15. You can see why this is so by examining the formula that Excel uses for the DB function:

Depreciation = (Cost - Total depreciation from prior periods) * Rate

where:

Rate = 1 - ((Salvage / Cost) ^ (1 / Life))

Excel rounds Rate to three decimal places. This can have a noticeable impact on the results when the costs are in the thousands range, and you can see it in cell F20. There's no way to use the DB function without subjecting yourself to this rounding problem.

You can duplicate the result of the rounding with this Excel formula:

=ROUND(1-((Salvage/Cost)^(1/Life)),3)

The latter formula rounds the formula that Excel uses to calculate the DB rate to three places. If you use it to calculate declining balance depreciation using a formula such as this one:

=(Cost–(Accumulated depreciation))*ROUND(1-((Salvage/Cost)^(1/Life)),3)

you'll duplicate the results of the DB function.

The formula that Excel uses for declining balance has not only a mathematical but a theoretical impact on how depreciation is calculated. The traditional approach does not begin by applying a depreciation rate to the difference between the asset's cost and its salvage value. The rate is applied to the original cost during the first period, and to the original cost less accumulated depreciation in subsequent periods. The result is that the traditional approach never fully depreciates the asset. This issue is mathematical in nature: no matter how many times you depreciate the current book value by 50%, it can never reach zero.

If you independently determine that the asset has a true salvage value of, say, $300. then depreciation must stop before it reduces the remaining book value of the asset below its true salvage value. This issue is a legal and regulatory matter: you're not *allowed* to depreciate an asset below its true salvage value, no matter how that value is determined.

Packing the Full Cost into the First Period

If you have an independent, credible estimate of an asset's salvage value, you might well prefer to use that instead of a value calculated through knowing the asset's original cost and its useful life. In that case, you would probably use Excel's DB function, supplying the estimate of the salvage value as DB's second argument.

Figure 8-4 also showed a presumably unanticipated effect of the formula behind Excel's DB function. Notice that the salvage value in cell B25 is zero, and that the entire original cost of the asset. $11,000, is depreciated in the first period, cell F25. Now *that's* accelerated depreciation!

Here's the reason. Combining the formulas for DB given earlier, according to Excel's documentation, gives this:

Depreciation = (Cost - Accumulated depreciation) * (1 - ((Salvage / Cost) ^ (1 / Life)))

If Salvage equals zero, then this factor:

(1 - ((Salvage / Cost) ^ (1 / Life)))

reduces to

(1 - ((0 / Cost) ^ (1 / Life)))

or

1 – 0 ^ .25

or 1. Because at the end of the first period the accumulated depreciation still equals zero, the full formula reduces to this:

Depreciation = 11000 * 1

And so the first period depreciation equals the cost. Subsequent periods base their depreciation on the undepreciated portion of the asset's value, but because it was fully depreciated during period 1, there's nothing left to depreciate.

Duh.

Supplying a Salvage Value

As a practical matter, you have three choices in Excel if you want to adopt the declining balance method of depreciation: using the traditional formulas, using DB with a calculated Salvage argument, and using DB with a Salvage argument determined independently of Excel.

Using the Traditional Calculations

If you structure it correctly, you need only one formula for declining balance; once entered in a cell, you just copy-and-paste it. The formula uses a mix of absolute and relative references so that a range can grow as you drag it down. Figure 8-5 gives an example.

	E3		▼		=	=(2/Life)*(Cost-SUM($E$1:E2))				
	A	B	C	D	E	F	G	H	I	J
1	Cost	Life	Period		Depreciation					
2	$8,000.00	4	1		$ 4,000.00					
3			2		$ 2,000.00					
4			3		$ 1,000.00					
5			4		$ 500.00					
6										
7				Total depreciation:	$ 7,500.00					
8				Salvage value:	$ 500.00					
9										

Declining Balance

Figure 8-5: You avoid a lot of problems if you build your own formula instead of relying on Excel's DB function.

Figure 8-5 shows the basic layout. There are two named cells: Cost in A2 and Life in B2. Cell E2 contains this formula:

=(2/Life)*(Cost-SUM($E$1:E1))

The expression 1/Life would be the depreciation rate used by the straight-line method. The expression used in the formula, 2/Life, represents the doubling of that rate for use in a declining balance calculation.

The expression Cost-SUM($E$1:E1) represents the original book value of the asset, less accumulated depreciation. It is this difference that is multiplied by the rate to result in a periodic depreciation amount. Because there is no numeric value in cell E1, the function SUM($E$1:E1) returns zero, and in the first period the depreciation is the rate (in this example, 2/4 or .5) times the Cost, or $4,000.

If you copy-and-paste the formula in cell E2 into E3:E5, the range used by the SUM function expands. The first cell reference in the $E$1:E1 address, $E$1, is an absolute reference and does not change regardless of where it's pasted. The second cell reference, E1, is a relative reference, so as the formula is pasted into E3, E4 and E5 the function changes to SUM($E$1:E2), SUM($E$1:E3) and SUM($E$1:E4). In this way, the depreciation in each period is based on the accumulated depreciation from all prior periods.

Use Excel's DB Function with a Salvage Value Calculated by Traditional Methods

One way around the problem induced by specifying the Salvage argument in the DB function is to use traditional methods to calculate depreciation at double the straight line rate to get a book value for the asset at the end of its useful life. Supply that salvage value as the second argument to the DB function. Figure 8-6 shows the results: it's identical to the ones returned by traditional methods.

	E5	▼	=	=(2/Life)*(Cost-SUM($E$3:E4))			
	A	B	C	D	E	F	G
1		**Declining Balance via Formula**					
2							
3	Cost	Life		Period	Depreciation		
4	$11,000.00	4		1	$ 5,500.00		
5				2	$ 2,750.00		
6				3	$ 1,375.00		
7				4	$ 687.50		
8							
9				Total depreciation:	$ 10,312.50		
10				Salvage value:	$ 687.50		
11							
12							
13		**Declining Balance via DB**					
14							
15	Cost	Life	Salvage	Period	Depreciation		
16	$11,000.00	4	$687.50	1	$5,500.00		
17				2	$2,750.00		
18				3	$1,375.00		
19				4	$687.50		
20							
21				Total depreciation:	$ 10,312.50		
22				Salvage value:	$ 687.50		
23							
24							

Declining Balance

Figure 8-6: Here, DB returns the same results as the traditional declining balance calculation.

Cells E16:E19 of Figure 8-6 use the Salvage argument that the traditional calculations arrive at in cell E10: $687.50. The only reason I can think of that you would want to use this two-step process, doing the traditional calculation to get a salvage value, and then supplying that value as an argument to DB, is that you find it both desirable and convenient to use the mis-named Month argument. But comparing the two approaches does shed some light on the DB function's mysterious innards.

Use Excel's DB Function with a Salvage Value Determined in Some Other Way

As noted earlier, you might have a better rationale than an asset's apparent useful life to specify the asset's salvage value. In that case, you should probably use that independent estimate. Perhaps the company has experience using similar assets and eventually establishing a fair market value. You're the best judge of that, and if you decide to use an independently derived estimate of an asset's salvage value, you can certainly use it in the DB function.

If you do so, just remember that the three-decimal rounding that Excel applies to the rate calculation will often cause a situation in which the total depreciation does not equal the difference between the original cost and the salvage value.

DDB Function

I have better news regarding Excel's DDB function than I did regarding its DB function – and it's not limited to the fact that the Period argument in DDB is *Period* instead of *Per*.

The DDB function allows you to specify a particular rate of depreciation, with reference to the SLN rate. That is, you can specify a Factor argument that is multiplied by the SLN rate, which is determined by the asset's useful life. (DDB is short for *double declining balance*.)

In contrast to the DB function, the rate of depreciation used by DDB is *not* determined by the salvage value. It *is* determined by dividing the Factor argument by the asset's useful life.

Furthermore, the DDB function does not base periodic depreciation on the asset's original cost less a salvage value – in fact, the only reason that the DDB function takes a Salvage argument is to determine when to stop calculating depreciation. Here's DDB's full syntax:

=DDB(Cost,Salvage,Life,Period,Factor)

The only optional argument is Factor. If you omit it, DDB defaults to the traditional approach of twice the straight-line rate. In other words, this:

=DDB(Cost,Salvage,Life,Period)

is equivalent to this:

=DDB(Cost,Salvage,Life,Period,2)

Figure 8-7 shows an example of the DDB function.

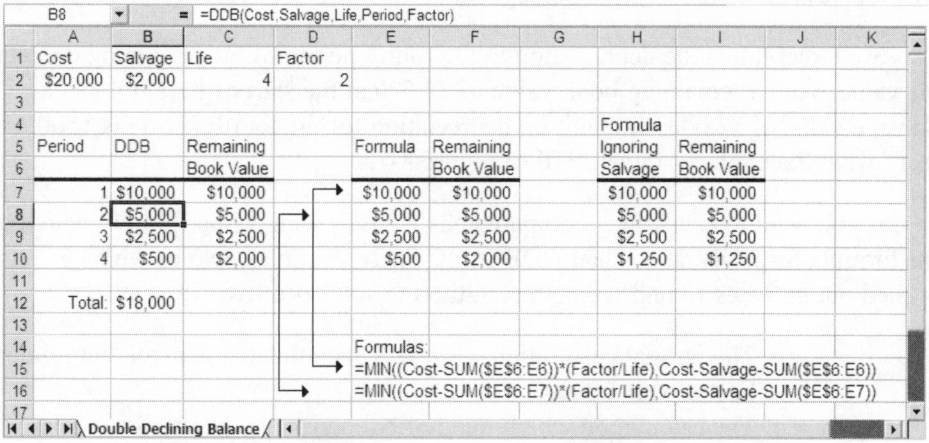
B8 = =DDB(Cost,Salvage,Life,Period,Factor)

	A	B	C	D	E	F	G	H	I	J	K
1	Cost	Salvage	Life	Factor							
2	$20,000	$2,000	4	2							
3											
4								Formula			
5	Period	DDB	Remaining		Formula	Remaining		Ignoring	Remaining		
6			Book Value			Book Value		Salvage	Book Value		
7	1	$10,000	$10,000		$10,000	$10,000		$10,000	$10,000		
8	2	$5,000	$5,000		$5,000	$5,000		$5,000	$5,000		
9	3	$2,500	$2,500		$2,500	$2,500		$2,500	$2,500		
10	4	$500	$2,000		$500	$2,000		$1,250	$1,250		
11											
12	Total:	$18,000									
13											
14					Formulas:						
15					=MIN((Cost-SUM($E$6:E6))*(Factor/Life),Cost-Salvage-SUM($E$6:E6))						
16					=MIN((Cost-SUM($E$6:E7))*(Factor/Life),Cost-Salvage-SUM($E$6:E7))						
17											

Double Declining Balance

Figure 8-7: The formula in E7 is shown in Row 15, and the formula in E8 is shown in Row 16. Cells E9:E11 follow the pattern.

The Cost, Salvage, Life and Factor arguments are given in cells A2:D2, and the cells in A2:D2 are named accordingly (for example, cell C2 is named Life). The range A7:A10 is named Period.

The DDB function is used in each of the cells in the range B7:B10 in this formula:

=DDB(Cost,Salvage,Life,Period,Factor)

(In this case, Factor could be omitted because it's been given the default value of 2.)

With a useful life of four periods and a factor of 2, DDB returns 50% of the remaining book value: four periods means that a 25% straight-line rate would be used in each period, and the factor of 2 doubles the 25% to 50%. So, the depreciation of $10,000 in Period 1 is 50% of the original book value; the depreciation of $5,000 in Period 2 is 50% of the $10,000 remaining book value; and similarly in Period 3.

However, note that the depreciation in Period 4 is only $500, although the remaining book value at the beginning of Period 4 is $2,500. If the depreciation in Period 4 were 50% of $2,500, the analysis would depreciate the asset by another $1,250. But that would reduce the book value at the end of Period 4 to $1,250, which is less than the specified Salvage value.

So, Excel limits the depreciation in the fourth period to the remaining depreciable value. With a remaining book value of $2,500 at the start of Period 4 and a Salvage value of $2,000, the limit on depreciation for the fourth period is $500 – and that's what Excel places in cell B10 of Figure 8-7.

If you want to check that, compare cells B7:B10 with ce3lls E7:E10, which use the formula for DDB rather than DDB itself. These formulas, two of which are spelled out in Rows 15 and 16, both result in the smaller of two values:

- The normal calculation: Cost less accumulated depreciation, times Factor over Life.
- The calculation which, in the final period, is the smaller of the two values: Cost less Salvage less accumulated depreciation. This is the remaining depreciable value when to continue with the normal calculation would eat into the Salvage value.

Again in Figure 8-7, cell H10 contains this formula:

=(Cost-SUM($H$6:H9))*(Factor/Life)

This is the normal calculation, extended into the fourth period. As you see, it returns $1,250. This would take the remaining book value down from $2,500 to $1,250, $750 less than the stated Salvage value. Therefore, one can't use the normal calculation willy-nilly, without attention to the asset's salvage value.

Notice in Figure 8-8 what happens if the Factor argument is changed from 2 (as it was in Figure 8-7), to 1.5.

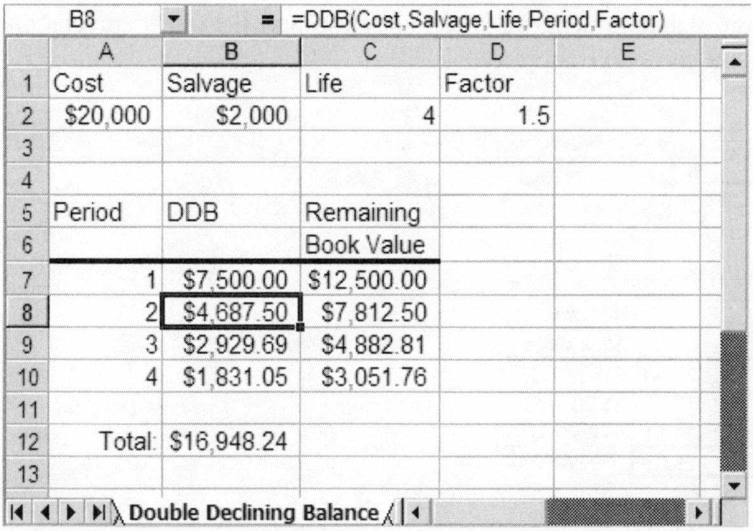

	B8	▼	=	=DDB(Cost,Salvage,Life,Period,Factor)		
	A	B	C	D	E	
1	Cost	Salvage	Life	Factor		
2	$20,000	$2,000	4	1.5		
3						
4						
5	Period	DDB	Remaining			
6			Book Value			
7	1	$7,500.00	$12,500.00			
8	2	$4,687.50	$7,812.50			
9	3	$2,929.69	$4,882.81			
10	4	$1,831.05	$3,051.76			
11						
12	Total:	$16,948.24				
13						

‖◄ ◄ ▶ ▶‖ \ Double Declining Balance / ◄

Figure 8-8: Here, the less aggressive depreciation rate fails to fully depreciate the asset.

With a Factor argument of 1.5 and a Life argument of 4, the rate of depreciation is 1.5 * .25, or 0.375. Therefore the early depreciation is less aggressive than when Factor is 2, and as a result there is still $3,051.76 remaining book value at the end of Period 4. This amount is greater than the specified Salvage argument, so you haven't fully accounted for the asset's depreciable value. You should probably increase the factor.

There is no Month (or Months, for that matter) argument in the DDB function. If you want to calculate depreciation on an asset that was put into use partway through the first period, you should consider using the VDB function (discussed in the VDB Function section of this chapter) or use a shorter period.

For example, if the asset was placed in use during April, you could measure periods in months instead of years, and subsequently sum the monthly depreciation for each year. If you take that approach, though, be sure to keep in mind the caveats discussed in the next section.

Watching the Cost to Salvage Ratio

Although the DDB function is generally a stronger one than the DB function, you still need to take some care with its use. In particular, if the Cost argument is much greater than the Salvage argument, DDB can underestimate the total depreciation to be taken. Figure 8-9 gives an example.

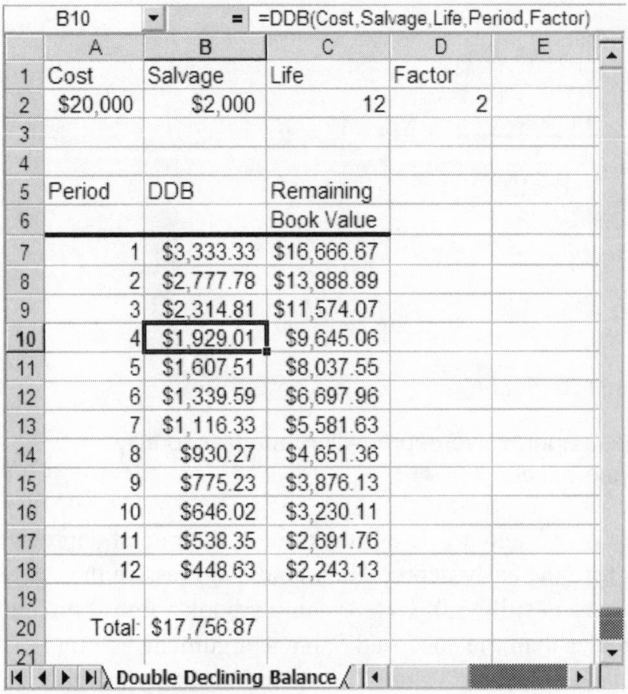

	A	B	C	D	E
	B10 ▼ = =DDB(Cost,Salvage,Life,Period,Factor)				
1	Cost	Salvage	Life	Factor	
2	$20,000	$2,000	12	2	
3					
4					
5	Period	DDB	Remaining		
6			Book Value		
7	1	$3,333.33	$16,666.67		
8	2	$2,777.78	$13,888.89		
9	3	$2,314.81	$11,574.07		
10	4	$1,929.01	$9,645.06		
11	5	$1,607.51	$8,037.55		
12	6	$1,339.59	$6,697.96		
13	7	$1,116.33	$5,581.63		
14	8	$930.27	$4,651.36		
15	9	$775.23	$3,876.13		
16	10	$646.02	$3,230.11		
17	11	$538.35	$2,691.76		
18	12	$448.63	$2,243.13		
19					
20	Total:	$17,756.87			
21					

Double Declining Balance

Figure 8-9: This cost to salvage ratio is too large for DDB to fully depreciate the asset.

On the worksheet shown in Figure 8-9, the Cost, Salvage, Life and Factor arguments are located in cells A2, B2, C2 and D2, respectively. The cells are named by selecting A1:D2 and using Insert → Name → Create.

In addition, there is a range named Period in A7:A18. With the setup as described, you can enter this formula:

DDB(Cost,Salvage,Life,Period,Factor)

in cell B7, and copy-and-paste it into B8:B18. The formula takes advantage of Excel's implicit intersection. For information on that feature, see the section named Defining an Implicit Intersection in Chapter 6.

With a Cost argument of $20,000 and a Salvage argument of $2,000, the sum of the depreciation amounts returned by DDB should be $18,000. But, as cell B21 in Figure 8-9 shows, it returns only $17,756.87. The problem has to do with the ratio of Cost to Salvage, as well as to the Life and Factor arguments.

It's a complex situation, but if you use the default Factor value of 2, DDB will return correct results up to the point that Cost is 7.7 times Salvage. Beyond that breakpoint, the sum of the depreciation amounts returned by DDB will be smaller than the asset's depreciable value. (Even then, if Life is less than 8 you'll be fine; a Life argument that's 8 or greater will cause problems.)

TIP: Suppose that the Factor value is 2, and the Salvage value is, say, one-fourth of Cost. This puts you in the region where you don't need to worry about underestimating depreciation, and Life can be a fairly large number such as 48. Now you can treat each month as a different period, and easily accommodate the placement of the asset into use during, for example, April. You simply treat April as Period 1, May as Period 2, and so on through 48 months.

And you should also watch the relationship between Factor and Life. Here's the formula used by the DDB function:

MIN((Cost – Prior depreciation) * (Factor/Life), (Cost - Salvage - Prior depreciation))

Suppose Cost is $20,000, Salvage is $4,000, and both Factor and Life are 2. Then, at the end of the first period, there has been no prior depreciation, and this is the calculation:

MIN((20000 – 0) * 2/2),(20000 – 4000 – 0))

works out to this:

MIN(20000,16000)

or $16,000. That means that the entire depreciable amount, Cost less Salvage, is taken in the first period. This might appeal to you or your client, but the Federal and state tax authorities are likely to take a dim view of it.

So, here are two recommendations to keep in mind if you use the DDB function:

- If you use the default value for Factor, 2, keep the Salvage value to at least 13% of the Cost value.
- Lay out your analysis as shown in Figure 8-9. This will put you in a position to see if the arguments you supply result in the full depreciation coming too early. You'll also be able to tell if full depreciation doesn't come during the final Period specified by Life (as shown in Figure 8-9).

Ignoring the DDB Help Documentation

Excel's Help documentation has, until Excel 2003, stated that the DDB function uses the following formula:

((Cost-Salvage) - Prior depreciation) * (Factor/Life)

This is not the case. Apart from the special handling used during a final period when the remaining book value would be less than the specified salvage value, the formula mis-describes how the current book value is calculated.

I'm going to repeat this because it's contradicted by the Excel Help documents, in all their awful majesty. The DDB function does not take the Salvage argument into account until the asset depreciable value has been exhausted. If you check Microsoft's online documentation for DDB, starting with Excel 2003, you'll find the formula given in the prior section:

Min((Cost - Prior depreciation) * (Factor/Life), (Cost - Salvage - Prior depreciation))

VDB Function

The VDB function is an extension of the DDB function. "VDB" stands for *v*ariable *d*eclining *b*alance. Its two additions to DDB are:

- A Start_Period argument and an End_Period argument. Using these arguments you can obtain total depreciation taken during several consecutive periods.

- A No_Switch argument, which causes VDB to switch to straight-line depreciation if and when SLN would return larger values than declining balance. (This argument is described accurately here, as far as I can tell for the first time in the Excel literature.)

The VDB function's full syntax is:

=VDB(Cost,Salvage,Life,Start_Period,End_Period,Factor,No_Switch)

The Cost, Salvage, Life and Factor arguments are treated exactly as they are in the functions that this chapter has already discussed, SLN, SYD, DB and DDB. Cost, Salvage and Life are required arguments.

The Start_Period and End_Period arguments are similar to the Period argument in the DB and DDB functions. They identify periods of interest during the asset's Life. Both Start_Period and End_Period are required. Here is an example:

=VDB(Cost,Salvage,Life,2,3)

With the given arguments, VDB returns the total depreciation that accrues from the end of the second period to the end of the third: that is, one period of depreciation, specifically the third. Another example:

=VDB(Cost,Salvage,Life,2,4)

VDB, with these arguments, returns the total depreciation accrued during the two periods from the end of the second period to the end of the fourth.

Figure 8-10 shows VDB used on a worksheet.

As in earlier figures in this chapter, the function's arguments are shown in the second row. Their cells are named according to the labels in the first row. The range A7:A16 is named Period.

The Factor argument is provided, although because the default value of 2 is used, it could be omitted.

The No_Switch argument is a little confusing, involving as it does a double negative. If you specify TRUE, VDB does *not* switch to straight-line depreciation. If you specify FALSE, or just omit the argument, VDB *does* switch to straight-line depreciation. Microsoft apparently decided that the normal course would be to switch to straight-line depreciation, so FALSE was made the default. In turn, that made it desirable to name the argument No_Switch instead of Switch.

	B11	▼		=	=VDB(Cost,Salvage,Life,Period-1,Period,Factor,No_Switch)		
	A	B	C	D	E	F	G
1	Cost	Salvage	Life	Factor	No_switch		
2	$2,400	$100	10	2	FALSE		
3							
4		VDB	Remaining		VDB	Remaining	
5	Period	(switch	Book Value		(Don't switch	Book Value	
6		to SLN)			to SLN)		
7	1	$480.00	$1,920.00		$480.00	$1,920.00	
8	2	$384.00	$1,536.00		$384.00	$1,536.00	
9	3	$307.20	$1,228.80		$307.20	$1,228.80	
10	4	$245.76	$983.04		$245.76	$983.04	
11	5	$196.61	$786.43		$196.61	$786.43	
12	6	$157.29	$629.15		$157.29	$629.15	
13	7	$132.29	$496.86		$125.83	$503.32	
14	8	$132.29	$364.57		$100.66	$402.65	
15	9	$132.29	$232.29		$80.53	$322.12	
16	10	$132.29	$100.00		$64.42	$257.70	
17							
18	Total:	$2,300.00		Total:	$2,142.30		
19							

Figure 8-10: You can supply fractional values for the period arguments to start the depreciation partway through a period.

Enough etymology. What happens when you specify FALSE for No_Switch, perhaps by default, is that Excel checks the sequence of depreciation amounts assuming declining balance, and compares it to the sequence assuming straight line depreciation. If the depreciation for the period using straight line for the remainder of the asset's Life is greater than the declining balance depreciation for the same period, VDB uses the straight-line calculation.

In Figure 8-10, each cell in the range B7:B16 contains this formula:

=VDB(Cost,Salvage,Life,Period-1,Period,Factor,No_Switch)

Substituting numeric values for the range names, the formula in cell B8 becomes:

=VDB(2400,100,10,1,2,2,FALSE)

or $384.00, the value shown in cell B8 in Figure 8-10.

Notice that the depreciation becomes a constant $132.29 in cell B13, continuing through B16. VDB has switched from a declining balance calculation to a straight-line calculation, per the FALSE value used for the No_Switch argument.

The range E7:E16 in Figure 8-10 contains formulas that are identical to those in B7:B16, except that the No_Switch argument is TRUE – that is, VDB is instructed *not* to switch to straight-line depreciation, but to continue with declining balance in all cases.

Notice, though, that in cell E13, that declining balance calculation results in depreciation of $125.83 during Period 7. The remaining book value at the end of Period 6 is $629.15. Dividing $629.15 by the four remaining periods results in a periodic straight-line depreciation of $132.29. This value is larger than the declining balance depreciation of $125.83 for Period 7. Therefore, because No_Switch is set to FALSE in B7:B16, VDB switches to straight-line depreciation as of Period 7. This also fully depreciates the asset as of Period 10, which VDB using TRUE for No_Switch fails to do – compare this situation with the earlier section, Watching the Cost to Salvage Ratio.

Chapter 9

Excel and QuickBooks

Importing lists to QuickBooks files

Updating lists with import files

Importing adjusting entries

Y ou can use Excel to import data into QuickBooks directly, using a tab-delimited text file created in Excel that has the filename extension .iif. The file must be configured properly for importing to QuickBooks.

About IIF Import Files

IIF import files are a bit complicated to create, but they are more powerful as an import tool than the Excel or CSV files that QuickBooks also supports for importing list data. You can create an IIF file in Excel, save it as a tab-delimited text file, and name the file, giving it the extension .iif.

Unlike its behavior when you import an Excel or CSV file, QuickBooks does not preview or error-check the contents of a tab-delimited text file. If the import fails at some point, it just fails. Therefore, you must be careful about the way you create the file.

On the other hand, using a tab-delimited file means you can import all the data you need to set up a company, instead of being restricted to the few lists provided in the Excel/CSV import feature, each of which is limited in the number of fields it accepts. An IIF file can contain data to populate every list in QuickBooks, including detailed information about each record in the list.

An IIF file is a great way for accountants to provide all the data required for a client's company file. It's like creating a perfect company file from scratch in QuickBooks, and delivering the file to the client.

Entering data in a spreadsheet is faster and easier than going through all the work involved in creating a company file in QuickBooks. Entering data in rows and columns in an Excel worksheet is faster than opening one QuickBooks list window after another, and then opening one dialog after another within each list in order to populate the list.

Most accountants are extremely comfortable working in a spreadsheet application, and after they've created a series of boilerplate import files for different types of companies, they can zip through the process of customizing a boilerplate for any particular client. Do your work in a regular spreadsheet file, saving it as an Excel file, so you can avoid all those reminders from Excel about text files not having all the features of a regular spreadsheet file. Then, when you're ready to create an import file for QuickBooks, save the file as a tab-delimited text file with the extension .iif.

Format of an IIF File

To get a spreadsheet to work correctly as an import file, you have to lay it out with a particular structure. Figure 9-1 shows an Excel worksheet with the chart of accounts in the right layout.

Notice the following characteristics of this sample IIF file:

- The list being imported is identified by that list's keyword in cell A1 (identified by the exclamation point): **!ACCNT**
- Each record (row) indicates the list into which the data is being imported (the keyword ACCNT in Column A, following the column header in row 1).
- Each category (column header) has the keyword for the field into which the data in that column is imported.

To create an IIF file from scratch, make sure you've set up your columns properly, with the appropriate headings, using keywords. When you enter data, remember that some data requires special handling, which again entails keywords. You'll find the documentation for the keywords is in this chapter.

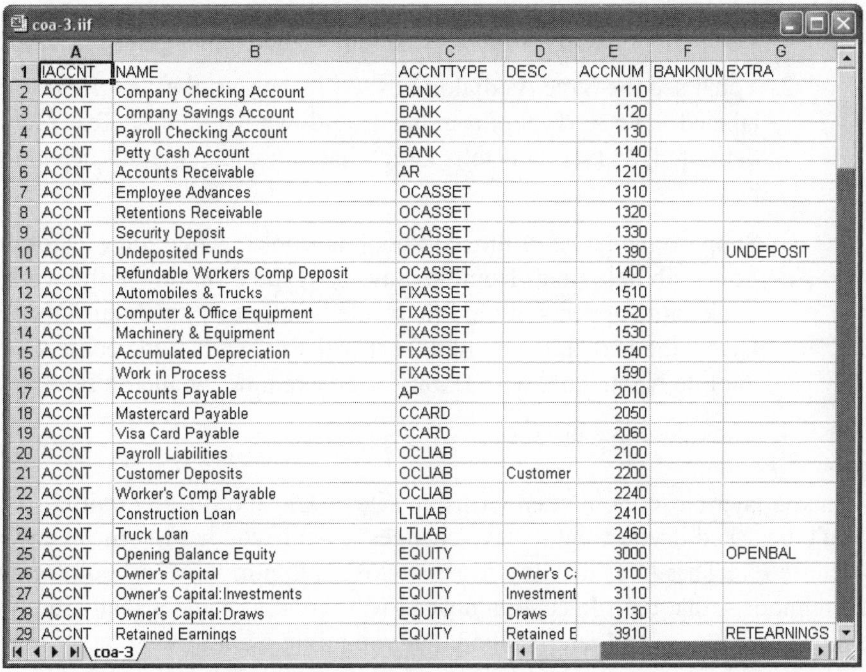
coa-3.iif

	A	B	C	D	E	F	G
1	!ACCNT	NAME	ACCNTTYPE	DESC	ACCNUM	BANKNUM	EXTRA
2	ACCNT	Company Checking Account	BANK		1110		
3	ACCNT	Company Savings Account	BANK		1120		
4	ACCNT	Payroll Checking Account	BANK		1130		
5	ACCNT	Petty Cash Account	BANK		1140		
6	ACCNT	Accounts Receivable	AR		1210		
7	ACCNT	Employee Advances	OCASSET		1310		
8	ACCNT	Retentions Receivable	OCASSET		1320		
9	ACCNT	Security Deposit	OCASSET		1330		
10	ACCNT	Undeposited Funds	OCASSET		1390		UNDEPOSIT
11	ACCNT	Refundable Workers Comp Deposit	OCASSET		1400		
12	ACCNT	Automobiles & Trucks	FIXASSET		1510		
13	ACCNT	Computer & Office Equipment	FIXASSET		1520		
14	ACCNT	Machinery & Equipment	FIXASSET		1530		
15	ACCNT	Accumulated Depreciation	FIXASSET		1540		
16	ACCNT	Work in Process	FIXASSET		1590		
17	ACCNT	Accounts Payable	AP		2010		
18	ACCNT	Mastercard Payable	CCARD		2050		
19	ACCNT	Visa Card Payable	CCARD		2060		
20	ACCNT	Payroll Liabilities	OCLIAB		2100		
21	ACCNT	Customer Deposits	OCLIAB	Customer	2200		
22	ACCNT	Worker's Comp Payable	OCLIAB		2240		
23	ACCNT	Construction Loan	LTLIAB		2410		
24	ACCNT	Truck Loan	LTLIAB		2460		
25	ACCNT	Opening Balance Equity	EQUITY		3000		OPENBAL
26	ACCNT	Owner's Capital	EQUITY	Owner's C	3100		
27	ACCNT	Owner's Capital:Investments	EQUITY	Investment	3110		
28	ACCNT	Owner's Capital:Draws	EQUITY	Draws	3130		
29	ACCNT	Retained Earnings	EQUITY	Retained E	3910		RETEARNINGS

coa-3

Figure 9-1: This sheet has the proper layout for importing the chart of accounts into QuickBooks.

Exporting Data into an IIF File

You can export data from another application and specify a tab-delimited file for the exported file format. The application could be another accounting software application, or a spreadsheet in which clients have been keeping customer information, inventory information, etc.

Saving the IIF File in Excel

Once you've structured an Excel worksheet as this chapter describes, you'll want to save it in the tab-delimited format. (That term just means that Excel will separate columns in the file with tabs instead of commas or spaces.)

But saving the file with an .iif extension poses a minor problem. When you specify a tab-delimited format, Excel by default gives the file a .txt extension. So, follow this sequence of events:

1. When you're ready to save the file in Excel, choose File → Save As.

2. You'll see the Save As dialog box. At its bottom there's a field labeled Save As Type. From the drop-down list, choose Text (Tab delimited) (*.txt). This tells Excel that you want columns separated by tabs.

3. Suppose the name of the workbook is Book1. After you've chosen Text (Tab delimited) from the Save As Type drop-down, the workbook name appears in the File Name box, with a .txt extension. Delete the text "txt" and replace it with "iif" so that the contents of the File Name box, with Book1 as an example, would be Book1.iif.

4. Click the Save button.

When you later close the file, either using File → Close or just by quitting Excel, you'll be asked if you want to save changes, even if you haven't made any. That's because Excel assumes that any file you close is in normal workbook format. When Excel notices that the file is not a normal workbook, it decides that you must have changed something, and reminds you that you might want to save the changes. If you haven't made changes since the last time you saved, click No.

Opening the IIF File in Excel

To open a tab-delimited file in Excel, right-click the file's listing in My Computer or Windows Explorer and choose Open With. Then choose Microsoft Excel from the list of installed applications. If you already have Excel open, you can choose Open from the File menu, and then choose All Files in the Files of Type drop-down. Navigate to the location where you saved the IIF file, click it and then click Open.

Excel responds by stepping you through a wizard, a sequence of dialog boxes where you specify certain preferences about how Excel should treat the file. When you're opening the IIF file, the only options that matter are:

- In Step 1, make sure that the Delimited option button is selected.
- In Step 2, make sure that the Tab checkbox is filled, and *only* that checkbox.

Step 3 has no options you'll need to change.

Creating Multiple Lists in One IIF File

You can actually create an entire company in one IIF file, by having all the entries for all the lists you want to import in one worksheet. This is a good way to deliver a "whole company in a worksheet" to your clients.

Each list must be in its own contiguous section of rows, with the appropriate keyword headings as the first row of each list. To make it easier to work with the file, insert a blank row between each section (list).

Many accountants who work in Excel save the file as a standard Excel (.xls) file while they're building import files. It's common to create a separate worksheet for each list being created. This method is more efficient, and lets you build boiler-plate worksheets for each QuickBooks list.

However, you can't save multiple worksheets when you save a document as a tab-delimited file. When you're ready to turn your Excel document into QuickBooks import files, you can either save each worksheet as a separate IIF file, or you can copy the contents of every worksheet into a single worksheet in a new Excel document. Then, save the new combined document as an IIF file.

This structure – that is, putting a blank row between each list so as to create different sections on the worksheet – does not lend itself to adding records using the Data Form (see the heading in Chapter 1, Using the Data Form). Excel won't shift subsequent lists down to make room for a new record in an earlier list. So, the recommendation is to use a different worksheet for each list while you're developing the data (which also lets you use the Data Form freely) and move all the data onto a single worksheet when you're ready to create the IIF file.

Importing an IIF File

Importing an IIF file is an uncomplicated process, and takes only a few easy steps. It's even easier if you copy the file to the folder in which the QuickBooks company file is located, so you don't have to navigate through the computer to find the file. Use the following steps to import an IIF file:

1. In QuickBooks, open the company that needs the imported file.

2. Choose File → Utilities → Import → IIF Files.

3. Double-click the IIF file you want to import.

QuickBooks automatically imports the file and then displays a message indicating the data has been imported. Click OK.

IIF File Keywords for Lists

In the following sections, I'll provide the keywords and instructions for building IIF files for QuickBooks lists. For many lists, I'll provide only the keywords for fields that are commonly imported, instead of covering the full range of possible keywords.

For example, all lists accept data in a field (column) named HIDDEN, and you enter Y (meaning "yes it's hidden") or N (meaning "no, it's not hidden") for each entry (row) to indicate whether the entry is active or inactive. It's normal to omit that column in an import file. In the absence of information about the active status, QuickBooks assumes the entry is N (not hidden.)

For lists that permit custom fields in the names lists and the items list, QuickBooks has keywords you can use to import that data. However, it would be unusual to take the trouble to create these in a worksheet. It would also be unusual for a file imported from another application to contain this information. Custom fields are usually specific to a particular company file, and are created within QuickBooks.

Profile Lists Import Files

Profile lists are the lists that contain entries to help you categorize and sort major lists. The entries in profile lists are fields in major lists, such as Terms or Vendor Type. You can see the profile lists by choosing Lists → Customer & Vendor Profile Lists.

I'm starting the discussion of importing lists with the profile lists, because if you import the profile lists, you can use their contents in other lists in subsequent imports. For example, if you import your Customer Type List, you can enter data in the Customer Type category of your customer import list, and QuickBooks accepts the data if the Customer Type category data exists. (I'm not covering all the profile lists; instead, I'll discuss those that are commonly imported.)

Customer Type List Import File

The Customer Type List has one keyword: Name. Your worksheet needs only two columns:

- Column A contains the list keyword !CTYPE in the top row, and the entry keyword in Column A for each row of data is CTYPE.
- Column B contains the data keyword NAME in the top row, and the data (the name you've created for a customer type) is in each following row.

Vendor Type List Import File

The Vendor Type List is almost exactly the same as the Customer Type List:

- The list keyword for the first row of Column A is !VTYPE and the entry keyword in Column A for each row of data is VTYPE.
- Column B contains the data keyword (NAME) in the top row, and the data (the name you create for each vendor type) is in each following row.

Job Type List Import File

The Job Type List is also similar to the Customer Type list:

- The list keyword for the first row of Column A is !JOBTYPE and the entry keyword in Column A for each row of data is JOBTYPE.
- Column B contains the data keyword NAME in the top row, and the data is in each following row.

Sales Rep List Import File

The Sales Rep List has four columns, using the following layout:

- The list keyword for the first row of Column A is !SALESREP and the entry keyword in Column A for each row of data is SALESREP.

- Column B contains the data keyword INITIALS in the top row, and the data (two initials) is in each following row.
- Column C contains the data keyword ASSOCIATEDNAME in the top row, and the data (the name of the sales rep) is in each following row.
- Column D contains the data keyword NAMETYPE in the top row, and the data (a code representing the list that the sales rep is a member of) is in each data row.

The NAMETYPE codes are:

- 2 if the rep is in the Vendor List
- 3 if the rep is in the Employee List
- 4 if the rep is in the Other Names List

NOTE: Because the list references other lists, import the Vendor, Employee, and Other Names lists before importing the Sales Rep list; or, place them above the Sales Rep list in a worksheet that contains multiple lists.

Ship Method List Import File

The Ship Method List (which supplies data for the Ship Via field in transactions) is also similar to the Customer Type list:

- The list keyword for the first row of Column A is !SHIPMETH and the entry keyword in Column A for each row of data is SHIPMETH.
- Column B contains the data keyword NAME in the top row, and the data (UPS, FedEx, Truck, etc), is in each following row.

Terms List Import File

The Terms List import file must contain all the information for each named set of terms. The terms you include must cover the terms you need for *both* customers and vendors (QuickBooks doesn't provide separate Terms files for customers and vendors).

- The list keyword for the first row of Column A is !TERMS and the entry keyword in Column A for each row of data is TERMS.

- The remaining columns contain the data keywords in the top row, and the data is in each following row. The data keywords for columns are explained in Table 9-1.

Keyword (Column Title)	Data
NAME	(Required) The name for the terms.
TERMSTYPE	The type of terms. 0 = standard terms (payment within a specific number of days). 1 = date driven terms (payment by a certain date of the month).
DUEDAYS	When TERMSTYPE = 0, t he number of days in which payment is due. When TERMSTYPE = 1, the day of the month by which payment is due.
DISCPER	The discount percentage earned for early payment. The data is a number and the percent sign (e.g. 2.00%).
DISCDAYS	The number of days by which the discount specified by DISCPER is earned.

Table 9-1: Import file keywords for the Terms list.

Standard Lists Import Files

The information in the following sections covers the commonly imported lists that are displayed on the Lists menu. After your profile lists are imported, the data in some of the "regular" lists can be linked to the data in the profile lists.

Chart of Accounts Import File

The chart of accounts (refer back to Figure 9-1) import file is not terribly complicated:

- The list keyword for the first row of Column A is !ACCNT and the entry keyword in Column A for each row of data is ACCNT.
- The rest of the columns contain the data keywords in the first row. The data is in each following row.

Table 9-2 shows the important column headings for importing a chart of accounts. If your clients don't use account numbers, you can omit the ACCNUM column.

Keyword (Column Title)	Text
NAME	(Required) The name of the account.
ACCNTTYPE	(Required) The type of account. The text must match keywords (See Table 9 -3).
DESC	Description of the account.
ACCNUM	The account number.

Table 9-2: Keywords for the chart of accounts.

The NAME entry is required, as is the ACCNTTYPE entry; also, your text in the ACCNTTYPE column must match the keywords in Table 9-3.

Section	Account Type	Keyword
Assets		
	Bank	BANK
	Accounts Receivable	AR
	Other Current Asset	OCASSET
	Fixed Asset	FIXASSET
	Other Asset	OASSET
Liabilities		
	Accounts Payable	AP
	Credit Card	CCARD
	Other Current Liability	OCLIAB
	Long-Term Liability	LTLIAB
Equity		EQUITY
Income		INC
Cost Of Goods Sold		COGS
Expense		EXP
Other Income		EXINC
Other Expense		EXEXP
Non-Posting Accounts		NONPOSTING

Table 9-3: Keywords for account types.

Account Numbers in Import Files

If the company file into which you import the chart of accounts has enabled account numbers, the numbers in the IIF file are displayed in the chart of accounts window and the drop-down lists in transaction windows.

If account numbers are not enabled in the company file, QuickBooks stores the account number data that was imported. When (or if) the user enables account numbers, the imported account numbers are displayed.

EXTRA Account Keywords

You can include a column named EXTRA to import accounts that QuickBooks automatically creates when such accounts are needed (when specific features are enabled).

For example, when a QuickBooks user enables the inventory feature, QuickBooks creates an account named Inventory Asset Account in the Assets section of the chart of accounts.

To use these accounts in an import file, the text you enter in the EXTRA column must match the required keywords. If the text doesn't match the required keyword, QuickBooks will create another account when the user enables the appropriate feature. Table 9-4 contains the keywords required in the EXTRA column when you create these special accounts.

Account	EXTRA Column Keyword
Inventory Asset	INVENTORYASSET
Opening Balance Equity	OPENBAL
Retained Earnings	RETEARNINGS
Sales Tax Payable	SALESTAX
Undeposited Funds	UNDEPOSIT
Cost of Goods Sold	COGS
Purchase Orders	PURCHORDER
Estimates	ESTIMATE

Table 9-4: Keywords for configuring the EXTRA column for special accounts.

Although QuickBooks adds these accounts automatically when needed, including them in the import file lets you control their account numbers. You can create boilerplate import files by client type, and include the appropriate EXTRA accounts. For example, product-based businesses need inventory and purchase order accounts, and some service-based businesses may need estimates.

Customers & Jobs List Import File

If you've been keeping a customer list in another software application, you can avoid one-customer-at-a-time data entry by importing the list into QuickBooks. This is possible only if your current application is capable of exporting data to a text file.

Use Excel to open the text file and use the instructions in this section to create an import file.

Although the IIF file that you import into QuickBooks must be tab-delimited, Excel is capable of importing text files that use other formats, such as .CSV (Comma Separated Values) files and .PRN files (.PRN files commonly align columns that have specific widths). Check to see what formats your current application uses to create text files, and then verify that Excel can open one of them. Then, you can save the file in Excel in the tab delimited format.

NOTE: *In QuickBooks 2006, Intuit changed the name of this list from Customer:Job to Customers & Jobs. However, drop-down lists still use the terminology Customer:Job. For consistency, I use Customers & Jobs.*

A QuickBooks Customers & Jobs List import file can contain all the information you need to fill out all the fields in the customer dialog, such as customer type, sales tax status, and so on.

However, it's unlikely your client kept records in a manner that matches these fields, so I'll provide the keywords and instructions for basic customer information. I'll include some of the additional fields so you can fill them in manually if you wish (or skip the keyword column for any data you don't want to import).

Customers & Jobs Import File Format

If you're dealing with data from another source, after you import the data to Excel, you need to format the worksheet as follows:

- To make room for the QuickBooks keywords you need, you'll need a blank row at the top of the list and a blank column on its left. If necessary, use Excel's Insert menu to get a blank Column A and a blank Row 1.
- Enter the text value !CUST (the exclamation point is required) in cell A1. This is the code that tells QuickBooks that this is a Customers & Jobs list.

- In the remaining cells in the first column, for every row that has data, insert the text CUST. This identifies the data in that row as data for a Customers & Jobs list.
- In the first row, starting with the second column (the first column contains !CUST), enter the QuickBooks keywords for customers.

NOTE: Use cell A1 to indicate the list if the Customers & Jobs list is the only list in the sheet. If the sheet holds multiple lists, the cell that contains !CUST must be in the upper left cell of the first row of the Customers & Jobs list

---

Table 9-5 describes the keywords and the text that belongs in the column under each keyword.

TIP: The only required entry is the customer name, which is linked to the keyword NAME. If that's the only information you have, use it to import the customer names. Your clients can fill in the rest of the fields as they use each customer in a transaction.

QuickBooks supports multiple shipping addresses for customers, and when you're creating customer records within QuickBooks you can name each shipping address. The import file can only manage one shipping address. When you import the file, the shipping address data becomes the default shipping address.

Importing Jobs

A job is linked to a customer, and the text must be in the format Customer:Job. Notice that no spaces exist before or after the colon.

To import jobs, you must make sure the customer is imported first so that there's a record to link the job to; the text for the customer must appear in the Name column before the text for the job. For example, if you have a customer named LRAssocs with a job named Consulting and another job named Auditing, enter the following in the rows in the Name column:

LRAssocs

LRAssocs:Consulting

LRAssocs:Auditing

Keyword (Column)	Text
NAME	The customer name (the code used for the customer).
COMPANYNAME	Name of the customer's company.
FIRSTNAME	Customer's first name.
MIDINIT	Customer's middle initial.
LASTNAME	Customer's last name.
BADDR1	First line of the customer's billing address, which is usually a name (customer's name or company name).
BADDR2	Second line of the customer's billing address, which is the street address.
BADDR3	Third line of the customer's billing address, which is either additional street address information, or the city, state, and zip.
BADDR4	Fourth line of the billing address, which is either additional street address information, or the city, state, and zip.
BADDR5	Fifth line of the billing address, which is either additional street address information, or the city, state, and zip.
SADDR1	First line of the default shipping address.
SADDR2	Second line of the default shipping address.
SADDR3	Third line of the default shipping address.
SADDR4	Fourth line of the default shipping address.
SADDR5	Fifth line of the default shipping address.
PHONE1	Phone number.
PHONE2	Second phone number.
FAXNUM	FAX number.
EMAIL	E-mail address of a contact.
CONT1	Name of the primary contact.
CONT2	Name of another contact.
CTYPE	Customer Type (must match text in the Customer Type import file).
TERMS	Terms (must match text in the Terms import file).
TAXABLE	Y or N
SALESTAXCODE	Tax code (must match text in the Tax Code import file)
LIMIT	Credit limit (e.g. 5000.00)
RESALENUM	Resale number for tax exempt customers

Table 9-5: Keywords for a Customers & Jobs import file.

Most jobs have the same basic information (address, taxable status, and so on) as the customer, so you don't have to enter text in the other columns. However, if any specific information is different, such as the name of the primary contact, or the job type, enter the text in the appropriate column.

Vendor List Import File

If you're exporting your vendor list from another software application, follow the formatting rules described earlier for the customer file.

- The list keyword for the first row of Column A is !VEND and the entry keyword in Column A for each row of data is VEND.
- The remaining columns contain the data keywords on the top row, and the data is in each following row.

The data keywords are explained in Table 9-6.

Keyword	Data
NAME	The Vendor Name (the vendor code).
PRINTAS	The Payee name that prints on checks.
ADDR1	First line of the vendor's address.
ADDR2	Second line of the vendor's address.
ADDR3	Third line of the vendor's address.
ADDR4	Fourth line of the vendor's address.
ADDR5	Fifth line of the vendor's address.
VTYPE	Vendor Type (must match text in the Vendor Type import file).
CONT1	Your primary contact.
PHONE1	Phone number.
PHONE2	Second phone number.
FAXNUM	FAX number.
EMAIL	E-mail address of a contact.
NOTE	The text you want to print in the Memo field of checks (usually your account number with the vendor).
TERMS	Terms (must match a name in the Terms import file).
TAXID	Tax identification number for a 1099 recipient.
SALUTATION	Salutation or title.
COMPANYNAME	Vendor's company name.
FIRSTNAME	First name.
MIDINIT	Middle initial.
LASTNAME	Last name.
1099	Specifies whether this vendor receives a 1099 -MISC form. Ente Y or N as the data.

Table 9-6: Keywords for importing vendors into QuickBooks.

Items List Import File

If your client has been keeping items in a software application (usually this means inventory items only), you can import those items to spare your client the chore of entering data by hand. Use the instructions earlier in this chapter to format the file.

The required keywords for items import files are the following:

- NAME—the item name.
- INVITEMTYPE—the item type.
- ACCNT—the income account to which you post sales of this item (must exist in the previously imported COA).

Some QuickBooks item types don't have an account (such as prepayments or tax items). However, because most imported items list originally were exported from another application, those item types are rarely imported (unless the application uses the same types of items as QuickBooks).

The keyword for the item list is !INVITEM on the heading row, and each record (row) must have INVITEM in the first column. Table 9-7 describes the keywords for the rest of the columns on the first row of the import file.

Keyword	Data
NAME	Item Name or Number
INVITEMTYPE	Item type. The data must match the keywords in Table 9-8.
DESC	The description that appears on sales forms
PURCHASEDESC	(Inventory part items only) The description that appears on purchase orders
ACCNT	The income account you use to track sales of the item
ASSETACCNT	(Inventory part items only) The inventory asset account
COGSACCNT	(Inventory part items only) The cost of goods account
PRICE	The percentage rate or price of the item (not for Group, Payment, or Subtotal type).
COST	(Inventory part items only) The unit cost of the item.
TAXABLE	Specifies whether the item is taxable —enter Y or N.
PREFVEND	(Inventory part items only) The vendor from whom you normally purchase the item.

Table 9-7: Keywords and data information for an Item List import file.

Keyword	Item Type
ASSEMBLY	Inventory Assembly item
COMPTAX	Sales tax item
DISC	Discount item
GRP	Group item
INVENTORY	Inventory part item
OTHC	Other charge item
PART	Non-inventory part item
PMT	Payment item
SERV	Service item
STAX	Sales tax group item
SUBT	Subtotal item

Table 9-8: Item Type keywords.

Employee List Import File

When you import an Employee List, you can import only basic data about the employee. In QuickBooks, you have to set up wage, tax, deductions, and other financial information manually in the Employee record. However, importing the basic information saves quite a bit of work.

The keyword for the employee list is !EMP on the heading row (Cell A1 for a sheet with only this list), and each record (row) must have EMP in the first column. Table 9-9 describes the keywords for the rest of the columns in the first row of the import file.

Keyword	Data
NAME	(Required) Employee's name.
ADDR1	First line of the address.
ADDR2	Second line of the address.
ADDR3	Third line of the address.
ADDR4	Fourth line of the address.
ADDR5	Fifth line of the address.
SSNO	Social Security number (XXX -YY-ZZZZ).
PHONE1	Phone number.
PHONE2	Alternate phone number.
FIRSTNAME	First name.
MIDINIT	Middle initial.
LASTNAME	Last name.
SALUTATION	Salutation (Mr., Ms., Mrs., etc.).

Table 9-9: Keywords for Employee List import file.

The Mystery of Employee Initials

QuickBooks' documentation says that the INIT data (employee initials) is a required entry for an employee list import file. It's not; I've imported many Employee Lists without it (and so I've omitted it from the keyword list in Table 9-9). In fact, the field doesn't appear in the employee record dialog when you create an employee in QuickBooks, or view an existing employee's record. If you've consulted the QuickBooks documentation to build IIF files and are worried about leaving it out, you can ignore the requirement you read there, and omit the column from your import file.

> *NOTE: I think it's probable that the INIT data requirement dates back to earlier versions of QuickBooks when sales reps had to be employees, and sales reps are listed by initials in drop-down lists.*

Other Names List Import File

Some companies never use the Other Names list, but this list is necessary for some company types, and handy for others. For proprietorships and partnerships, or any business in which a draw occurs, the owners should be in the Other Names list instead of the Vendors list.

Companies that occasionally issue non-payroll checks (such as loans) to employees must add the employees to the Other Names list. That entry is the payee for loans, or other non-payroll disbursements.

The keyword for the Other Names list is !OTHERNAME on the heading row (Cell A1 if this is the only list in the sheet), and each record (row) must have OTHERNAME in the first column. Table 9-10 describes the keywords for the rest of the columns on the first row of the import file.

Price Level List Import File

Price levels are assigned to customers and sales transactions, and the IIF file has the following format:

- The list keyword for the first row of Column A is !PRICELEVEL and the entry keyword in Column A for each row of data is PRICELEVEL.

- Columns B and C contain the data keywords NAME and VALUE in Row 1 of the list.

The data is percentages, such as 10.00%, or 5.50%. A discounted price level is a negative percent, such as –5.00%.

Keyword	Data
NAME	(Required) The name.
BADDR1	First line of the address.
BADDR2	Second line of the address.
BADDR3	Third line of the address.
BADDR4	Fourth line of the address.
BADDR5	Fifth line of the address.
PHONE1	Phone number.
PHONE2	Alternate phone number.
FAXNUM	FAX number.
EMAIL	E-mail address.
CONT1	Primary contact (if a company).
SALUTATION	Salutation, or title (Mr., Ms., Mrs., etc.).
COMPANYNAME	Company Name (if a company).
FIRSTNAME	First name.
MIDINIT	Middle initial.
LASTNAME	Last name.

Table 9-10: Keywords for the Other Names List import file.

Sales Tax Code List Import File

Sales tax codes are assigned to customers and items, and indicate whether sales tax should be imposed. These are *not* the sales tax items, which determine the rate and the tax agency (those are in the Item List).

Sales tax codes need to be imported only if you need more tax codes than QuickBooks provides automatically. QuickBooks preloads the entries Tax and Non, which suffice for many businesses. However, for businesses in states that require explanations for nontaxable sales, you need additional codes. Here are some examples of sales tax codes you can assign to customers:

- NPO for nontaxable nonprofit organizations.
- GOV for nontaxable government agencies.
- RES for customers who are nontaxable because they resell products (your customer record should include the resale tax number).

The list keyword for the first row of Column A is !SALESTAXCODE and the entry keyword in Column A for each row of data is SALESTAXCODE.

The following keywords are used in this import file:

- CODE is the name of the sales tax code (and is required data). Data entries cannot exceed three characters.
- DESC is an optional description of the code.
- TAXABLE specifies the taxable or nontaxable status (and is required data). The data is Y or N.

Class List Import File

Classes are assigned to transactions in order to track income and expenses by class. The list keyword for the first row of Column A is !CLASS and the entry keyword in Column A for each row of data is CLASS.

The column heading for Column B is NAME and the data in the rest of Column B is the class name.

Summary of List Headers

Table 9-11 contains the HDR keywords for importing lists via IIF files. The data in the column labeled HDR must be in cell A1 of your IIF import file if the file contains a single list. If the file contains multiple lists, each list must begin with a row with the HDR keyword in Column A.

Updating Lists with Excel Import Files

Do any of these scenarios seem familiar?

- A client needs to track certain information about customers, and you've suggested a custom field. You created the custom field for the Customers & Jobs list, and added it to sales transaction windows by customizing the templates. The client has 500 customers to update with data for the new field.
- A client has created price levels and wants to assign a price level to many of the 200 customers in the system. Or, instead of price levels, it's sales reps (or both).

- A client tracks jobs and doesn't have the same rep on every job for the same customer. QuickBooks doesn't provide a Rep field for jobs; instead, the Rep for the customer is automatically the Rep for the job.

HDR	List
!ACCNT	Chart of accounts.
!CUST	Customers & Jobs List
!VEND	Vendors List
!EMP	Employees List
!OTHERNAME	Other Name list.
!CLASS	Class List
!CTYPE	Customer Type List
!INVITEM	Items List
!INVMEMO	Customer Messages
!PAYMETH	Payment Method L ist
!SHIPMETH	Shipping Method List
!TERMS	Payment Terms List
!VTYPE	Vendor Type List

Table 9-11: Header keywords that identify the list you're importing.

Tweaking and updating information in lists is a common practice as users become more familiar with QuickBooks, and the additional data can be the solution for producing more sophisticated detailed reports.

Performing these tasks on a customer-by-customer, vendor-by-vendor, or item-by-item basis means opening each record, moving to the appropriate tab, entering the data, closing the record, opening the next record, and ... you get the picture.

Not only is this time consuming, but the user is likely to be inconsistent about data entry in the custom field, making it hard to track the needed information. The fastest, most accurate method for upgrading data in lists is to import the information from an application that's more cooperative about entering a large number of records.

Any field in any list can be updated with an IIF file. For example, your client may create a Customer Type to use for sorting customers in reports, or to prepare mailings. Or, your client might create a custom field and have to enter data in that field for most (or all) of the entries in a list. Working in QuickBooks means opening the record for each entry in the list, moving to the right tab in the record's window, typing in the data, closing the record, selecting the next record, and so on. This could take days if the list is a long one.

For some lists, you can use either an IIF file or an Excel XLS file. Only the following lists can accept XLS imports:

- Customer
- Vendor
- Items
- Chart of accounts

However, not all fields are available for import when you use an XLS import file. For example, you cannot import data for custom fields, which is a severe limitation. As a result, I use IIF files for all of these tasks.

Creating Import Files to Update Existing Lists

Start by having your client export the appropriate list from the company file and send it to you:

- Tell the client to choose File → Utilities → Export → Lists to IIF Files.
- Remind the client not to export multiple lists, even if more than one list needs updating; instead, export the lists one at a time.

Open the IIF file in Excel and look for the first row of "real" data, which has the list name preceded by an exclamation point. Select all the rows above that row and choose Edit → Delete to remove those rows from the worksheet. This data isn't necessary in an import file, and removing it makes it easier to work with columns (because the column names for the rows you're deleting are not the same column names you'll work with as you add data). Figure 9-2 displays a customer list where all the rows above !CUST (in cell A21) have been selected for deletion.

To add data, you must be able to see the NAME column. Freeze the column that holds the names so that as you scroll through the columns the NAME field stays visible. Use the following steps to freeze the column:

1. Click the column heading of the column to the right of the NAME column to select it.

2. Choose Window → Freeze Panes.

(If you want to unfreeze the worksheet later, just choose Window → Unfreeze Panes. You don't need to select a column first.)

Adding and Modifying Data

Except for data going into custom fields (covered in the next section), the data you enter in any column must match the data already in the QuickBooks file. For example, if you're adding Customer Type data to the Customers & Jobs list, the data must match the Customer Type entries in the Customer Type list. If there's a Customer Type named Stmnt (to indicate customers who should receive statements), the text you enter must be Stmnt; you cannot enter Statement, Stamnt, or any other text. The same is true for Terms, Price Level, and other data contained in QuickBooks lists.

wedoitallcustsand reps.IIF

	A	B	C	D	E	F	G	H	I	J
1	!HDR	PROD	VER	REL	IIFVER	DATE	TIME	ACCNTNT	ACCNTNT	SPLITTIME
2	HDR	QuickBooks Premier	Version 17	Release R	1	#####	1.16E+09	N	0	
3	!CUSTNAN	INDEX	LABEL	CUSTOME	VENDOR	EMPLOYEE				
4	!ENDCUSTNAMEDICT									
5	CUSTNAN		0	ContractRe	Y	Y	N			
6	CUSTNAN		1	RequiresD	N	Y	N			
7	CUSTNAN		2	Backorderl	Y	N	N			
8	CUSTNAN		3		N	N	N			
9	CUSTNAN		4		N	N	N			
10	CUSTNAN		5		N	N	N			
11	CUSTNAN		6		N	N	N			
12	CUSTNAN		7		N	N	N			
13	CUSTNAN		8		N	N	N			
14	CUSTNAN		9		N	N	N			
15	CUSTNAN		10		N	N	N			
16	CUSTNAN		11		N	N	N			
17	CUSTNAN		12		N	N	N			
18	CUSTNAN		13		N	N	N			
19	CUSTNAN		14		N	N	N			
20	!ENDCUSTNAMEDICT									
21	!CUST	NAME	REFNUM	TIMESTAN	BADDR1	BADDF	BADDR3	BADDR4	BADDR5	SADDR1	SAD
22	CUST	RetailCustomer	89	1.16E+09						
23	CUST	GrantJohnCnsltg	88	1.17E+09	John Grant	John G	845 N. Wa	Philadelphia	PA 19177	
24	CUST	House	80	1.14E+09	House					
25	CUST	testpledge	79	1.13E+09						
26	CUST	Accounting Systems Plus	73	1.09E+09	Accounting Systems Plus					
27	CUST	Accounting Systems Plus:on-si	74	1.09E+09	Accounting Systems Plus					
28	CUST	Accounting Systems Plus:softw	76	1.09E+09	Accounting Systems Plus					
29	CUST	Accounting Systems Plus:traini	75	1.09E+09	Accounting Systems Plus					
30	CUST	Adam's Consulting	38	1.09E+09	Adam's Consulting					

CustList

Figure 9-2: Find the first row of real data, and eliminate every row above it.

To make sure you enter data correctly, open the list and press Ctrl-P to print the list. Then, with the entries in the Customer Type, Price Level, etc. list in front of you, you'll be able to enter the text correctly.

WARNING: *If the data you're entering or changing is a QuickBooks Keyword you must use the keyword. All the keywords for all the list files are documented earlier in this chapter.*

There's a way to get drop-downs into individual Excel cells, where the items in the drop-down list are limited to the items from the entries in an existing list. This ensures accuracy, and is accomplished with the following steps:

1. Copy a list such as the Customer Type list onto the active worksheet.

2. Select the cells where you want the data to conform to one of the items in the Customer Type Name column.

3. Choose Data → Validation and click the Settings tab if necessary.

4. Choose List from the Allow drop-down.

5. Click in the Source box and then drag through the cells, in the copy of the Customer Type list, that contain the items you want to choose from.

6. Make sure that the In-cell Dropdown checkbox is filled.

7. Click OK.

Now, when you select one of the cells to be filled in, a drop-down arrow appears. Click the arrow to display the available items, and select the item you want for that customer.

You can also give the source list a range name, using Insert → Name → Define or Insert → Name → Create. In the Data Validation Source box, enter an equal sign followed by the range name: for example, **=CustomerNameList**. (This is the only way to manage it if the source list is on a different worksheet from the list you're building.)

When you're working in Excel, you can take advantage of the Windows clipboard and the Excel data entry tools to enter data.

1. After you enter data in the first row (record) for which you're entering or modifying text, select the cell and press Ctrl-C (or right-click in the cell and choose Copy) to copy the text to the clipboard.

2. Find the next row that needs the same data, and press Ctrl-V to paste the text (or right-click in the cell and choose Paste).

3. Move to the next row that needs the same data and press Ctrl-V to paste the text there. Continue to paste until you've pasted this text into all the records that should have it. (Once you have text in the Windows clipboard, you can continue to paste it endlessly, as long as you don't stop pasting to perform another task that clears the clipboard.)

4. Enter the next data text into the appropriate row, and follow the same pattern to paste that text into every row that should get that particular value.

If you have a section of contiguous rows that require the same data (e.g., all the jobs listed below a customer), enter the data in the first row, and then select that cell. Position your mouse in the lower right corner of the cell over the fill handle (the small black square in the lower right corner of the active cell). When your pointer turns into crosshairs, drag down to fill all the cells with the same data.

Working with Custom Fields

The Custom Field columns do not have the name of the custom fields that were created in the list. The columns are labeled CUSTFLD1, CUSTFLD2, and so on. Have your client open the custom field list in QuickBooks and write down the names of the custom fields so you know the type of data you have to enter as you update the list. The top custom field is CUSTFLD1, the next is CUSTFLD2, etc. Here's how to instruct your clients to find the custom fields:

- In the Items list, open any item, and click the Custom Fields button to see the custom fields.

- In a Names list, open any entry in the list and move to the Additional Info tab to see the custom fields.

When you enter data into custom fields, you must be consistent, or else it will be difficult to create accurate reports on the contents of the fields. For example, if you have a custom field in the Customers & Jobs list named Backorder (to indicate which customers will accept backorders), devise a protocol for the data. For customers that do not accept backorders, if you use the text NoBO (see Figure 9-3), don't mistakenly enter text No BO (note the space), or just No. Ensuring this consistency is another reason to use the Data Validation approach described earlier in this section.

	A	B	C	D	E	F	G
1	ICUST	NAME	CUSTFLD3	BADDR1	BADDR2	BADDR3	BADDR4
2	CUST	InHouse	NoBOs				
3	CUST	RetailCustomer	NoBOs				
4	CUST	GrantJohnCnsltg	ShipSeparately	John Grant Consulting	John Grant	845 N. Wa	Philadelp
5	CUST	House	ShipSeparately	House			
6	CUST	testpledge	ShipSeparately				
7	CUST	Accounting Systems Plus	ShipSeparately	Accounting Systems Plus			
8	CUST	Accounting Systems Plus:on-site set-up	ShipSeparately	Accounting Systems Plus			
9	CUST	Accounting Systems Plus:software	ShipSeparately	Accounting Systems Plus			
10	CUST	Accounting Systems Plus:training	ShipSeparately	Accounting Systems Plus			
11	CUST	Adam's Consulting	NoBOs	Adam's Consulting			
12	CUST	Adam's Consulting:Jan 04	NoBOs	Adam's Consulting			
13	CUST	Adam's Consulting:March 04	NoBOs	Adam's Consulting			
14	CUST	Adam's Consulting:Year End 04	NoBOs	Adam's Consulting			
15	CUST	Bellevue Bistro	Hold Until Filled	Bellevue Bistro			
16	CUST	Bellevue Bistro:4th Street Restaurant	Hold Until Filled	Bellevue Bistro			
17	CUST	Bellevue Bistro:Kelly Drive	Hold Until Filled	Bellevue Bistro			
18	CUST	Bellevue Bistro:Main Street	Hold Until Filled	Bellevue Bistro			
19	CUST	BillsCafe	NoBOs	Bill's Cafe			
20	CUST	GarretArtists	ShipSeparately				
21	CUST	Computer Warehouse	NoBOs	Computer Warehouse			
22	CUST	Computer Warehouse:Set-Up	NoBOs	Computer Warehouse			
23	CUST	Gotham	ShipSeparately	Gotham Computers			
24	CUST	Gotham:Audio	ShipSeparately	Gotham Computers			
25	CUST	Gotham:On-Site Wiring	ShipSeparately	Gotham Computers			

wdia-3custlist custom fields

Figure 9-3: Entering data for the custom field for backorders keeps customer preferences straight (the field appears on transaction templates to make it easy to track the information).

Saving the Import File

I always use the Save As command in Excel to save the file in order to retain the original exported data (in case I have to repair a mistake I made). I usually add a dash and a number to the original filename (such as SmithCustList-1, if the original exported file was named CustList and came from the client named Smith).

For information on saving the file as an IIF file, see the section headed Saving the IIF File in Excel, earlier in this chapter.

Importing Updated Data into QuickBooks

Before your clients import data, make sure they back up the company file. If anything goes amiss, they can restore the backup and continue to work in the file. Later, examine your import file to find any errors, and try the import once again (and also backing up the company file again).

To import the file, tell your client to choose File → Utilities → Import → IIF files. Select the file you created and click Open. QuickBooks automatically imports the data. Open the list that was tweaked with the import file to make sure everything is as expected.

Importing Adjusting Entries

You can import transactions into QuickBooks with IIF files, but except for journal entries, the process is fraught with danger and frustration. For most transaction imports, it's better (and easier) to have your clients purchase a third party program to manage the processes. Usually, transaction imports are used to copy transactions from one company file to another (in order to start a new file when the original file has grown too large), or to import sales data from a Web site shopping cart. There are many third-party applications for these tasks, and you can check them out at the Intuit Marketplace Web pages (www.marketplace.intuit.com).

Before QuickBooks 2007, the Accountant's Copy feature was easy to use (for accountants) and easy to import back into the company file (for clients). Essentially, the copy that the accountant returned to the client was an IIF file, although it had the extension .AIF (which Windows confused with a media file, but QuickBooks understood what to do with it). The file contained journal entries, and sometimes contained new accounts that the accountant created in order to make all the journal entries needed.

Starting with QuickBooks 2007, the Accountant's Copy changed drastically in several ways:

- The file is a full working copy of the company data file and accountants can use all the features in QuickBooks, which means accountants can act as data entry clerks (although I've found very few accountants who want to perform basic data entry tasks).

- The restrictions regarding the tasks accountants and clients can perform while an Accountant's Copy exists are convoluted and complicated.
- Accountants cannot open an Accountant's Copy file in any QuickBooks edition except Premier Accountant Edition.
- Creating the accountant's changes file is more complicated and requires more keystrokes and mouse clicks.
- Transmitting the accountant's changes involves the transfer of a very large file, and you may not be able to send it to the client via e-mail (depending on the mail size restrictions imposed by the client's ISP).
- For the client, importing the accountant's changes is a multi-step task instead of a simple import.

Even if you only want to make adjusting entries in your clients' files, both you and your clients have to go through all these steps. The workaround for accountants who want to send adjusting entries only is to create a separate, easy-to-import IIF file. The file is tiny (easy to e-mail) and your client can import it easily. You have to tell your client to change the state of the company file, which is configured for an outstanding Accountant's Copy (and restricting the tasks your clients can perform), and instructions for your client are included later in this section.

Creating a Journal Entry Import File

You can create an IIF file in Excel that results in journal entries being recorded when the client imports the file. In order to create the JEs you must know the names of the accounts, and you can obtain that information from either of these sources:

- An Accountant's Copy file that your client sent you.
- A Chart of Accounts export list that your client sent you.

The easiest (and most accurate) way to create JEs is to copy and paste account names, because if you have a typo in the account name, QuickBooks will not import the file. I find the best way to do this is to use an exported copy of the COA (you can export it from the Accountant's Copy if your client didn't send you the list), and load that file in Excel.

Then, create a new worksheet in the Excel file for the JEs, copying the account names from the worksheet that holds the exported list. When you save the IIF file, make sure the JE worksheet is the active worksheet (Excel only saves the active worksheet, not the entire file, when you save using a file type of Text.)

As explained earlier in this chapter, an IIF file must have one or more header lines that tell QuickBooks about the information in the file. This is true for transaction import files as well as list import files.

As you can see in Figure 9-4, the HDR entries (which contain exclamation points) indicate that the file contains transactions, splits (the posting accounts) and a keyword that announces the end of the transactions. In addition, each row (transaction item) has a Keyword to indicate what the row contains.

	A	B	C	D	E	F	G
				wedoitall3JEs-5.IIF			
1	ITRNS	TRNSTYPE	DATE	ACCNT	AMOUNT	DOCNUM	MEMO
2	ISPL	TRNSTYPE	DATE	ACCNT	AMOUNT	DOCNUM	MEMO
3	IENDTRNS						
4	TRNS	GENERAL JOURNAL	12/31/2006	Operating Account	-100	7	xfer out
5	SPL	GENERAL JOURNAL	12/31/2006	Payroll Account	100		xfer in
6	SPL	GENERAL JOURNAL	12/31/2006	Employee Advances	-50		move advances
7	SPL	GENERAL JOURNAL	12/31/2006	Travel & Ent:Travel	50		apply to travel
8	SPL	GENERAL JOURNAL	12/31/2006	Salaries-Officers	500		
9	SPL	GENERAL JOURNAL	12/31/2006	Salaries and Wages	-500		
10	SPL	GENERAL JOURNAL	12/31/2006	Licenses and Permits	100		xfer
11	SPL	GENERAL JOURNAL	12/31/2006	Cost of Goods Sold	-100		xfer
12	ENDTRNS						
13							

Figure 9-4: A transaction import file must contain the appropriate keywords in addition to the data.

TIP: Select the cell below the last data in the AMOUNT column and click the AutoSum icon on the Excel toolbar to make sure the resulting total is zero. You don't want to import an out-of-balance JE to a QuickBooks file.

Note in Figure 9-4 that the first row of the JE has the Keyword TRNS and the following rows have the Keyword SPL (for "split"). The first row also contains data in the DOCNUM column, and the data is the JE number.

This keyword setup is related to the way QuickBooks saves JE transaction data, using a source account (for JE's, the first line) and target accounts (all other lines). The source/target paradigm in QuickBooks is important to understand in order to generate reports accurately, but it's beyond the scope of this book. You can learn more about the source/target problems by reading *Running QuickBooks Premier Editions*, available in your favorite bookstore or from the publisher, CPA911 Publishing.

Adding Accounts for Journal Entries

Sometimes, an account you need for an adjusting entry isn't in the client's Chart of Accounts. You can remedy this in either of two ways:

- Contact the client and provide instructions for adding the account to the COA (be sure to be absolutely specific about spelling, spaces, etc. to match the way you entered the account name in the IIF file). The account must exist before the client imports your transaction file.
- Add the account to the COA in the IIF file, so it's available when the transaction is imported.

To add an account to the client's COA, you must make sure to place the account data before the transaction data. In that way, the COA contains the account when the transaction is imported. Follow the rules (keywords and data) enumerated earlier in this chapter for importing accounts, as seen in Figure 9-5.

Figure 9-5: You can add an account when you're making a JE that needs that account.

In Figure 9-5, I added an Expense account to track officer salaries, and then moved the appropriate total out of the Salaries account the client was using into the new account. (I could instead have called the client to instruct him to add the account.)

In Figure 9-5 I inserted a blank row between the account import and the transaction import to make it easier to understand the figure. You don't have to create a blank row between import types, but if you do QuickBooks ignores it and imports the file's contents properly.

NOTE: You can add any type of list item to your JE import file, but it's not common to need to add a customer, vendor, employee, etc. to create adjusting entries.

Importing Auto Reversing JEs

You can enter a JE that auto-reverses so that the client's reports are accurate by date. If you create an adjusting entry for the last day of the fiscal year (or any other ending period) and then reverse it in the following rows of the IIF file with a future date, QuickBooks will report the totals properly when the report dates are selected. Figure 9-6 displays the data needed to import an auto-reversing JE.

	A	B	C	D	E	F	G	H
	SmithCoAdjJE-reversals.iif							
1	ITRNS	TRNSID	TRNSTYPE	DATE	ACCNT	AMOUNT	DOCNUM	MEMO
2	ISPL	SPLID	TRNSTYPE	DATE	ACCNT	AMOUNT	DOCNUM	MEMO
3	IENDTRNS							
4	TRNS		GENERAL JOURNAL	12/31/06	Accounts Receivabl	500.00		8 Adjustment
5	SPL		GENERAL JOURNAL	12/31/06	Cash Advances	-500.00		Adjustment
6	SPL		GENERAL JOURNAL	01/01/07	Accounts Receivabl	-500.00		Adjustment
7	SPL		GENERAL JOURNAL	01/01/07	Cash Advances	500.00		Adjustment
8	ENDTRNS							
9								
10								

SmithCoAdjJE-reversals

Figure 9-6: Imported auto-reversing JEs result in accurate reports because QuickBooks is date-sensitive when creating reports.

Canceling an Outstanding Accountant's Copy

If your client sends you an Accountant's copy and you opt to use an import file for the adjusting JEs instead of returning an Accountant's Changes file to your client, you must instruct the client to cancel the Accountant's Copy. Otherwise, the client is restricted in the types of tasks that can be performed.

NOTE: *When a client creates an Accountant's Copy, the QuickBooks title bar changes to indicate the fact that the company file is waiting for a file from the accountant. A parenthetical phrase such as Accountant's Copy Exists, or Accountant's Changes Pending appears along with the Company name.*

The steps required to cancel an outstanding Accountant's Copy vary depending on the version of QuickBooks.

- In QuickBooks 2007, choose File → Accountant's Copy → Cancel Accountant's Changes.
- In QuickBooks 2006 and earlier, choose File → Accountant's Review → Cancel Accountant's Changes.

The company file is returned to its normal state (users can perform all tasks) and your client can import your IIF file.

Appendix A

From the Web to Excel

Why Bother?

Establishing a Connection

Finding the Data

Understanding the Macro

From time to time I find it helpful to log on to the World Wide Web, if only to ego-surf by Googling myself. One of the useful aspects of the Web is that you can put your hands on real time data – information that changes from day to day, hour to hour or even by minute. Stock prices are an example, as are indices like the Dow industrials. This Appendix shows you how to extract that information into a workbook.

Why Bother?

If you're interested only in what the present level of an index is, there are thousands of Web pages you can check for information, accurate to the last few minutes at worst.

With an index, or any indicator, that you're familiar with, a current value might be as much information as you want or need. You know that the Dow industrial average, since the 1990s anyway, tends to stay within a 100 point trading range on any given day. Yesterday's close and today's gain or loss is often enough to tell you what's going on with that particular basket of stocks.

If you're interested in a longer view, the Web pages that carry a current snapshot also tend to carry longitudinal information. Typically you can call for a chart showing the last month, year, five years, or longer for the indicator you want.

But what if you're interested in an indicator whose properties you're not familiar with? Or one that doesn't have a history that you can get at with a couple of mouse clicks? In that case, you might have to build your own history of the indicator, so that you can get – on a going forward basis at least – data on maxes, mins, a measure of central tendency such as the mean, median or mode, and so on. With that sort of information, you're in a position to interpret the meaning of, say, the number 873; without that information, you can't tell if 873 is good, bad, or a typographical error.

Here are a few examples of the sort of information that you or your client might want to pick up automatically on a regular and frequent basis:

- Company credit cards when a bunch of people have them. This is a good way to keep a running tally of charges by user.
- Bank accounts, to keep track of posted payments.
- Electronic invoices. Quite a few firms, particularly general contractors, receive electronic invoices from their subs and post them to an intranet in XML.
- Online stock and price levels maintained by suppliers (especially useful for drop shipping).

I've written several books about Excel. A while back, some knuckle-dragger posted a negative review about one of my books on Amazon. He complained that the book didn't have an accompanying disk with Excel workbooks on it, workbooks that would contain the data on which the book's examples were based.

And he was right. The book did not have a CD bound into it. What he didn't say, because he apparently didn't know, was that few if any such books have had "companion CDs" for years now. It's too expensive to supply them when the cost of downloading the workbooks from the publisher's Web site is almost no cost at all. And that's how you get the files for that book as well as thousands of others.

So this guy gets to badmouth the book, in a narrow sense accurately, but wildly off base on any rational interpretation. Although I was thoroughly p.o.'d, there wasn't anything I could do. Amazon wouldn't take the review down, and they were right not to.

Nevertheless, I wanted to know what effect that review would have on sales of my book on Amazon. It happens that Amazon posts information, updated hourly, on a book's Amazon sales ranking; the lower the number, the better the sales. I watched that number each day for a couple of weeks, like scratching a mosquito bite. Then I realized that I was acting like a nincompoop.

I found that I needed to check the sales ranking hourly. Those rankings can and do change by tens of thousands of ranks in a 24 hour period. If I looked at the ranking once daily, I could very easily get a wildly discrepant value for that day. But it would be crazy to try to make sense of hourly data, so I'd have to summarize the rankings somehow – a daily or weekly summary would make good sense.

So, I wrote a VBA macro to pick up the data from the Web site on an hourly basis. Once the data is retrieved into an Excel workbook, the macro adds the ranking to a list, along with the date, and then updates a pivot table based on that list. A chart then redraws itself based on the most recent data. I never have to touch it – I just look at the chart from time to time. The whole process is automatic, untouched by human hands. Eventually, I determined that the sales of the book had fallen off after that review.

Now I'm going to show you how to do the same sort of thing with any Web-based data source you like. In return, I'd really appreciate it if you'd post a review of *this* book on Amazon, declaring how wonderful it is that there's no CD bound into it.

Establishing a Connection

The first item on the agenda is to establish a connection between an Excel workbook and the Web site that you want to get data from. Depending on the version of Excel you're using, the instructions might differ slightly – for example, "Get External Data" versus "Import External Data" – but you should be able to work your way through it.

Start with a blank worksheet, and choose Data → Get External Data → New Web Query. The dialog box in Figure A-1 appears.

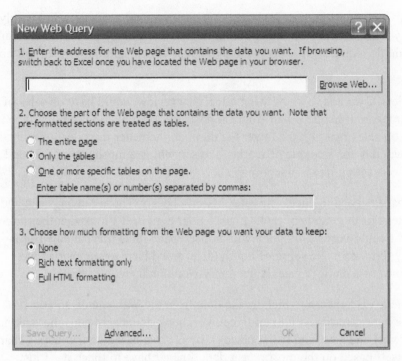

Figure A-1: The appearance of this dialog box differs according to the version of Excel you're using.

Unless you know the Web site's address off the top of your head, click the Browse button instead of typing in the site's URL. When you click Browse, your default Web browser (such as Internet Explorer or Firefox) opens. Use it to navigate to the site that you want to get data from. Once you've arrived there, do either of the following:

- If you're using Internet Explorer as your default browser, Excel will automatically put the site's address into the New Web Query window for you when you switch back to Excel.
- If some other application such as Firefox is your default browser, Excel might not be so user friendly. In that case, just copy the URL from the browser's address box and paste it into the New Web Query window's edit box. (As noted in Chapter 5, Ctrl-C and Ctrl-V are handy for this.)

When the New Web Query edit box has an address in it, the OK button is enabled and you can proceed if you want. Before you do, though, consider setting these options:

- In part two on the New Web Query window, choose to retrieve the entire page.
- In part three, choose None to indicate that the data should be retrieved as plain text.

The reason for the first choice, the entire page, is that if you choose only tables, or a particular table or tables, you can run into problems at a later date when the tables might have been replaced or renamed or re-tagged. Then, Excel will have trouble finding the specified table or tables.

And you have no need for the Web site's formatting. You're interested only in the data, and you really don't care to have 98.6 enter your workbook as *98.6*.

NOTE: *In Excel 2002 and Excel 2003, you're given the opportunity to click arrows on yellow backgrounds, which mark the upper left corner of each table in the Web page. You can select the entire page by clicking the arrow in the page's upper left corner.*

When you click OK, Excel pulls the data from the Web page and onto the active worksheet. Control returns to you when the import has finished. The worksheet is also provided a new range name, by default the last portion of the URL. The number of columns and rows used in your worksheet depends on the number of elements in the Web page. A commercial site could easily take up 400 rows and 30 columns.

The named range is "live" – that is, you could click any cell in that range and choose Data → Refresh Data. Excel would then import the current information on that Web page into the worksheet. The approach I outline here makes use of that.

Finding the Data

With the current data from the Web page captured on a worksheet, you would then want to isolate and save the information you're interested in. In the case of my book's sales ranking, the information looks like this, in one of the worksheet's cells (by no means always the same cell):

Amazon.com Sales Rank: #24,183 in Books (See Top Sellers in Books)

(Not bad for a book published in 1995.) While I can depend on finding the text string "Sales Rank: " and for it to be followed by the book's sales rank, I can't depend on that information being in the same worksheet cell time after time. And I can't depend on finding the string "24,183" time after time – if I could, there'd be no point in updating the information.

The sequence of events is:

1. Decide on something unique but constant to search the Excel worksheet for. In this example, "Sales Rank: " is a good choice.

2. Search the worksheet for the cell that contains that unique item – again, in this case, "Sales Rank: "

3. Strip the contents of that cell until only the useful data remains.

4. Write the data to a list on another worksheet, along with an identifier such as the system date.

5. Update a pivot table's cache from the list.

All this can be automated by using a macro. You can even set things up so that after the macro has finished running, it will wait a period of time – an hour, say – and then run itself again.

Understanding the Macro

You can download the following macro code from cpa911publishing.com/downloads.htm, but it helps to understand what it does. I've put some explanatory notes in with the code.

The first two statements set options. The *Option Explicit* statement is just good programming practice. It forces the code to explicitly declare, or *dimension*, the variables used in the code. It is a major help in the prevention of spaghetti code – code that is unintelligible – as well as outright errors. The *Option Base 1* statement isn't strictly necessary here. It forces all VBA arrays to begin with element number 1, instead of the default element number 0. I have Excel set up to slug both those statements into every VBA module I open.

```
Option Explicit
Option Base 1
```

Then, the first of two subroutines is initiated, and five variables that the code uses are declared. The SalesRank variable is declared as Long, which is an integer variable type with a much higher upper bound than the Integer data type, which maxes out at 32,767. A sales rank, sadly, can be much larger than 32,767.

```
Sub PickUpData()
Dim Sales As String, SalesRank As Long, WhichRow As Integer
Dim StartPoint As Integer, StopPoint As Integer
```

The code assumes the presence of a worksheet named QuerySheet in the active workbook. This worksheet contains the results of the Web query in what VBA refers to as a QueryTable. The next statement causes Excel to refresh the results of the Web query. The setting for BackgroundQuery means that the code will not continue running until the query has finished executing.

```
ThisWorkbook.Sheets("QuerySheet").QueryTables(1).Refresh BackgroundQuery:=False
```

The next statement finds a cell that contains the string "Sales Rank: " and assigns its contents to a variable named Sales. The statement makes use of the (only) range name in QuerySheet, which identifies the range of data extracted from the Web site. That is the range that Excel searches for the "Sales Rank: " string.

```
Sales = ThisWorkbook.Sheets("QuerySheet").Names(1).RefersToRange.Find("Sales Rank: ", LookIn:=xlValues)
```

As noted before, I expect the cell found by the code to look like this:

Amazon.com Sales Rank: #24,183 in Books (See Top Sellers in Books)

with the only difference from query to query being the rank itself. The next two statements locate the first character in the sales rank (here, the number 2) and the last character (here, the number 3).

```
StartPoint = InStr(Sales, "#") + 1
StopPoint = InStr(Sales, " in") − 1
```

Then, the code finds the string in the middle (using the Mid function) of the Sales variable that begins with the rank's first character, and is as long as the inclusive difference between the positions of the rank's first and last characters.

```
SalesRank = Mid(Sales, StartPoint, StopPoint - StartPoint + 1)
```

The code now makes use of a With block. Everything between the With and the End With statements is assumed to belong to the item named by the With statement. Here, the worksheet named "Book Rank" is named in the With, and when the code encounters something preceded only by a dot (such as .Cells) it is taken to belong to the Book Rank worksheet.

```
With ThisWorkbook.Sheets("Book Rank")
```

Inside the With block, the code finds the final cell in column A that has a value in it. It does so by the combination of End and xlUp. This is the VBA equivalent of selecting, in this case, cell A65000, holding down Ctrl and pressing the up arrow. Then, the number 1 is added to that cell's row, to return the row number of the first unused cell in column A.

```
WhichRow = .Cells(65000, 1).End(xlUp).Row + 1
```

The book's sales rank is written to column B in the first unused row, and the date and time (by means of the Now function) are written to column A in the same row. The pivot table on the Book Rank worksheet is refreshed. See the section called Using Named Ranges as Data Sources in Chapter 2 for information on linking a pivot table to a list.

```
.Cells(WhichRow, 2) = SalesRank
.Cells(WhichRow, 1) = Now
.PivotTables(1).RefreshTable
```

The code ends the With block and saves the workbook.

```
End With
ThisWorkbook.Save
```

Then, the code calls a subroutine named DoItAgain (discussed next), and the subroutine named PickUpData terminates.

```
DoItAgain
End Sub
```

The subroutine named DoItAgain has one statement only, and it uses the OnTime method. This method specifies a particular time of day. It then names a subroutine that is to run at that time of day. In this case, the Now function is used to determine the current time. One hour is added to that time, and the subroutine just discussed, PickUpData, is named. The result is that one hour from the time that DoItAgain is run, PickUpData is run once again.

This means that if you want, you can just leave Excel running the code for days on end, updating the information retrieved from a Web site once an hour, saving the data in the workbook, and updating a pivot table (and a chart) at the same time. Here's DoItAgain:

```
Sub DoItAgain()
Application.OnTime Now + TimeValue("01:00:00"), "PickUpData"
End Sub
```

Figure A-2 shows what the worksheet named Book Rank might look like.

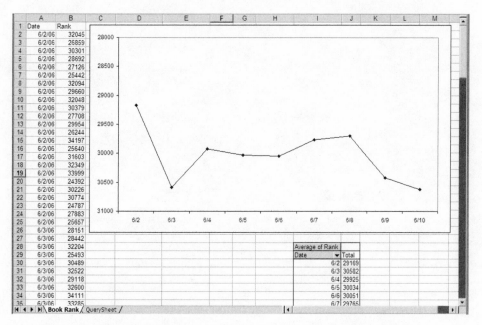

Figure A-2: The chart updates automatically when the pivot table is refreshed.

Index